Waldringfiel

To, Iain,
With Very Best Wishes and Many Thanks
for your valuable help with certain parts of
this Book. From Gareth

To Joe Clark, Founder and now President of the Waldringfield History Group

Waldringfield

A Suffolk Village beside the River Deben

The Waldringfield History Group

First published 2020 by Golden Duck (UK) Ltd.

golden-duck.co.uk

Golden Duck (UK) Ltd
Sokens
Green Street
Pleshey
nr. Chelmsford
Essex
CM3 1HT

A CIP catalogue record for this book is available from the British Library.

ISBN: 9781899262434

Printed and bound in Great Britain by Biddles Ltd.

biddles.co.uk

WALDRINGFIELD WALKS

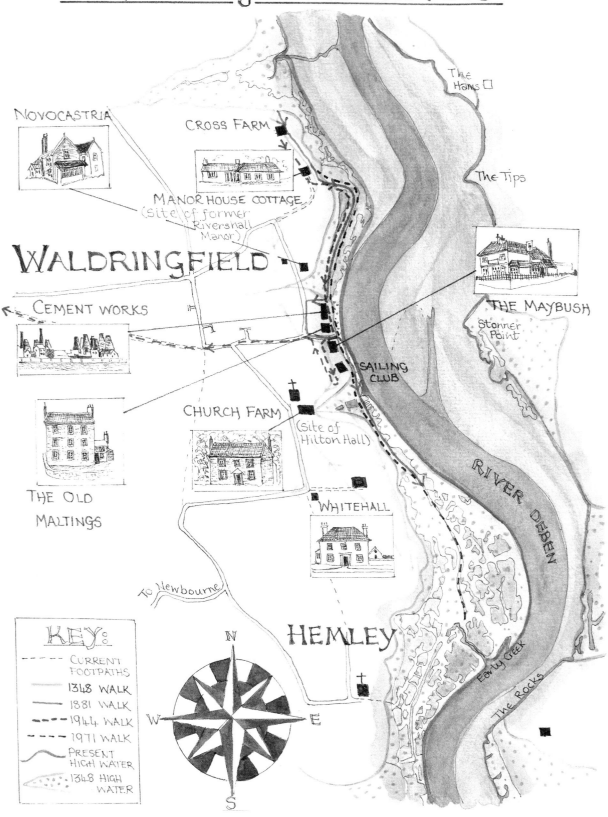

NOVOCASTRIA

CROSS FARM

The Hams

The Tips

MANOR HOUSE COTTAGE
(Site of former
Rivershall
Manor)

WALDRINGFIELD

THE MAYBUSH

Stonner
Point

CEMENT WORKS

SAILING
CLUB

THE OLD
MALTINGS

CHURCH FARM

(Site of
Hilton Hall)

RIVER DEBEN

WHITEHALL

To Newbourne

HEMLEY

Early Creek

The Rocks

KEY:
- - - - CURRENT
FOOTPATHS
———— 1348 WALK
——— 1881 WALK
- - - 1944 WALK
— — 1971 WALK
〜〜 PRESENT
HIGH WATER
〜〜 1348 HIGH
WATER

N
W — E
S

Wonderful Waldringfield

'High marks in the competition of curious local mispronunciations of place names may fairly be claimed for the case of Waldringfield, near Ipswich. If you do in Suffolk as the Suffolkers do, you must call it "Wunuerfl," which is also their pronunciation of "wonderful," a favourite Suffolk word.'

Evening Star, 23rd September 1904

Signposting the way to the river [7]

'To the river!' First one, then another signpost, entices the visitor onwards through this 'wunerful' Suffolk village, now largely a collection of idiosyncratic 19th-century and 20th-century dwellings, home to a living, developing 21st-century community which has not lost touch with its past.

The first documented reference to 'Waldringfield' dates back to circa 951, when mentioned in the will of Bishop Theodred, close ally of the great King Æthelstan. Theodred granted his nephew, Osgot, his estate at 'Waldringfeld'.

Waldringfield is mentioned again in the 11th-century Little Domesday Book (spelt then 'Waldringafelda') when it had a population of 12 households. It is likely that the 'Wald' element of Waldringfield comes from the name 'Waldhere', modern English 'Walter'. 'Wald' means might, power and authority, and 'here' signifies army leader, commander or warrior. There is an old English epic poem called 'Waldhere' and there was an earlier Bishop of London with that name, but no definitive connection between them and this wonderful village. The 'inga' element in 'Waldringafelda' refers to the people or tribe, whilst 'feld' refers to open country. So, in summary, the village name of Waldringfield derives from Old English, meaning 'the open land of Waldhere's people'.

Wonderful Waldringfield is many thousands of years older than its name. Neolithic artefacts have been found here and, when former resident Audrie Fitzjohn designed the village sign for the Queen's Silver

Audrie Fitzjohn (1912-1995) designed the village sign. She lived in Sunnyhill. In addition to her design skills, she was a keen sailor with her neighbour Joan Andrews in the Dragonfly Class and had a love of natural history. Audrie's design was cast by Jacobs, the blacksmiths at Kirton, and cost about £150 [8]

Jubilee in 1977, she curled a plesiosaur round a trading barge to symbolise the importance of ancient geology in village history. The sign was topped with a naval crown as Waldringfield has associations with wider sea-faring as well as river transport. Sir Peter Vanneck, who was Lord Mayor of London in 1977, and owned a house opposite the village shop, unveiled the sign dressed in his mayoral regalia accompanied by Lady Cordelia Vanneck. They toured the village in an old hay wagon loaned by the Rector, Rev John Waller.

This book is a celebration of village history and Waldringfield's association with the River Deben, Suffolk's loveliest and most unspoiled river. We cannot offer an explanation for the

Rev John Waller, Lady Cordelia Vanneck, and Sir Peter Vanneck [9]

name 'Deben'. Language experts tell us that it does not mean 'the deep one' (from the old English 'deop') and sailors, caught by the shifting shingle that bars its entrance or the mudbanks uncovered by the ebb tide, would probably agree. In 1577 the Deben was referred to as the 'Deue' and in 1618 as the 'Deane'. We are content to remind ourselves that the river was in existence long before there were words and let the mystery of its name remain … unfathomable.

Suffolk is where 'south-folk' live, in contrast to the 'north-folk', in the kingdom of the East Angles (East Anglia). Trollope may have used the phrase 'silly Suffolk' in its pejorative sense, in his novel *The Way We Live Now*, but 'silly' is actually a variant of 'seely' originating from the Anglo-Saxon word 'selig' meaning holy. Perhaps this is not surprising for a county with so many ancient churches?

And there is beauty – in our eyes at least. Surely, we say to one another, there can be no spot in the whole of Suffolk more evocative to the senses than the wide, flat, far-reaching expanse of the Deben at Waldringfield. The open skies, the call of the curlew, the ebb and flow of the river, the taste of the salt, the smell of the seaweed, the ever changing light. This iconic scene keeps us connected to our history; a constant and reassuring thread for uncertain times.

Wonderful Waldringfield indeed!

Sunrise [10]

Table of Contents

A teal [11]

Seagull in flight [12]

To Begin at the Beginning

'I didn't have time to write a short [book], so I wrote a long one instead.'

Mark Twain

In the Autumn of 2016, the members of the Waldringfield History Group (WHG) decided that such was the wealth of material on the group's website it should be shared in the form of a book. Opinions were varied about what sort of book this should be, ranging from a fully referenced historical record through to a popular visual experience with more pictorial content than text. What has evolved, we hope, is a book which is intended to inform and stimulate further interest whilst also providing easy reading and entertainment.

The book has been produced primarily for the benefit of the Village and its inhabitants, for posterity and as a basis for continuing investigation. The WHG is immensely grateful to all those people who have contributed in one way or another to the production. The greatest thanks of all go to Joe Clark, founding Chairman and now President of the WHG, for recognising the extreme importance of Thomas Naunton Waller's glass plate photographs taken in the later part of the nineteenth century.

Although there are three editors (Jane Hall, Gareth Thomas, Alyson Videlo), this book is the result of considerable team effort on the part of all members of the WHG and their friends, some writing original chapters and panels, others rewriting, editing, reviewing, providing critiques, finding photos, checking facts, illustrating and advising in presentation and design. As a consequence, the writing style varies between the chapters, rather depending on how and by whom each individual chapter was started.

The reading experience is enhanced not only by photographs but by paintings from local artists Kitty Moss and Kit Clark, by sketches and maps drawn by WHG member Jackie Brinsley and by sketches drawn by the late David Ruffle. The editors are very grateful to the Ruffle family for allowing his series of sketches to be used in this way in memory of both him and his late wife, Audrey, a WHG member and, for some time, the Hon Treasurer.

The IT involved in the production of this book and the requirements of the publishing world have been challenging. The editors are immensely grateful to Bertie Wheen for his IT and typesetting skills and to Julia Jones for her copy-editing and for her publishing advice. A five-generation link between Julia's family and Waldringfield has made her contribution doubly empathetic.

We are also extremely grateful to our generous sponsors. Without them publication would not have been possible. They are listed on a separate page.

The book does not pretend to cover all aspects of the village history. From the early stages of writing it became apparent that there was too much material for one book. A decision was made to concentrate on the association between the village and the river. Consequently, there is little written about the detail of the oldest building in the village, All Saints Church. There is very little about agriculture and next to nothing about the Baptist Chapel and the social history afforded by the graveyards of the Church and the Chapel. There is very little about local transport and the road links with surrounding villages, with Ipswich and with Woodbridge. That material remains on the website for future consideration.

It may be argued that by adopting this thematic approach we have created a false division of the village because each of the listed omissions carries some association with the river. For instance the association of All Saints Church with the river might not be obvious to the modern observer. However, when the first stones were laid in the thirteenth century it is likely that they were hauled up directly from vessels which had accessed the inlet below. It is likely that the 600 year old font was delivered in the same way. The steep cliff face is there today. Just take a quiet sojourn through the graveyard and imagine how it might have been all those years ago, before the construction of river walls.

The book is structured mainly upon a riverside walk taken from the northern extreme of the village, the Parish boundary with Martlesham, to the southern extreme, the boundary with Hemley. This walk is taken on four different occasions, 1348, 1881, 1944 and post WW2, circa 1971. In 1348 there were no river walls to contain the tide; in 1881 the village was a hive of industry; in 1944 security was tight and the beach was inaccessible; in 1971 the shore was much as it is now although the craft on the river were beginning to change.

Naturally there are features of the village, past and present, which require chapters of their own and these will become obvious during the course of the walks. Some individual topics are presented as panels.

When the Waldringfield History Group was formed many kind people provided old photographs and, very quickly, a vast selection accumulated on the website. Many of them are included in this book. Every effort has been made to acknowledge the sources of the material or to contact copyright holders. In many instances it has proved difficult to know whether copyright is an issue. Obviously the WHG is very apologetic if there prove to be instances where the position has been misunderstood; the editors would appreciate notification of any such instances so that they can be corrected in future reprints or editions.

No claims are made for this work being totally correct but every effort has been made to confirm the facts and to expose certain mythologies, some created by previous writers. That having been said, there remain, still, some unanswered questions. But that is no bad thing, surely, as it gives the Waldringfield History Group a continuing 'raison d'être'?

Some readers may wish to learn more about the Waldringfield History Group, its origins, its foundation in 2007, its activities, its website and its membership. For its origins it is recommended that those readers go first to 'The Story of the Glass Plates' and then to the appendix entitled 'The Waldringfield History Group'. In that appendix there is reference to the activities of an earlier group of people, 'The Bygones' who created a 'History scrapbook' and recorded several interviews on tape. These are now accessible on the WHG website along with many more modern interviews and presentations.

This book, although essentially a history book, does not finish in the past. Instead it describes a fifth walk, 'a Walk toward the Future', armed with lessons of the past and with memories too. We hope that you enjoy the whole experience.

Gareth Thomas. Chairperson, Waldringfield History Group

Reflection of aircraft contrails at dawn (the village sits under a major flight path to Northern Europe) [13]

The Story of the Glass Plates

'A good photograph is knowing where to stand.'

Ansel Adams, American photographer

Thomas Naunton Waller [14]

Thomas Naunton Waller was born in 1863, the 3rd son and 6th child of Thomas Henry Waller, Rector of Waldringfield, and his wife, Jane. His older brothers, five years older than he, were twins. The older of the two went on to work for a bank whilst the younger of the two farmed White Hall and Church Farm, the family farms.

Thomas, at first, decided to follow his oldest brother into the world of banking and spent time following that career in Walthamstow. However, he discovered that it was not for him; he decided, instead, to study engineering and chose to become, for a fee, a Premium Apprentice Engineer at the ship-builder Hawthorn Leslie in Newcastle.

He was also a skilled amateur photographer at a time when photographic techniques were developing rapidly. Thomas designed his own camera and became prolific with his hobby, mainly in and around Waldringfield and on the River Deben, but also in Walthamstow where, evidently, there is a collection of his photography in that area. His work was much appreciated in photographic circles, so much so that in 1992 it accounted for ten percent of the photographs in Humphrey Phelps' book entitled *Suffolk of One Hundred Years Ago*.

In 2007 Waldringfield resident Joe Clark rediscovered a large box of photographic glass plates which had been inherited by his wife Kit (née Waller) to whom Thomas Naunton Waller was a great uncle. A dilemma presented itself as to how these plates could be developed for the greater good.

The problem was solved once he had consulted with Stan Baston, a village resident well known for his skill with both cameras and computers. After a period of experimentation Stan found that it was possible to align the plates on a lightbox and photograph them with a Digital SLR camera mounted on a tripod. By so doing he was able to produce negative images which, following conversion to positive, provided an intriguing collection of photographs representing life in Waldringfield in the last decade of the nineteenth century.

Woodbridge Ferry by TN Waller [15]

Not surprisingly there were imperfections although many proved correctable by modern computer techniques and Stan Baston's expertise.

An outstanding characteristic of this 'Waller collection' is the artistic composition of many of the photographs. Like his grandniece, Thomas Naunton Waller 'had an eye' for a picture but, of course, he was not in a position with his hobby to demonstrate the eye for colour which she enjoys with her art.

Although these glass plates had lain dormant for several years it is clear that some, at least, had been processed before as Stan, another man with an eye for a picture, recognised them as photographs he had seen before. His favourite is a photograph of the Woodbridge Ferry.

In the autumn of 2007, armed with the images so painstakingly reproduced from the glass plates by Stan, together with some other old postcards and photographs, Joe presented to the village a talk entitled 'A Walk around Waldringfield 100 years ago'. The current Waldringfield History Group was formed as a consequence of that talk.

Joe Clark became the Chairman but is now the President of the Group. It gave him and Kit Clark great pleasure to see the camera being prepared for display at the new Woodbridge Museum in the autumn of 2019.

In 1886 Waller had used his budding engineering skills to design and build his own camera and some of the highly technical 'paraphernalia' to go with it. Naturally the camera was used with a tripod. Nevertheless, one of the problems encountered was the movement induced when removing the lens cap

Joe Clark, President of the Waldringfield History Group, with Thomas Naunton Waller's camera, the lens cap, the shutter mechanism and, immediately in front of Joe, a goniometer. The shutter mechanism needs to be seen to appreciate the precision which must have been involved in its construction. A goniometer is a tool used to set an angle for cutting gems or precision tools but the three dimensional appearance of this particular gadget makes one wonder if it was used as a goniophotometer which measures the distribution of light at specific angular positions, usually covering all spherical angles [16]

in order to expose the glass plate at the back of the camera. Undaunted, he went on to design and build a shutter system which, although still ahead of its time, might have been modelled on an earlier design patented in 1881 by Sands.

The reader can only imagine the weight and the cumbersome nature of the equipment involved in obtaining these photographs. The tripod, camera and glass plates were heavy and difficult to carry so it is remarkable that a considerable number were taken either from the river or from locations on the eastern shore such as Stonner Point. The most stable platform for pictures from the river would have been an anchored barge of which there were plenty about, at least until 1907 when the Cement Works closed.

In addition to the camera, lens cap and shutter the Woodbridge Museum also holds the tripod, a darkroom oil lamp, a beautifully made viewer and a goniometer. How grateful we must be to those earlier pioneers of photography such as Thomas Naunton Waller for their sheer determination in perfecting their art. How different it is today when with a quick point of the digital camera or the smartphone one can acquire multiple images of a subject and, in the event of dissatisfaction with the images, acquire dozens more in a mere flash. It's the difference between taking a photograph and making one, to quote more thoughts from Ansel Adams.

The goniometer (or was it used as a means of deciding the best angle of illumination – as a goniophotometer?) [17]

The Ever Changing River

'I thought how lovely and how strange a river is. A river is a river, always there, and yet the water flowing through it is never the same water and is never still. It's always changing and is always on the move.'

Aidan Chambers, *This is All: The Pillow Book of Cordelia Kenn*

The Anchorage by David Ruffle [18]

Like most rivers the Deben has changed over the years, in fact, it changes also from day to day, hour to hour. Natural forces such as the tides and weather patterns shape the channels and foreshore gradually, whereas man can have a more rapid effect. In this chapter, we begin to explore some of the more obvious features which might prompt a visitor to ask: 'How did that come to be?'

In the Medieval period before river walls, the saltmarshes would have extended further and small streams and inlets would have existed where currently there are none. At the time of writing, a period of lockdown due to the coronavirus epidemic, the sounds heard are probably similar to those of much earlier centuries; sounds of the wind, the birds and other creatures. The sounds of modern-day living have all but disappeared; no boat engines, no aeroplanes, no motor cars.

The river walls were most likely built in the sixteenth century probably starting at the seaward end and working upriver towards Woodbridge. The walls around Waldringfield probably date to between 1540-1734 except for the stretch between Waldringfield and Hemley which is most likely later.

The weather affects the river; storms can temporarily affect the Beach and the waters, leaving mud deposited on the sandy Beach; even freezing can occur, as seen in 1963. Occasional dredging can also have a similar effect. This happens less frequently now as fewer large boats are sailing to Woodbridge which used to be such a busy port when most cargoes were transported by water.

The building of the river walls changed the shape of the river but not forever as the water has a way of reclaiming the land eventually. Breaches occurred due to high tides in the Methersgate and Hemley walls in 1937 and for at least the Hemley section the dispute between the landowners and local water board as to who was responsible for them caused a lack of repair and an ever-widening breach. (The officials of the Water Board stated that the river walls were their responsibility but that they could not afford to repair them; they were not prepared to permit any other agency to carry out repairs so the breaches remained.) A jettisoned World War II bomb also caused a breach near Cross Farm, but in wartime there would have been other more important things on which to focus.

A heavy storm in 2016 [19]

Waldringfield's stretch of the river now flows from Cross Farm and just below Methersgate Quay downriver to Hemley Hall and just below Shottisham Creek which is now walled off. The drone photographs show the extent of the Waldringfield part of the river as well as a good view of the 'cuttings' and our 'island'.

A few local landmarks have changed little over the last hundred years or so but some have changed dramatically especially the Cement Works of which little remains.

These Works needed mud for the manufacturing process and much of this was dug from the saltmarshes downriver of Waldringfield and loaded onto barges. Walter Tye tells of the mud that was dug for the works between 1875 and 1907.

The Manor House Cottage jetty looking north towards Woodbridge in 2013 [20]

'During their twenty-five years of mud shovelling, they cleared over ten acres. Going out with the ebb tide, they waited, till the bottom was visible, then one loading fore and the other aft, they shovelled up twenty-five tons of mud before the tide returned, taking from three to four hours.'

Starting from the north and working downriver the main landmarks to be seen are described further in this chapter.

The Manor House jetty was built in the 1960s by the owners of Manor House

Labelled drone picture looking upriver [21]

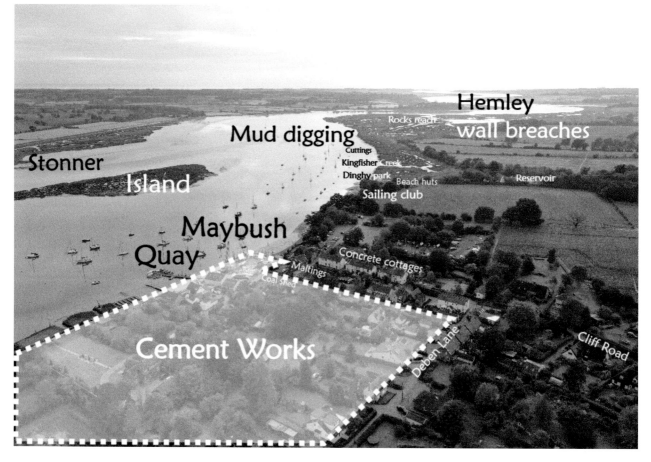

Labelled drone picture looking downriver [22]

2020 overhead picture of the Tips and Hams showing the erosion [23]

Cottage for their private use and is one of the furthest north landmarks on the Waldringfield shoreline. The riverside path towards Woodbridge is breached just above here and impassable. It is situated on an area of river described as 'Ham Point' on an 1845 naval survey map as it is opposite the 'Hams' and the 'Tips' which is an area of higher ground on the eastern bank that has quite a large and noisy heronry and is on a bend in the river.

wall just one tide before completion. His men worked for 10d a day and he stopped this pay when they came over for the annual ploughing match. Jim Turner, in 1996, mentioned that the Tips were twice as long in the 1930s. This was confirmed by Jill Atkins and a comparison with early-20th-century OS maps shows this to be true for both the Hams and Tips.

The Hams and Tips

The Hams and Tips are areas of higher ground with a dip between them, the 'Hams' slightly upriver of the 'Tips'. There was a failed attempt by Robert Knipe Cobbold of Sutton in the 19th century to embank 150 acres of foreshore by linking these two higher areas together, which was thwarted by a storm that destroyed the

2019: Golden sunrise over the island and Stonner Point beyond [24]

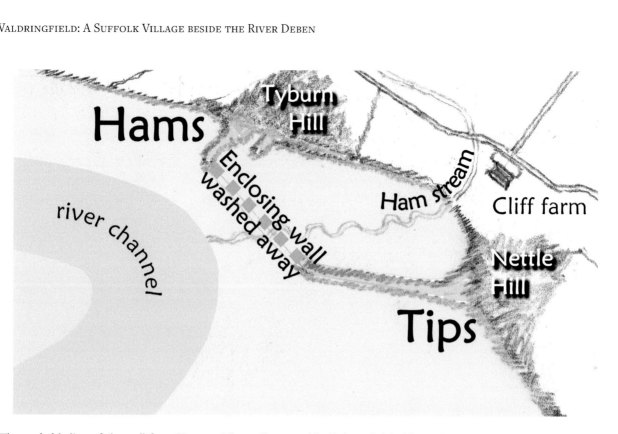

The probable line of the wall from Hams to Tips walls erected by Robert Cobbold (see the 1805 map for more detail) [25]

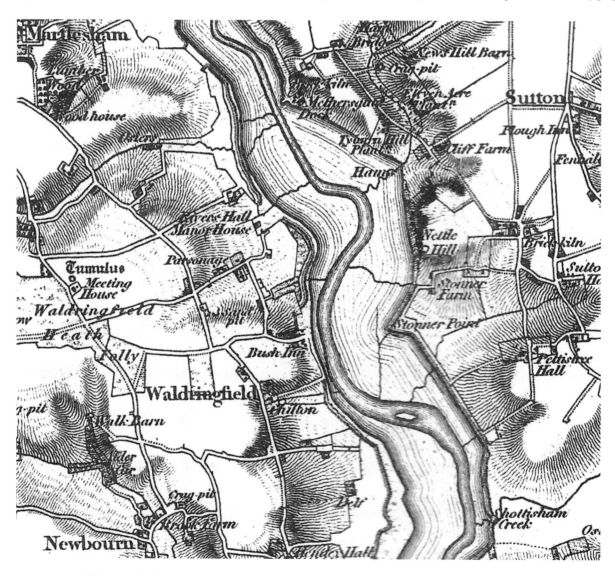

1805 map clearly showing Stonner and the 'Horse' just downriver of the current island [26]

A dramatic view of the remaining stumps in 1980 [27]

The Boatyard and Quay from upriver in 2013 [29]

The Island

The island doesn't have a name although many have tried to give it one in the past. In truth it isn't really an island as at high tide it is often completely covered and the channel on the far side of it dries out at low tide. It then becomes part of the Parish of Sutton. Many workers used to be ferried across the river from Stonner Point (referred to as Woodhall Stonnor in 1625 and Stoney Point in 1796 but clearly as Stonner Point in Ordinance Survey maps from 1805) to work on the farms and estates around Waldringfield as well as coprolite pits and the Cement Works.

The ferry ran from the point just north of the island to the area of the slipway by the Maybush. At one point there was a channel and a Quay at Stonner formed around the 1880s to allow the loading of coprolite and possibly the unloading of manure from London for the fields by the local landowners, the Waller family. The Quay at Stonner Point was a large structure (possibly similar in size to the existing one at Methersgate) as can be seen from the earlier picture but all that remains of the Quay today are the stumps.

Waldringfield Quay

On the 1839 Tithe map, the land was described as either shore or saltings so the Quay wasn't there at that time. With the coming of the Cement Works in around 1865, there was most likely some form of quay created for the unloading of clay and the loading of the manufactured cement. The Cement Works soon made large cement blocks for the external walls of the Quay enclosing the rammed chalk structure. John Frost of Woodbridge may have done some preliminary work on a quay, as he managed to recover £3 12s 6d from the then owners of the Cement Works, Messrs Coles & Shadbolt. After the Cement Works closed and was demolished the Quay continued to be used for loading and unloading of coal and to remove the rubble from the site. It was largely unused for some years until 1925 when it was purchased from Frank William Mason by Alfred William Stollery, who was a family friend. By AW's contact with Harry Nunn during WW1, he then rented it to the Nunns' Boatyard business. The Boatyard grew on the site of the Cement Works which had closed in 1907.

Stonner Point Quay in 1980 [28]

Postcard of Waldringfield Quay [30]

The Beach in the 1950s [31]

The Beach in 2019: Compare the lack of sand at the far end of the Beach with the amount in the 1950s photo [33]

The Slipway

There is a record from 1931 of a discussion between the Boatyard and the Board of Trade regarding the installation of a pontoon. In 1938 there was an application by Nunn's Boatyard to build a concrete slipway and a year later they paid an annual fee of 2s 6d to the Waldringfield Fairway Committee (WFC) for its use. In 1975 the Crown Estate regularised the 'unauthorised' Boatyard slipway. The Sailing Club purchased the slipway land twice, once from the Maybush and once from the Church Commissioners when they were selling off all their land along the river bank. There was a dispute over who owned it and WSC, not unreasonably for them, wanted to ensure they couldn't be denied access for launching and retrieving of their boats.

The post visible to the right of this picture was a mooring post for securing boats. Today it is in an area of thick mud but earlier in the 20th century it was shown as an area of sand and shingle. There were a further four large posts spread along the Beach; these date from the time when sailing barges were loaded and unloaded whilst laid up on the Beach. Waldringfield Beach was especially suitable for this type of flat bottomed boat due to its cant edge. Even at low water you can get very close into the Beach – very useful from many a yachtsman's point of view.

The Cliff

Most of the Cliff is owned by the Sailing Club having been purchased by them along with all the land not purchased by a company called the Waldringfield Hut Owners Ltd (each Hut owner purchasing a share), when the land was sold by the Church Commissioners in 2002.

It has suffered from erosion over the years but there was a Robert de Clyff living here in the 14th century which would seem to indicate that it was a prominent feature then. The Maltings was previously known as Cliff House, the Maybush Inn has also been named the Cliff Inn or the Bush Inn in the past and the main road changed from Maybush Lane to Cliff Road which would all seem to reflect the prominence of the 'cliff'. Of course, being Suffolk which is a relatively flat county the title of 'cliff' might be seen as a little ambitious. The dip in which the Sailing Club was built was a place for washing coprolite in the nineteenth century.

The steps are a relatively new feature of the cliff, having been

WALDRINGFIELD

The cliff path around 1920 [32]

1963

The river froze in 1963 [34]

enhanced with volunteer labour in the 1950s at a similar time to the river wall in front of the Waldringfield Sailing Club. You can see the path is split into two and whereas adults would go down the narrow path on the left, the children used to have great fun going down the route on the right, under the roots of the tree and sliding down. Although the modern steps are often a cause of complaint as to their unevenness this is nothing compared to the situation before they were constructed.

The Scrubbing Posts

The Scrubbing Posts are an important tool for owners of yachts and small boats that spend most of the season afloat. Algae and barnacles grow on the bottoms of these boats, especially during the warmer weather, and these need to be regularly removed, otherwise damage can be caused to the underside of the boat and it would also suffer from increased drag through the water. The owners would book a time slot on the posts with the Harbourmaster, where they can tie up alongside and wait for the tide to drop allowing access to the underside. They then have a few hours before the water returns, to scrub the bottom clean.

These were first erected before 1938 as they are mentioned in the minutes and the reports to the Parish Council.

- **1938:** A warning notice was placed on the Scrubbing Posts so they existed at this time. There was an application by Nunn's to build a 10ft to 12ft concrete hard for the Boatyard.
- **1939:** August minutes show that it was decided to have a notice board warning that the scrubbing posts were 'owners' risk'. A draft letter explaining the objects of the Fairway Committee was discussed.

In 1963 they were pushed over by ice. Presumably, they were replaced shortly afterwards. In 1978 greenheart (a very dense and strong wood) posts were installed in a concrete pad.

The famous Albert Strange-designed yawl *Sheila* on the scrubbing posts [35]

The Boatyard now offers a more expensive cleaning option during the summer, where the boat can be craned out and pressure washed underneath. A lot easier but possibly less fun!

The Dinghy Park Slipways

The first 'Admiralty' slipway was built in 1944 for the launch of the large dummy landing craft, called 'Bigbobs'. Locals describe there being a large grassy area with a pond before World War II.

The Sailing Club received permission from Canon Waller for a dinghy park in 1952, and a 'causeway' was built down to the river in 1958.

The dinghy park was later extended and new concrete slipways laid. In 2004 mesh (eco structure) was then laid between the two downriver slipways to trap mud and sand and to try and combat erosion, as shown in photo [40] on page 24.

During the winter months, the land would have been used for yacht storage. Wooden yachts have to be removed from the water during the winter to avoid being damaged by ice. This winter storage is now undertaken by the Boatyard either on the Quay itself or on overflow land behind the Cement Cottages

Winter boat storage near the slipways about 1950 [36]

More winter boat storage around the top of the Admiralty slipway probably taken in the 1960s [37]

The reservoir in 2020 looking towards the river [38]

and Maybush Inn and although many boats are now made from GRP rather than wood most owners still prefer to take them out for the winter to undertake maintenance.

The Reservoir

This was constructed in the 1960s for Dr Tom Waller although it was previously walled off to some extent to prevent Farmer Everard's cattle from straying onto the marshes. A spring and stream run from the grounds around Church Farm Cottages to a pond deep in the old river inlet. The pond then feeds into the reservoir which overflows into a continuation of the stream. This may have been the site of a mill (water) for the main Medieval Manor of Waldringfield Hilton.

Cuttings

These cuttings have been a source of debate within the history group as they obviously look man-made. Some reports say that they were the remains of the cuttings made from extracting mud for the Cement Works. They may have been mud berths for boats during the winter months and during World War II when access to the river was severely restricted, although access to them would have been difficult this far from the Beach. Or, they may simply have been left behind when mud was extracted to build or repair river walls, but again this seems unlikely as mud was normally cut from the landward side. The reservoir was not built until at least the 1960s and these cuttings were there before then. Another possibility is some form of fish trap or shellfish/oyster bed but this seems unlikely as they are not the same as any others.

They are not depicted on maps until 1925 or thereabouts; either they did not exist or they were deemed to be of no importance to the surveyors, so after much research and debate their creation and intended function remains a mystery.

In the far distance is Early Creek. This was the area where the farmers used to swim their cattle across the river to the Rocks and back when droving to market. In between can be seen the old river wall in front of White Hall and Hemley Hall farms which breached in 1937, flooding the lower farmland.

The river then slowly meanders out of the Parish on its way past Ramsholt and Kingsfleet towards the sea at Felixstowe Ferry in the far distance.

The cuttings [39]

The 'Admiralty' Slipway today showing the eco matting in place [40]

A mullet swirl [44]

Dragonfly [41]

A black-headed gull watching by the water [42]

A cormorant [45]

A rabbit on the Quay [43]

A young swallow [46]

Waldringfield before the Written Word

'There is evidence also that there were lions, bears, mammoths and woolly rhinos here. Bit of a shock in the Maybush car park on a dark and windy night.'

[47]

From 'The Early Years' presentation by
Waldringfield History Group in 2008

Coming up the River Deben in a boat or walking the river walls close to Waldringfield, one cannot avoid wondering how it must have appeared to early invaders and settlers. What would the river have looked like? Where would they have put ashore?

Of course, the river would have been completely different from that of today. Without river walls there would have been extensive marshland and deeper inlets. There would have been no island opposite Waldringfield. But, as today, there would have been sharks' teeth!

The results of a recent major archaeological exploration, carried out between 2016 and 2019

Sharks' teeth collected by Jackie Brinsley on Waldringfield Beach over the years [48]

prior to the laying of cables from an offshore wind farm, have yet to be released. However, one of the most important findings has been that of a Neolithic trackway at Seven Springs, close to Woodbridge and approximately four miles from Waldringfield. The trackway dates as far back as 4,300 BCE – showing there was human habitation in this locality then.

The East Coast and the entrance to the river would have been vastly different in times past; perhaps less easily navigated than the River Orwell. It is feasible that the Angles, who came here from North West Europe in the fifth century CE, accessed the land around Waldringfield not from the river but overland from Gippeswyk (Ipswich), at the head of the Orwell, where a vast number of Saxon artefacts have been gathered through archaeological digs. In contrast, the evidence for Anglo-Saxon settlement in and around Waldringfield is sparse.

On the other hand, Waldringfield is no more than three miles across the water from Sutton Hoo (or Haugh) where a wooden boat measuring 27m long and 4.5m wide was buried in a royal Anglo-Saxon grave (probably Raedwald, King of East Anglia) about 625 CE. It is thought that this boat had been hauled up to the Haugh from the river below, which more than suggests that the Angles were using the River Deben, as it is now known, for access to the land.

The Angles began to arrive here when the Roman governance of Britain had collapsed, and when Roman military forces had withdrawn along with many of the elite Romano-British landowners. There is evidence of Roman habitation in Waldringfield, mainly in the fields either side of Mill Lane beyond All Saints Church. Once the Romans had left, the land was sparsely populated by native Britons (by then Romano-British) who are said to have welcomed the arrival of the Angles as they had the wherewithal

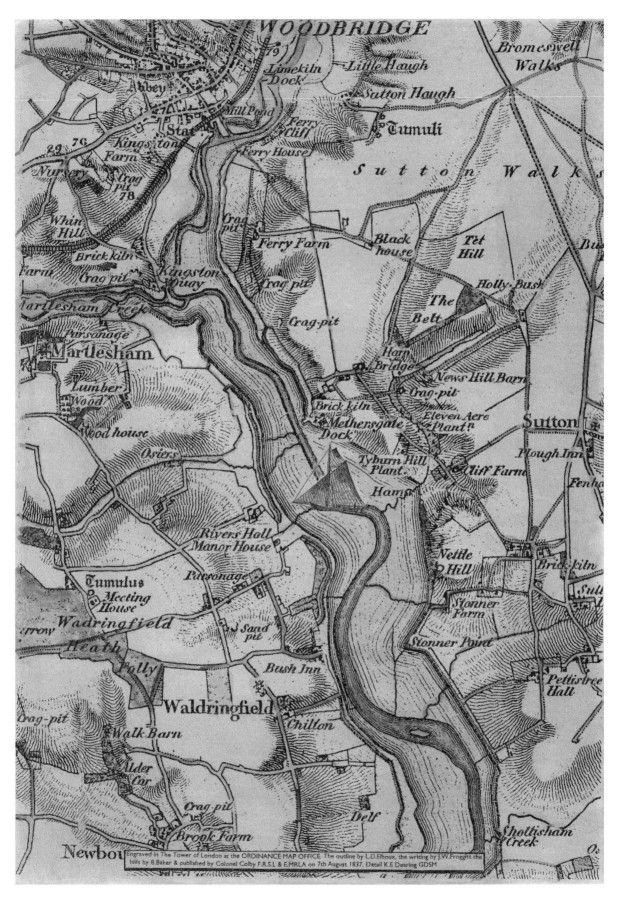

Chart of the River Deben 1837. This chart was engraved in The Tower of London at the Ordnance Map
Office and published by Colonel Colby on 7th August 1837. This chart is very important in that it shows
Waldringfield only 3.5 miles from Sutton Haugh as the crow flies, or as the navigator might traverse the
river. It also shows the similarity between the terrain on the two shores with tumuli and multiple crag pits
and sand pits. A small island is shown but it lies further south than the island which we see today [49]

to protect against attacks by Saxon pirates and other raiders.

Relatively little is known about human activity in the Waldringfield area in the period between the departure of the Roman forces and the arrival of the Normans in the 11th century except, of course, that Vikings, mainly from Denmark, began invading the East Coast in the 9th century. Those invasions took place further north than this part of East Anglia. The mouth of the Deben was so far south for them that the Vikings may well have come overland from the north or by boat past the marshes of the Wash.

Initially, the River Orwell formed the southern border of the Viking East Anglian territory although this extended later as far as the Thames. Waldringfield, at that time, was in the Kingdom of the Viking Guthrum who was christened Æthelstan when he converted to Christianity in 878 CE. He died in 890 CE after ruling East Anglia for ten years. He was succeeded by other Vikings who, interestingly, chose to continue featuring St Edmund on their coins.

There is little direct evidence of Viking influence in this part of Suffolk. Instead, it is the Court Rolls of the eleventh century which determine the nature of the settlements which gave rise to Waldringfield as we know it today.

Archaeological findings from the Waldringfield area cover all periods of history and prehistory. The river has been a major influence on human habitation and activity; it has acted as a highway for trade and the movement of people. There have been chance finds in gardens and fields (particularly after ploughing) and, more recently, through metal detecting. Features such as ditches from field systems or barrows have shown up through aerial photography. Also, the aforementioned major dig has taken place. At 48m wide and extending over 37km from Falkenham through Newbourne, Hemley, Waldringfield, Martlesham, Seckford and Bealings it was, at its inception, the largest archaeological dig in Europe.

The Prehistoric Origins of Waldringfield

100 million years ago	The chalk and flints which underly most of Suffolk were raised from the Cretaceous seabed and deposited above sea level. The amount of carbon dioxide in the atmosphere was four times greater than it is today. Most of the British Isles as we know them were covered by sea.
70 million years ago	The chalk bedrock was pushed from below and folded to form the inland hills. Clays and estuarine shelly sands such as those found at Sutton Hoo – and also inland from Waldringfield – were deposited on the surface as the eastern side of Suffolk as we know it submerged below sea level. Also submerged was the land-link to mainland Europe – what is now known as the Dogger Bank. (This land was re-exposed during the glacial and interglacial periods of the Pleistocene ice age and only re-submerged 7000 years ago.)
66 million years ago	Dinosaurs (and more than 75% of all species) went with the Cretaceous-Paleogene extinction event, following the impact of an asteroid or comet between about 7 and 50 miles wide.
2 million years ago	The start of the Lower Palaeolithic period. Early humans (genus Homo) were to be found in East Africa. The evidence suggests that they used early stone tools.
1½ million years ago	Descendants of these early humans reached Southern Europe. Simple stone tools recently excavated from Pakefield in Suffolk and Happisburgh in Norfolk show that these early humans appeared in Britain between 700,000 years ago (Pakefield) and 1.1 million years ago (Happisburgh). They arrived on foot because Britain, then, was a peninsula of the European mainland, the Dogger area having risen once again above sea-level, as described above. The connecting landmass was not the only major difference from today's geography; a pre-cursor of the River Thames flowed eastwards from its current source and then north-eastwards from the area of St Albans over much of Suffolk (including Waldringfield). Ancient gravels from this river are to be found at Waldringfield, Kesgrave and Sproughton. Another large river known as the Bytham, not now in existence, flowed out from the midlands through East Anglia, reaching the sea at Pakefield.

470 thousand years ago	The period of Anglian Glaciation. An ice sheet covered all of Suffolk except the very south-eastern part. The melting of this ice sheet left thick boulder clay known as Lowestoft Till, together with outwash gravels. The meltwaters drained east to south-east thus forming the Waveney, Gipping, Deben and Stour valleys and the basic Suffolk landscape. That landscape has been modified continuously by thawing, erosion, changes in sea level and, at the south-eastern end, subsidence. Worked flints found in the river gravels and at intact sites such as Hoxne show that early humans (directly ancestral to Neanderthals) were hunting big game in this area all those years ago.
60 thousand years ago	Members of the species to which we belong, Homo sapiens, migrated from Africa via the eastern Mediterranean. By 43,000 years ago these modern humans were colonizing Europe, including Britain, albeit intermittently, because there were several further glaciations. The last started around 28,000 years ago, reaching its zenith about 8,000 years later. This was followed by a series of rapid fluctuations of temperature. Between glaciations the land was forested. There is little evidence of human activity in Suffolk at that time – it was probably too cold! There is evidence of human activity elsewhere in central and southern Britain from 18,000 years ago and after.
15 thousand years ago	Britain was still connected physically to Denmark and the Low Countries. The river valleys were deeper and the sea level was 60 metres lower than it is now. There was even more glacial outwash gravel over most of the southern Suffolk peninsula. All the eastward flowing rivers would have joined the Thames and the Rhine and then flowed westwards into the English Channel. More hunters came by land from the Low Countries. Complex, highly organized hunting societies lived in areas which have since been identified. One such area has been found near the lower reaches of the River Gipping, near Bramford Road in Ipswich. Distinctive flints have been found. There have been isolated finds from this period at Martlesham Creek and on the Foxhall Road.
6500 BCE	Britain became an island. One thousand years later the sea level rose further. There were mixed oak and evergreen forests over most of the island. Humans of this Mesolithic period continued a complex hunter-gatherer existence. They hunted locally at this time as evidenced by isolated local finds, including a stone axe just inland from Waldringfield. These hunters seem to have exploited riverside and lakeside environments, using them for spearfishing and as a source of flints. The first boats were carved-out tree trunks. The New Stone Age (Neolithic) and its associated culture which developed 6 ½ thousand years ago, about 4500 BCE, was markedly different in that arable and animal husbandry had been introduced to Britain from the European mainland. Humans lived in stone huts with turf roofs in protected communities or settlements. They made ceramic pots and kept dogs and herd animals. Settlements were mainly in regions of light soils – within a mile or so of watercourses and river valleys and in the sandlings of south-east Suffolk. It is very likely that the area represented by Waldringfield was populated by then as it fulfils all those criteria. However, the population would have been sparse.

The most common artefacts from the past are the shark teeth which may be picked at random from amongst the stones on the Beach. Shark teeth are arranged in rows inside the mouth. These rows move forward continually until they reach the front of the mouth. The teeth in the front row are then shed after about ten days, or following an attack on prey. As a consequence, shark teeth are common on any seabed where sharks exist. The majority of the teeth found on the Beach will date from the time within the last 10,000 years when the area was under the sea. Older, fossilised specimens may be as old as 50 million years; if one such is found then it is likely that it has been released from sedimentary red crag, either by erosion or by the digging for coprolite.

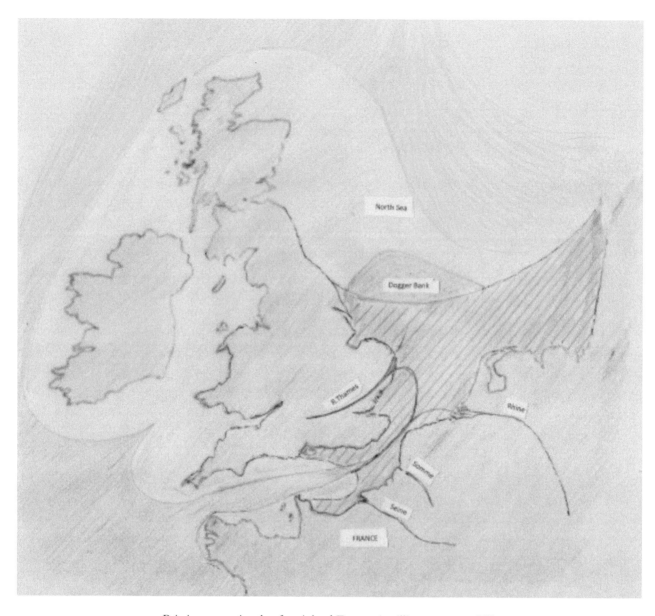

Britain as a peninsula of mainland Europe 1 million years ago [50]

A list of archaeological finds in Waldringfield derived from the Proceedings of the Suffolk Institute of Archaeology and History between 1903 and 2007 shows items from the Neolithic to the Medieval. They include: a Neolithic flint chisel and arrowhead; the base of a Bronze Age urn; Iron Age pottery and clay mould fragments; various Roman coins, brooches and a bronze figurine of Hercules; Saxon brooches; and Medieval bronze harness fittings. The Suffolk Heritage website refers to two Neolithic finds – a polished stone axe in the (Basalt)-Moore collection and a flint axe in the Hancox collection. Both these finds appear to have been made in the fields immediately to the west of the Newbourne Road.

Finds made by a local metal detectorist show a similar spread of dates and include: a Bronze Age chisel; an Iron Age coin; Roman brooches, coins and a bronze harness pendant; Medieval coins, a key and a spur; plus Georgian and Victorian coins, thimble and belt buckles.

Prior to the archaeological dig referred to previously there had been only one official excavation within the Parish of Waldringfield. This took place in October 1985, in the churchyard of All Saints Church. It followed the discovery in 1984, during the digging of a grave, of a number of fragments from fired clay moulds used to cast items of Iron Age horse harness (see [54]). The fragments were subsequently submitted to the British Museum for recording and study. To date, Waldringfield is the only site where the moulds for crescenteric terrets and quadrilobe strap unions have been found. These items were inlaid with rare coloured glass which would have been imported from the Mediterranean area. There are bird-head motifs on some of the fragments and it is these which make the artefacts 'a rare find'.

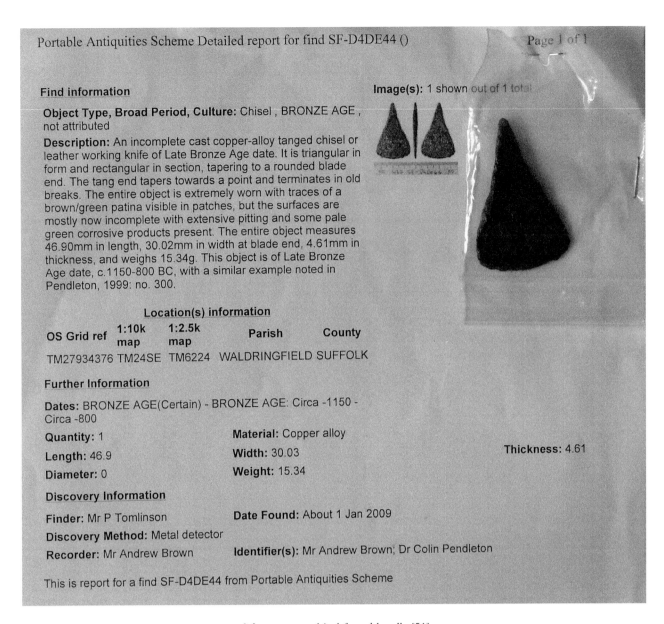

Find information

Object Type, Broad Period, Culture: Chisel , BRONZE AGE , not attributed

Description: An incomplete cast copper-alloy tanged chisel or leather working knife of Late Bronze Age date. It is triangular in form and rectangular in section, tapering to a rounded blade end. The tang end tapers towards a point and terminates in old breaks. The entire object is extremely worn with traces of a brown/green patina visible in patches, but the surfaces are mostly now incomplete with extensive pitting and some pale green corrosive products present. The entire object measures 46.90mm in length, 30.02mm in width at blade end, 4.61mm in thickness, and weighs 15.34g. This object is of Late Bronze Age date, c.1150-800 BC, with a similar example noted in Pendleton, 1999: no. 300.

Image(s): 1 shown out of 1 total

Location(s) information

OS Grid ref	1:10k map	1:2.5k map	Parish	County
TM27934376	TM24SE	TM6224	WALDRINGFIELD	SUFFOLK

Further Information

Dates: BRONZE AGE(Certain) - BRONZE AGE: Circa -1150 - Circa -800

Quantity: 1

Length: 46.9

Diameter: 0

Material: Copper alloy

Width: 30.03

Weight: 15.34

Thickness: 4.61

Discovery Information

Finder: Mr P Tomlinson

Discovery Method: Metal detector

Recorder: Mr Andrew Brown

Date Found: About 1 Jan 2009

Identifier(s): Mr Andrew Brown; Dr Colin Pendleton

This is report for a find SF-D4DE44 from Portable Antiquities Scheme

A bronze age chisel found locally [51]

The Bronze Age started between 2700 BCE and 2500 BCE; immigration from the east brought the 'Beaker people', named after their distinctive ceramics. It also brought skills with metal, first copper and gold and then bronze. This was immigration by sea and Bronze Age finds, as with Neolithic, show extensive trading networks with the continent. The River Deben and its various tributaries and landing points would have come into their own. It is very likely that there were settlements in or around Waldringfield. Again, it had all the criteria, as well as being one of the very few places where new arrivals could beach their boats. There are barrows from this time all over the south Suffolk peninsula including at Kesgrave, Foxhall, Waldringfield Heath and Newbourne. They are usually a mile or so inland from the river. Three local Round Barrows are recorded in the Suffolk Historic Environment Record, two on the junction of the Martlesham, Brightwell and Waldringfield parishes and one on Waldringfield Heath. The recent archaeological exploration, referred to before, revealed two bronze urns near to Low Farm which is situated at the entrance to the village. In the Bronze Age, boats would have been similar to coracles whilst, on land, man was using wheels.

The Iron Age started about 700 BCE when Britain experienced an influx of Celts from the Franco-Germanic borders and, possibly, from Iberia. These Celts, known to us now as Britons, and later, Romano-Britons, would eventually be pushed westwards by people of other Germanic and Eastern European stock (Angles, Saxons, Jutes and Vikings). The proximity to water was all important to the Britons and their metalwork skills. It is known that there were settlements in the Waldringfield area.

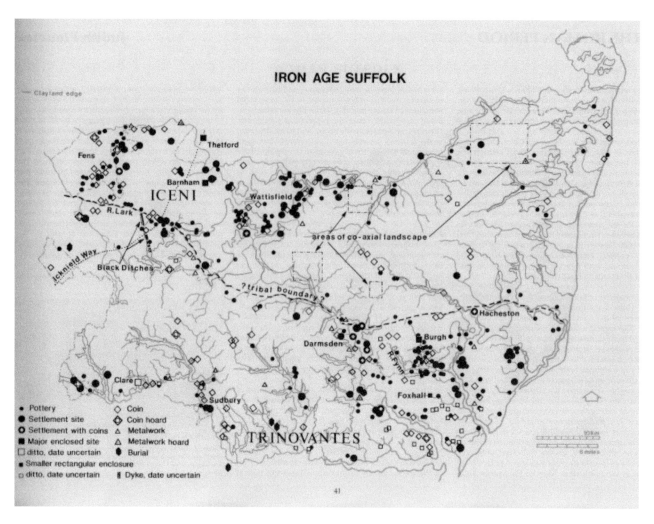

This map shows the settlements of Iron Age Suffolk including two situated either in Waldringfield or close by [52]

At first, all this immigration might have been peaceful but as the population increased so, too, did the feuding which is so often associated with the monarch-led tribes of the Ancient Britons. The Iron Age map shows very clearly the tribal boundary between the Iceni to the north and the Trinovantes to the south. That boundary passed close to Hacheston which is approximately 12 miles north of Waldringfield.

Although the Romans had come to Britain with hostile intent in the first century BCE it was not until 45 CE that they arrived in earnest with the intention of annexing Britain into the Roman empire. They made their capital initially in Colchester but gradually they spread their wings and there is no doubt from the available evidence that some of them lived in and around Waldringfield. As a civilization, the Romans were more advanced than the Britons, and once the initial conquering stage was complete they were able to teach the locals many skills. Gradually, over the generations, there developed a Romano-British culture which would only change when the Anglo-Saxons arrived.

Roman pottery – another local find [53]

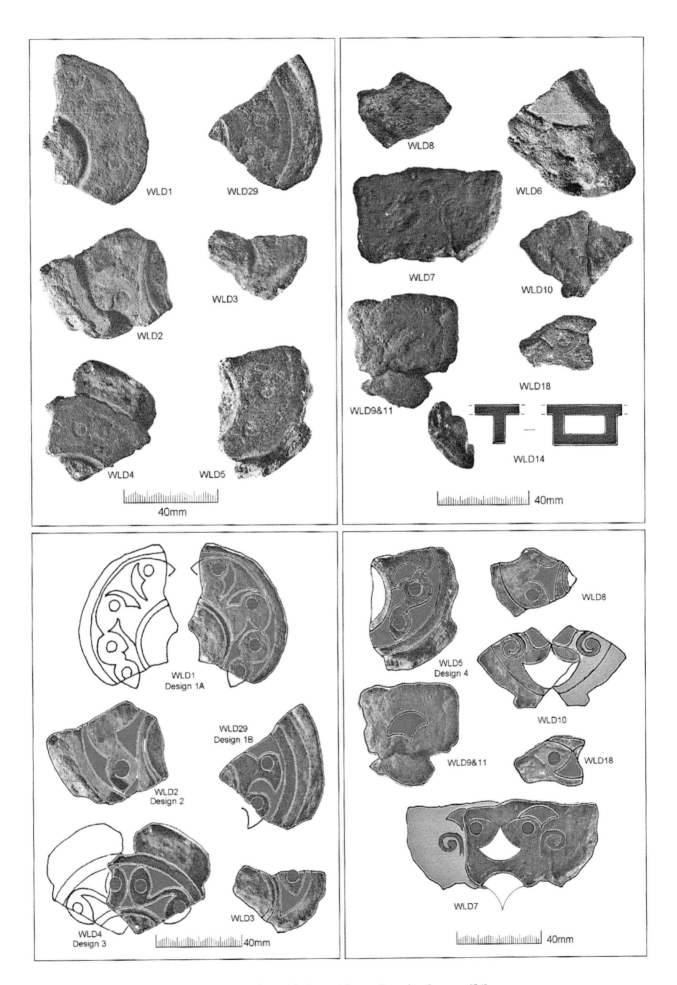

Fragments of moulds for making an Iron Age harness [54]

The Little Domesday Book, the Subsidy Returns of 1327, Court Rolls and the Manors of Waldringfield

The Little Domesday Book, covering the counties of Essex, Suffolk and Norfolk, was completed in 1086. It describes 'Waldringafelda' and 'Waldringafelda Minima'. It gives details of ownership and governance both before and after the Norman Conquest of 1066. Although all land was ultimately held for the King, part of the Waldringafeldas was also owned, pre-Conquest, by the Abbot of Bury. There were three other landholders; Beorhtmaer and his mother, Cwengifu, and a sokeman, a freeman with extensive rights. Beorhtmaer and Cwengifu were the major stakeholders in Waldringafelda Minima, although most men answerable to Beorhtmaer are recorded as having lived and worked in Newbourne and Preston. After the Conquest both the Abbot and Cwengifu retained their ownership. According to the records within the book, Robert Malet and Ranulf, both Normans, were also landholders.

The settlement of Preston, near to Cross Farm, appears to have been larger than Waldringfield. Nowadays it is nothing more than the name of a field.

The details about the Waldringafeldas suggest no more than a dozen households, say fifty inhabitants, still divided into two manors.

There are no further records until the Subsidy Returns of 1327. These provided a combined assessment of Waldringfield, Martlesham and Newbourne for the purposes of one-off taxation to finance the war in France; there were 31 registered taxpayers in the three villages and their level of tax was less than the average for the Carleford Hundred, suggesting, perhaps, that this area of Suffolk was less wealthy than other parts. The Carleford Hundred was one of twenty-one in Suffolk. About ten miles long and four to six miles wide it extended from Hasketon in the north to the Colneis Hundred in the south and from Witnesham and Tuddenham in the west to the River Deben and the Wilford Hundred in the east.

Court Rolls

There is a Court (or Manorial) Roll, dated 1356, which relates to the Manor of Waldringfield Hilton, a manor not listed before the Norman Conquest. Another Court Roll, dated 1561, refers to the Manor of Waldringfield Rivershall with no known prior reference to such a manor. It is impossible to equate with any certainty the Waldringafeldas and these two manors but on the balance of probabilities the Manor of Rivershall is the more modern version of Waldringafelda Minima and the Manor of Waldringfield Hilton is, by implication, the larger manor of Waldringafelda with its water mill and its church.

The debate is of a specialist nature which goes way beyond the scope of this book. George Arnott suggested that Lesser Waldringfield was Waldringfield Heath but cartologists would beg to differ.

It may or may not be coincidental that the name 'Rivershall' appears in documents for the first time in the sixteenth century when there is a Will, made about that time, relating to a family called Rivers.

Regarding Hilton Manor, it is stated by Copinger that in 1305 Sir Robert Hilton was the patron of the living at Waldringfield and probably Lord of the Manor. The author refers to the Manor of Rivershall being the estate of Brihtmar (Beorhtmaer), a freeman, in the pre Domesday days of Edward the Confessor and being the estate of Ranulf at the time of the Little Domesday Book.

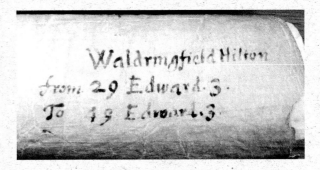

Court Roll of Edward III. Edward III was on the throne for fifty years from 1327 until his death in 1377 [55]

The 1783 map has 'Chilton Hall' marked on the site of the present-day Church Farm Cottages. The current buildings are sufficiently old to have been there at the time the map was drawn and the extra 'C' is likely to have been an error caused by the style of writing and perpetuated in subsequent publications such as the 1805 Ordnance Survey map. It may be supposed, quite reasonably, that Hilton Hall occupied the site of what is now Church Farm Cottages.

Personalities of the Manor of Hilton from the Court Roll of 1356

Manor of Hilton 1356	Inhabitants
Lord of Manor (non resident?)	William Lampet
Priest (non resident?)	Richard Taverner (of Newbourne)
Native tenant	Simon Genew Augustus Austyn Robert Koc John Seweyn/Sekeyn Edmund Wat
Landholders	John [Lawn] John [Oslok] Robert de Clyff John Gerard Richard Herman Hugh le Lytel William Pye

* A degree of poetic licence has been necessary with regard to the personalities of Hilton Manor in 1348 simply because there are no specific manorial records available prior to 1356. By then, of course, the Black Death had taken its toll although some of the names in 1356 are the same as those which appear in the subsidy returns of 1327. Interestingly the name of Richard Taverner (of Newbourne) appears in the 1356 Court Roll despite his reputed death from the Black Death and despite his replacement as the village priest by Thomas le Soler in 1349.

A Walk along the River in 1348

'Honi soit qui mal y pense.'
Edward III upon forming The Most Noble Order of the Garter on 24th June 1348

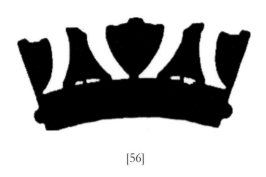

[56]

It is said that the name of the Order, and hence its motto, derived from an incident at a ball the previous year when the King's mistress supposedly dropped her garter, leading the King to pick it up and to tie it around his knee whilst saying 'May evil come to the one who has impure thoughts.'
In French of course.

Why Choose a Walk in 1348?

Although there are various opinions about the dates of origin of the river walls it is reasonably safe to assume that they were not in existence before the 14th century. On balance it is likely that in 1348 the River Deben would have been in its natural state with a wide entrance to the sea and inland navigability beyond Melton. The geography would have been so different that both Newbourne (Newebourne) and Brightwell (Brythwelle) would have been navigable for ships.

In 1347 the traffic on the river is likely to have been extraordinarily busy as the year-long siege of Calais did not end until August of that year and the garrisons were supplied from Goseford, the busy port at the mouth of the river. Inevitably the port of Woodbridge and various access points along the river, including Waldringfield, would have been involved in the supply chain.

By June 1348 the second pandemic, the Black Death, reached the south coast of England, ready to spread in all directions north including East Anglia. The world would never be the same again.

In the Spring of 1348 matters political and social were relatively stable. Edward III had been on the throne for 21 years but, still only 35 years old, he was a young and enthusiastic King. He was born at Windsor Castle in 1312 and acceded to the throne at the age of fourteen by which time he was already married to Queen Philippa who was of similar age. Edward ruled England, Wales, parts of Scotland and parts of France. He was a good leader of men with a very supportive Queen.

There had been major battles at both ends of the Kingdom with the Scots fighting for independence since 1332 and the French fighting over succession to the French throne since 1337. Only two years before our walk King Edward, aided by his teenage son (later referred to as the Black Prince), led his men to an impressive victory at Crécy. Then, very soon after, they went on to lay the siege at Calais. All this warfare led to high levels of taxation. Weather extremes and crop failures also contributed to quite a lot of hardship. Nevertheless, in the early months of 1348 most citizens had a feeling of reasonable well-being.

The great famine of 1315-1317 and Edward II's disastrous reign were history. There was encouraging news from abroad. Things were looking relatively good.

It seems, therefore, that the first half of 1348 would be an opportune time to take a representative look at this very special shoreline.

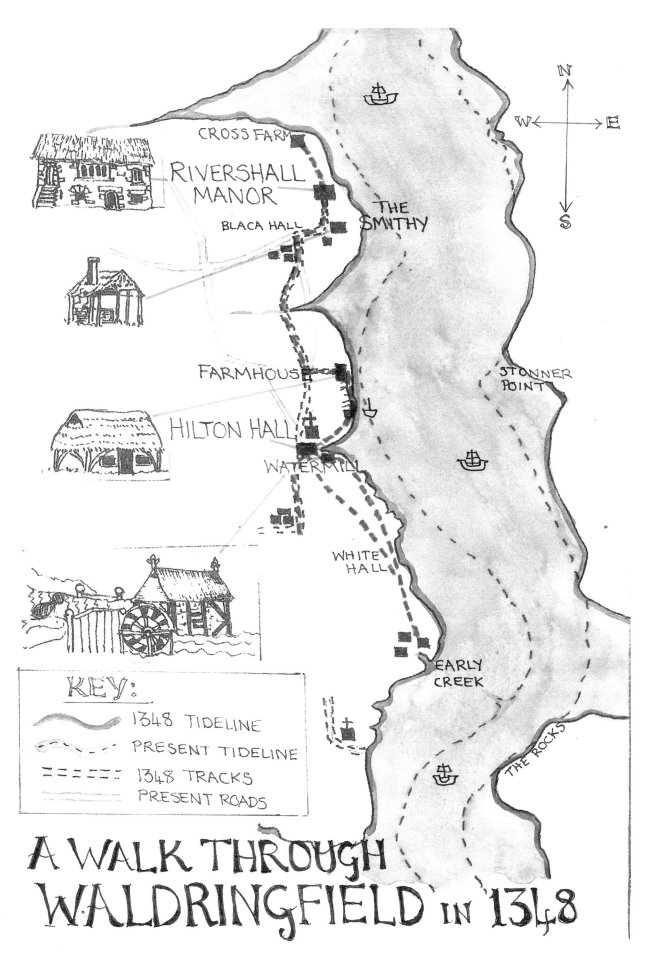

CROSS FARM

RIVERSHALL MANOR

BLACA HALL

THE SMITHY

STONNER POINT

FARMHOUS

HILTON HALL

WATERMILL

WHITE HALL

EARLY CREEK

THE ROCKS

KEY:

1348 TIDELINE

PRESENT TIDELINE

1348 TRACKS

PRESENT ROADS

A WALK THROUGH WALDRINGFIELD IN 1348

[57]

A typical medieval manor house [58]

Time for a Stout Walk

It is 1348; almost three hundred years have passed since the Norman Conquest and the recordings of the Little Domesday Book. There are no maps or documents on which to base our observations; a certain degree of speculation is required. Certainly, the village and its shoreline are not as they will be in 2020. There are no walls (mud banks) to contain the great river. The mouth of the river is wide so that tidal flows are vastly different to what they will become in the future. The natural shoreline makes for creeks and bays where there will be none once the river walls are built. For Waldringfield this means a creek to the immediate north, a creek toward the south, just below the church and, in the middle, a wide bay encroaching on an area which will, one day, be called Lower Road or Sandy Lane.

We have put ashore on the southern side of a creek about half a mile north of the northern boundary of the Waldringfield manors. Let us call it Preston Creek as the area is known as Preston (Priests' Town). There are a couple of settlements here, one just out of sight at the top of the hill, the other actually very close to the manorial boundary and only a short distance from the shoreline. It is called Cross Farm, or it will be in the future, if not now.

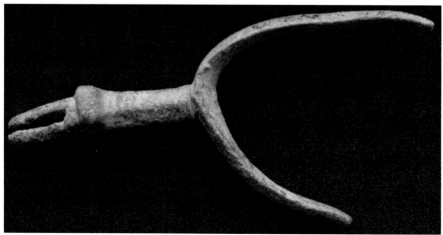

Medieval spur [59]

Edward III Seal with Hulc [60]

From the settlement, close to the riverbank there is a commanding view back up-river to Wudebrige where, for almost 200 years, there has been a mill run by Augustinian canons. Directly across the half-mile width of water are the cliffs of Sutton, recently eroded to some extent by the ravages of repeated violent storms which, only last year, caused almost half of the town of Dunwich to slip into the sea.

Turning back on to our intended path, across the field to the south, in a dip in the land we can just see the thatched roof of the Manor of Rivershall. Here, coming towards us, is a young man in his twenties who greets us in unfamiliar language. He has just returned from a military posting in Calais so his 'middle English' is very heavily corrupted by Norman French. The official language of the English Parliament and the Courts is currently French but the King is intent on changing that to English. The people here tend to speak in a very local dialect of middle English which is a mix of Anglo-Saxon and Norman French. The young man has many tales to tell of Crécy and Calais. He invites us into the Manor House to take ale with his father.

In order to reach the Manor we have to cross a stream which drains water from the heathlands into the main river. What an ideal situation they have here with access to fertile land, to grazing and to fishing in the river. We take ale and bid 'God spede' to the master and his son whose names we did not catch

– perhaps it was 'Rivers'? Even from our privileged position of being able to see into the future we do not know when this settlement was first called Rivershall – we do know that there are, in later records, references to Rivershall Way (1579) and to the will of Thomas Rivers (1675).

From the Manor we continue in a southerly direction along a bridle path which turns sharply to the west just beside a small smithy. The blacksmith is busy so we will not disturb him – again we do not know his name but we are aware that the above-mentioned Thomas Rivers left some money to Thomas Rivers, the son of Anthony Rivers, blacksmith. We know also, from census information and newspaper advertisements, that there was a wheelwright living and working at this very spot in the 19th century. Perhaps, instead, the blacksmith was Roger Tidy who, together with Juliana Tidy, was obliged in 1367 to do 'horse carrying works' for the Lord of the next manor, the Manor of Hilton. Various pieces of metal are lying around by the smithy including a spur, a belt mount and a Germanic counter. Lo and behold, there scattered on the ground are a few coins; there are two Edward III silver pennies and a half groat. It is very tempting to pick them up but we had best leave them for the blacksmith to find. Perhaps they dropped from the pouch of Richard Taverner, the priest. He often passes this way – so does William Lampet, Lord of the Manor of Hilton.

1839 Tithe map extract showing the position of Blaca's Hall (34) and the Wheelwrights (smithy) (43) [61]

An artist's impression of the creek to Hilton by Kit Clark [62]

To our right as we walk in a westerly direction from the smithy, there is a field once known as 'Blaca's Hall' (Blaxhall in more modern times). This is an Anglo Saxon name indicating that Blaca had his home here. To our left, to the south of the bridle path the field slopes very gently toward a wide bay, the waters of which extend inland to cover an area which, in future centuries will be dry land, traversed by the afore-mentioned Lower Road / Sandy Lane.

Our route takes us toward what will one day be called The Street and, later still, Fishpond Road. Even in the 21st century this will be the area of the village where the oldest domestic properties (Rose Cottage and Dairy Farm) stand but they will not be built for another two to three hundred years. There are homesteads there now, benefiting from easy access to the river and a constant source of fresh spring water. We leave them to our right as we walk around the edge of the bay, crossing a widespread stream which drains into the waters of the Deben. The land is marshy and we have to pick our way carefully. One day, a gentleman by the name of Joe Lubbock will describe this stream as it courses down from School Road close to four cottages that will be built there in the 20th century.

A typical water mill in Medieval Times. It is probable that the mill wheel at Hilton was under-shot like above and maybe driven by the tides [63]

Water mill pond in summer [64]

A glance into the bay shows a 'cog' at anchor waiting to be loaded with bales of wool bound for Flanders. These cogs, and hulcs too, are vessels which trade not just from busy ports like Dunwich and Goseford but also from trading posts in the river including, of course, Wudebrig and Waldringafelda. The river can be busy at times especially when King Edward gathers his fleet at Goseford. Occasionally we will see a balinger out there. With its single sail, complemented by thirty oarsmen, speed is its trademark. They are used as frigates by the navy but they are also used by pirates. Although we use the term 'navy' it has to be said that there are very few ships in it; the major part of King Edward's fleet is made up of commandeered cogs.

Cogs have been plying European waters since the ninth century but they have become much more commonplace in the last two centuries. There is one depicted on the seal of Ipswich which dates from 1200 CE. Features may vary but, essentially, cogs are built, not on a frame but by planking first. The planking is clinkered (overlapping) as shown so clearly in the Ipswich seal. The vessel is double ended or, for landlubbers, sharp at both ends. There is a single mast which is stepped amidships (i.e. arising from the centre of the vessel). The bow and the stern post are straight raked and there is a centreline rudder.

Hulcs tend to be larger in that they can carry greater volumes of cargo. The main difference between hulcs and cogs lies in the planking which, in a hulc, does not stop at the bow and stern posts but curves upward to end at a horizontal line well above the waterline.

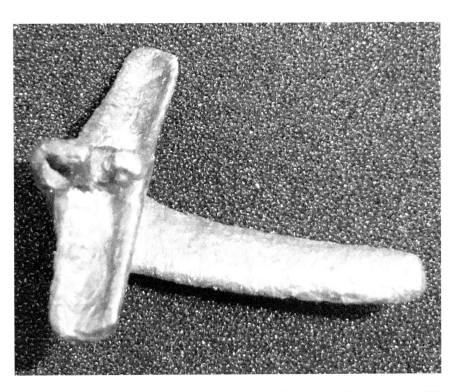

First century Roman brooch [65]

The seal of Ipswich (c. 1200) [66]

This tends to give the vessel a more curved shape. There is one depicted on the King's new seal.

But best to get on with our walk. The wide stream emptying into the bay occupies the bottom of quite a wide valley which divides the Manor of Rivershall from the Manor of Hilton. Once over the stream we ascend the southern side of the valley as far as a track which, one day, will be called Cliff Road. A track leads off to the south west toward All Saints Church which is now just over fifty years old.

William Lampet, Lord of the Manor of Hilton, has sent John Gerard to greet us; he holds land in the Hilton Manor. He gives us the choice of going toward the Church which stands atop the steep northern bank of the Hilton inlet or going eastwards to re-join the shoreline at the edge of the bay. We choose to walk eastwards to the shore.

At the end of the track, to our right and at the edge of the river is a farmhouse, also the home of the ferryman who is able to take passengers over to Stonner Point or other destinations on the eastern shore, such as Methersgate, Ramsholt or Shottisham Creek. It may even be the home of Robert de Clyff

839 Edward III half Groat and Penny [67]

Medieval belt mount [68]

about whom, in due course, we will have information from Court Rolls. We have a sixth sense that one day this farmhouse will be an alehouse and that it will be called 'Bush Inn' or 'The Maybush'. To our left, there is saltmarsh. Beyond, in the shallows, there are fish traps which are flat bottomed baskets woven from brown withies.

Further upstream, around the point, there is a kiddle or wooden weir used to trap fish on the falling tide.

As we walk along the edge of the river just below the farmhouse, the land to our right rises so that there is proper cliff formation. There are one or two small storage huts at the base of the cliff and on the Beach there is a vessel being loaded with hemp. This will be taken up-river to Wudebrig where there is a good market for it. The early harvest is used for the making of linen whilst the rougher, later harvest may be used for cordage and for the making of canvas.

John Gerard is proud of his native Waldringafelda but sees it as no different to any other agricultural village. He makes no reference to its nautical connections. The smallholding peasants who live here produce hemp, barley and rye; they rear sheep mainly for the wool and, of course, there is always the family cow.

Passing along the top of the low cliff in a southerly direction we can see the Church on the horizon to our right. To our left, again, a wide expanse of water with shallows but no island between here and Stonner Point. After a few hundred yards the cliff top, albeit lower than it was at the farmhouse, passes around to the right in a south westerly direction thus marking out the northern side of Hilton Creek. This goes inland right up to the base of the steeply sloping land next to the Church and Hilton Manor.

Here there is a spring and close by a watermill, which was mentioned in the Domesday Book.

We linger awhile to see how the mill works and how the miller uses an eel trap in the water course, but then we decide to climb the creekside path up to Hilton Manor, a building not dissimilar to the one in which we took ale earlier in our walk. Time perhaps for another.

But, wait, as we pass the edge of the churchyard we can see the priest, Richard Taverner, conducting the burial of a small simple coffin – another infant death. They occur so frequently. What we know from our ability to predict is that Richard, himself, will be dead within 12 months, taken by a pandemic known as the Black Death which by June of this year had made its way from China to Continental Europe and was now about to devastate the population of England, Wales, Scotland and Ireland.

From Hilton Manor we can re-access the water's edge by walking down the southside of Hilton Creek. It is far less steep which makes for easier walking. As we round the corner to face south we see ahead of us a vast expanse of water bounded on the east by the creek at Shottisham and a beach, later to be called the Rocks, and on the west by the muddy shore of Hemley Bay and Early Creek, the latter marking the southern extent of Hilton Manor.

We reckon that by the nineteenth century the western shoreline will have been marked by trees and that by the twentieth century they would have died because of repeated exposure to the elements and to the waters of the Deben. There are scattered dwellings

Paul Tomlinson, local metal detectorist who has been responsible for several significant finds around Waldringfield. All detecting is carried out with the permission of the relevant landowner with whom any finds are discussed [69]

in this area. It is possible that, in the future, artefacts such as a Roman brooch, a fourteenth century key and coins, including an Iron Age Norfolk Wolf coin, will be found here.

There are alternative routes to the one we have taken to the southern boundary of the Manor. The most direct would have been down Hilton Way (to be named Mill Road in later centuries) as far as the track to Hemley and the Manor of Hapsley. There is a small community of dwellings on the right hand side of Hilton Way just before it intersects the boundary. Alternatively we might have taken a south-easterly track across the fields towards an area later to be called White Hall where, incidentally, more artefacts will be found, and then across more fields to the river's edge at Early Creek.

The Parish Church of All Saints

All Saints Church circa 1917 [70]

The Parish Church of All Saints is the oldest surviving building in the village. However, it is the site of the building, as much as the building itself which warrants attention. Standing about ½ mile south of the main part of the modern village, it is immediately adjacent to the site where Hilton Manor once stood. It is likely that a thousand years ago, or even more, early Christians took over a pagan burial-site in order to build a place of worship. The findings of a Bronze-age burial-urn and Roman shards in the churchyard indicate activity on the site long before the arrival of Christianity.

Once a decision had been made to build a place of worship it is likely that the materials would have been transported by boat into the creek which, then, before the construction of river walls, lay immediately below the site.

Construction is likely to have commenced in the second half of the thirteenth century. The tower, with its small, mellow Tudor bricks, was added in the late 1400s / early 1500s. There is but one bell, three of the original four having been sold in 1811 to raise funds for repairs and the provision of box pews.

The building of the present church was started in the late thirteenth/early fourteenth centuries, as evidenced by the single trefoil-headed window of the late 1200s in the nave to the west of the porch and, on the south side of the chancel, two windows dating from the early 1300s. The font, still in use today, is thought to be about 600 years old. It is very likely that the heavy stones and other materials involved in the construction were lifted from boats by a block and pulley system.

The Parish and its Church are documented in ecclesiastical records from the 13th century. The clergy who have served the Parish can be traced back to 1305 and there is a list of recorded Rectors on the north wall of the nave. Little is known about those listed before the middle of the eighteenth century. Since 1744 there have been only ten Rectors of whom five have borne the surname 'Waller'; four of those were successive generations of the same local land-owning family.

The Reverend Thomas Henry Waller was the first of these, being the incumbent from 1862 to 1906. He was responsible for an extensive restoration of the Church in 1864 during which the current east wall and its window were constructed. The East window is sometimes known as the Coprolite Window because the restoration was largely funded by proceeds from the extraction of coprolite from pits in and around Waldringfield.

Thomas Henry kept a perennial diary which has served to inform local historians on many matters including the coprolite extraction. He retired to the Old Rectory (now Rivers Hall) and lived until 1920. The glass in the tower's west window was given in 1923 in memory of him, his wife Jane who predeceased him in 1916 and their grandson, Lieutenant Thomas Waller who was killed in action near Ypres in 1917 (although the window mistakenly records the place of death as Arras).

13th-century single trefoil window in south wall of the nave [71]

Thomas Henry's son, the Rev Canon Arthur Pretyman Waller, took over the incumbency in 1906 and saw the Parish through two World Wars, retiring in 1948 to Mill Cottage where he lived until his death in 1964. His great interest was entomology and his collection of moths is kept at Ipswich Museum.

In 1935 the Rev Canon Trevor Waller, Arthur's son, became vicar of Debenham, but in 1948 he moved down-river to take over from his father. He was a keen and expert sailor who kept a 4-ton sloop on the Deben. He retired in 1974 to White Hall Cottage and died in 1994. It was the Rev Trevor who commissioned his Churchwarden, Mr EA Nunn, to extend the chancel three feet into the nave in order to accommodate the choir, such was its size.

Trevor Waller's son, John, became the incumbent in 1974 and remained so until his death in 2013. Described by the Rev Roy Tricker as a '...one-off' priest, who ploughed his own eccentric furrow throughout his ministry, with his gruff Suffolk voice, his wealth of hilarious stories, his love of the sea and of his boat *Jesus*, touched the lives of thousands – ruffling the occasional ecclesiastical feather, but warming many a churched and non-churched heart!' There is now a wetlands bird sanctuary to his memory behind the river wall to the north of the village.

The earliest memorial in the Church is a ledger slab in the chancel floor – placed in memory of Richard Frost who died in 1741. Commemorations in the Church include coprolite merchant and farmer, William Kersey (died 1887), the Rev Thomas Henry Waller and parishioners who served in the two Great Wars. Also commemorated are four parishioners who died in the First World War. There are memorials to Captain Francis Waller (1855), Major Bertram Glossop (died 1941) and his wife, Helen, Rear Admiral George Cresswell (died 1967) and his wife Katherine and Sir William Lawrence Bragg, eminent physicist and Nobel Laureate Scientist (died 1971) and his wife Alice.

The Maybush

*'No pleasanter spot can be found than in the old bar-parlour with its heavy oak beams
…and the quaint spinner on the ceiling.'*

WG Arnott, 1968

[72]

The village pub, 'The Maybush', was originally a farmhouse, probably just 30ft x 14ft with great thick walls according to Arnott. Standing in the road alongside the pub, one is able to see a central section of wall built of little red bricks which suggest an origin around the middle of the 15th century. It is likely that this is one end of the rectangular structure described by Arnott. Once inside the building, close to the bar, it is easy to trace the 'thick' side-walls, even today after many extensions to the building.

Almost certainly the Maybush was an Inn when it was first licensed around 1745. For a century it had remained the 'Cliff Inn' but by 1844 it had mysteriously become known as 'The Bush'. Then by stages it became the 'The May Bush' and 'The Maybush' as it is today.

The first recorded landlord was Daniel Button, in 1833, but he was already 62 years of age and may well have been in post for some years prior, possibly some decades, thus taking the history back into the 18th century. He was followed in 1845 by Robert Salter whose two children were christened in Waldringfield All Saints Church. The subsequent landlord, William Gooding (1848 – 1855) was described not only as an innkeeper but also as a coal merchant, perhaps

providing the first recorded hint of commercial waterborne transport. Certainly, within twenty years there was a building erected near the Quay for the purpose of storing coal.

The next tenants, George and Caroline Hunt, were to set a tenancy record which still stands: 48 continuous years between them. George Hunt was the landlord from 1856 until his death in 1891; he was followed by his wife, Caroline, who continued in post for another thirteen years until 1904. The couple had eleven children over the course of 21 years.

On one occasion, early in their tenancy, in 1857, the normal function of the Bush Inn was set aside for an 'Inquisition' (Inquest) to be held before a 'Most Respectable Jury'. A warrant had been issued for the exhumation of the remains of one David Rush, labourer of the Parish, following the dissemination of a report that he had been poisoned by his wife. Examinations had been carried out both locally and at Guy's Hospital in London; sealed glass specimen jars were presented in evidence, their contents being described in gory detail, and with some suspicion, by the press. A dramatic climax was anticipated but the verdict was 'death by natural causes'.

The last twenty years of the nineteenth century were, according to Walter Tye, probably the most exciting days for the Maybush. Coproliters, cement workers and bargemen were its chief patrons and Caroline Hunt was the hostess. The pub was open all day and, at night, Mrs Hunt provided sleeping accommodation for twelve workers, some of whom travelled considerable distances over land and water to work in Waldringfield. The busiest time of the day was said to be 11am when dusty-throated workmen would crowd into the tap-room where three dozen pints of ale would be waiting. At weekends lively competitions of quoits or skittles would often end with fights outside; Jack Stebbing, skipper of the barge *Kingfisher* and champion bruiser of Waldringfield was the usual winner.

The Maybush c. 1910. The pile of bricks below the bay window and the pantiles stacked on the ground suggest recent renovation at that time [73]

Punch-up outside the Maybush by Kitty Moss (member of the Waldringfield Thursday Art Group) [74]

The Ipswich Journal

25 Jul 1857

In consequence of a report having been spread about that David Rush, a labourer in that Parish, who had died very suddenly on the 6th and buried on the 8th instant was supposed to have been poisoned by his wife, Mr Wood on the 10th inst., at the request of the minister and churchwardens of that Parish, issued his warrant to have the body exhumed and instructed Mr George Washington Tailer and Mr John Stearn Gissing, surgeons, to make a post mortem examination of the body. On the 15th instant the inquest was held upon the body at the Bush Inn at Waldringfield before a most reasonable jury: when William Moles, a Waldringfield labourer deposed that he knew the deceased and had done so for several years [[...]].

The three medical men agreed in their opinion that deceased died from the effect of intense inflammation of the stomach and intestines; how that inflammation was produced they were not prepared to say, but recommended that the stomach and some other portions of the

inside of the deceased should be analysed by some eminent man. The inquest was therefore adjourned until the 22nd inst., and in the meantime the portions of the body chosen by the surgeons were inclosed in jars, and taken, by the direction of the Coroner, to Dr Alfred S Taylor, Professor of Chemistry, at Guy's Hospital, for analysis.

On the 22nd instant the adjourned inquest was held when the report from Dr Taylor was read to the jury on their re-assembling. In his report Dr Taylor stated that ...he had tested the same for mineral and other poisons, but could not detect the presence of either. ...Mr John Stearn Gissing was then examined, and stated that he fully concurred in the statement of Mr George W Tailer, and in the report of Dr Alfred S Taylor, and was of the opinion that the deceased died from natural causes.

The jury being of the same opinion returned a verdict accordingly.

The late George Turner's sign in the Maybush bar [75]

The Twizzler [76]

George Turner and daughter Peggy in one of
his rowing boats on the beach [77]

Jimmy Quantrill, with his wife, Edith May, took over from Mrs Hunt. Jimmy had been skipper of a Paul's barge (The *May*); frequently he would bring supplies to the Cement Works and take coprolite and farming products such as grain and straw to other destinations on the east coast, or to London. He would recount the experience of bargemen fighting for a cargo at the London dockside. It is not surprising that, like Jack Stebbing, he was reputed to have pugilistic skills which enabled him to keep strict order at 'The Maybush'.

Jimmy and Edith had a daughter, Hilda May.

Jimmy Quantrill left the Maybush after ten years to take over the Butt and Oyster at Pin Mill. He was succeeded at the Maybush by Walter Thompson who was there as tenant from 1916 until 1922. He was followed by George Thomas Turner – 'Uncle George' to all and brother to Hilda's first husband, Edward Cecil Turner. This George Thomas Turner arrived with his own nautical connections, having been a crewman, possibly the cook, on King George V's record-breaking J-class yacht *Britannia*. His father and his brother were also crew members.

Uncle George retired to 'The Guesthouse' (now called Deben House) in Cliff Road where his wife, Grace, served cream teas on the lawn. George hired rowing boats from the beach and there is testimony to that activity in a sign which still hangs above the bar, not far from the aged Twizzler.

Fun was to be had spinning the Twizzler which still remains mounted in the ceiling in the oldest part of the pub. The Twizzler was used as a points scoring game with three goes each. It is said to have been George Turner's party piece to be able, from standing, to spin it with his foot. Younger generations of the Turner family are able to make similar claims – it must be in the genes!

Then came another Grace – Gracie Hill, with her husband, Albert. They ran the Maybush as tenants for 34 years from 1934.

In the days of Albert and Gracie Hill the pub was virtually a second sailing-club-house, most especially during the Easter week-end and Deben Week. Sailing Club winter committee meetings were held in the tenants' private living room. This was all to do with licensing and Sunday restrictions on the Sailing Club. The pub was also the social club for the beach huts' 'Arab Quarter' and for the touring caravans parked on the slopes above the pub – the post-industrial days. Those were the days when Carl Giles, the famous cartoonist, was a regular at the bar.

During the Hills' tenancy (and during that of their successors, the Dearings) it was usual on Christmas Eve for the locals to gather for a sing-song and a Xmas Club raffle. There would be a buffet and a free round of drinks provided by the landlord.

Part of Albert Hill's poster campaign [78]

This photograph, brought back from Holland by Mike Nunn, shows Gracie and Albert Hill together with Albert's parents, Bob and Elizabeth and a lady who has not been identified. The picture was taken, probably in 1947, by the late Siem Kroes, a Dutch yacht builder from Kampen on the IJsselmeer; he was a regular visitor to Waldringfield, by boat of course, for over 60 years, and his family still visit [79]

The Bush Inn, circa 1880 [80]

The Maybush pile of pennies. This was very heavy and customers were asked to hold a surrounding
blanket when it was knocked over. Such was the weight that the four blanket holders lurched forward
and collapsed in a heap, much to the amusement of all those assembled, including Giles [81]

Albert and Grace Hill [82]

Albert and Gracie Hill were the last of the non-catering landlords at the Maybush. They retired in 1968 to the 'Moorings' on Cliff Road.

They were followed at the Maybush by Bob and Ron (Veronica) Dearing who were responsible for the introduction of, first, the toasted cheese or ham sandwich and, later, meals cooked in-house.

Peter and Marjorie Broughall took over in 1980

and continued the expansion of the Maybush kitchen. They introduced a loudspeaker system which was relayed outside and was known sometimes to disrupt the Saturday dinghy racing. The story goes that an announcement from the bar that 'Number 42 – your meal is at the food counter' caused the skipper of Dragonfly 42 to up his helm and recross the start line despite having made a perfectly timed start to a race.

1996 was not the finest year for the Maybush but the history of the establishment would not be complete without mention of it. A feud between the new landlord, Richard Farley, and some people of the village was reported in the press and Waldringfield was falsely labelled by the said landlord as an 'evil village'.

Fortunately the episode was brief and in 1997 the current tenants (now known as Deben Inns) took over and led the Maybush back to sunnier times with menus today which would have left the old guard totally amazed.

RETURN OF THE TALL SHIPS
PAGES 14 & 15

BATTLE FOR THE ASHES
TEST MATCH PREVIEW PAGE 41

A SUPERB COMPETITION FOR COUNTRY GARDEN OWN

I'M QUITTIN 'EVIL' VILLAG

Landlord resigns as pub conservatory bid denied

by JON WELCH

A PUB landlord is quitting picturesque Waldringfield, branding it "the most evil village in the world", after receiving a succession of malicious calls and letters

Richard Farley announced his resignation as licensee of the Maybush yesterday after councillors threw out proposals to build a £30,000 restaurant extension at the historic riverside pub.

The chocolate-box village, with its gently bobbing sailing boats and views across the River Deben, is not the sort of place one might associate with evil, but Mr Farley yesterday insisted dark forces were at work in Waldringfield.

Mr Farley, 45, claims he and his wife Michelle have received abusive phone calls in the early hours of the morning during the past two weeks, as well as anonymous letters.

His claims that the village is evil were last night dismissed as "absolutely ridiculous nonsense" by district councillor June Metcalfe.

She condemned the letters and phone calls, calling them "thoroughly unpleasant and totally unnecessary", but said they were likely to

be from a "sick" person rather than part of an orchestrated hate campaign.

"I find the people of Waldringfield extremely easy to talk to, but you can't bully them. I find them very courteous. I have got a lot of friends there and they all help each other," she said.

Mrs Metcalfe said Mr Farley's decision to quit Waldringfield was a matter for him alone, but said the restaurant application would have been approved had it not been for its riverside frontage.

Michael Atkins, chairman of Waldringfield Parish Council, also denied villagers were evil

Continued on Page 10

LEAVING FOR GOOD: Richard Farley, landlord of the Maybush at
Photo

The *East Anglian Daily Times* reports dissent between the 'Evil' Village of Waldringfield and the then landlord of the Maybush in 1997 [83]

It is easy to visualise that solid little farmhouse presiding over a scene in which, for four hundred years, the only things to change were the tides, the skies and the seasons. Perhaps it provided a base for a ferryman.

Then, suddenly, there was industrialization – the recovery of coprolite, the manufacture of cement and the carrying of bulk cargo by barge. This was followed, almost immediately, by the internal combustion engine which not only powered the movement of goods but also brought undreamed-of mobility to an ever expanding Suffolk population, some of whom were into sailing and other water-based pastimes. Others, of course, were into walking, bird-spotting and even caravanning.

Whatever the pastime there was a strong possibility that a visit would involve the Maybush.

"There's always something sad about the last Sail of the Season."

The cartoonist Giles donated many of his cartoons to local causes [84]

The Maybush today – from the water [85]

Owd Boys

Dick Elvin [86]

George Jones had left Waldringfield on August Bank Holiday 1939 with no idea that it would be several years before he returned. Early in 1944 he managed a brief visit after his return from Sierra Leone, where he had been serving at Freetown, before taking up his new post at HMS *Badger* (Harwich). He found the Deben oddly empty, the beach defended with barbed wire, soldiers in the pub yard and the yachts laid up on the saltings. Some of the older men, First World War veterans, were undertaking local defence and patrol duties. It was good to meet them again and listen to their rich Suffolk accents and their stories.

In this fragment, typed up immediately after his visit (possibly for *Yachting Monthly*), George is careful not to mention place names. In fact he amalgamates his drinks in the Maybush with what must have been a separate visit to Woodbridge. The ferry man who is said to have been having 'a slow quick one' is almost certainly Dick Elvin and his pub would have been the Anchor, not the 'Bush'. The incident is included here partly as an additional example of 'owd' Suffolk speech, but also as exemplifying the characteristic humour with which these river folk listened to German accounts of their successes. (Deutschlandsender was the German long wave radio service.) The other men are likely to have included Jimmy Quantrill, Harry Nunn and Bob Button who had been a Chief Petty Officer in WWI.

'Take Harry for instance. He's changed. The last time I saw him, he was dressed in an old Norfolk jacket with some very, very old grey trousers, mending our trawl net. He still has the trousers, the very, very old grey trousers, but there the link with the past ends, for a peaked cap, crossed anchors and brass buttons proclaims him a Petty Officer in the Royal Navy.

There are others too, mostly longshoremen. There's a Stoker Petty Officer and a Chief with last war ribbons and good conduct badges. When they saw me they all crowded round, shaking me by the hand and patting my arm in contempt of the King's Regulations and Admiralty Instructions for the Maintenance of good order and discipline: "Hew are ye Jargie bor?" "Hew ye a-doin' on in Nivy?" and "Dew yew come an' have a drop o' Nelson's blood in owd Bush."

The Bush Inn was much the same except there was no bread and cheese and the yard was full of soldiers, eating their lunches. There was plenty of rum however and it was soon flowing as the old chaps

Jimmy Quantrill (left) in his Pin Mill days – 1924? [87]

Bob Button [88]

got into their stride. They told how bombs and magnetic mines had fallen into the river and on the saltings. "They explosions gave all the owd wimmin' hiccoughs for a fortnight, that they did." Slowly I realised that something else had changed – the yarns were taller and more hair-raising than in the piping days. I listened tensely while mines exploded beside me and innocent cows were blown to pieces on the local meadows. Visibility was much reduced by tobacco smoke so that it was difficult to make out the prickly tropical fish dangling in the corner near the dart board. Tall story followed tall story as "Nelson's Blood" did its work. "Oi remember when Oi was in the owd Abominable down in the Red Sea…"

It was nothing like this before the war. Of course there were tales I had some difficulty in believing, such as the two hundred mullet caught in one seine net in Pilots' Reach or the barge out of London River that took the wrong turning to the left past Harwich and arrived with her cargo in the Deben instead of Snape Mills…

The funniest story of all was provided by the German "News". A lone Nazi "Knight of the Air" had been over yesterday and had dropped one of those aimless bombs that causes the old ladies so much discomfort. It fell just off the ferry steps with a great splash, throwing mud about and sinking the ferryman's rowing boat. The ferryman was luckily in the Bush having a slow quick one and nobody was hurt. Years ago a barge unloading at the Maltings might have been embarrassed but there is nothing on the river nowadays.

Deutchlandsender would have none of this, however. "This is Jarminy calling! Shipping in the port of Rumblesbridge was successfully bombed. Our airmen covered themselves with honour and glory."

I turned to the Ferryman, who was drinking his usual pint of Two Beers in the corner, "What do you think of that, Dick?" He paused, put down his glass, "Well bor, Oi don't know about honour an' glory, but leastways Oi reckon he covered hisself with dutty owd river mud!"'

The Old Maltings
also known as Cliff House

[89]

'The peace of this place, the damp smells of mud and October mist, the rust and slate colours all around, and the cronk! cronk! of the Heron wading his solitary way across the marshes, is a breath of heaven after London.'

Dirk Bogarde

Situated behind the Boatyard, facing the River Deben and on the opposite side of Cliff Road to The Maybush, The Old Maltings stands in perhaps the most prominent position of the four listed buildings in Waldringfield today. The building was listed in 1983 and is described by Historic England as 'early 19th century. Red brick and black glazed pantiles. "T" plan with 20th-century wing to rear which replaced earlier wing.' There are 'brick stacks to the ridge at gable ends. 3 storeys with 2 storey wing to right and glazing bars; gauged flat brick arches.' Also described, is an 'entrance doorway with flat canopy on slender wood columns; fluted pilasters with frieze and a 6 raised and fielded panelled door.'

The house is clearly visible on the 1805 OS map and was probably constructed at the turn of the century. A detailed description is given in a Bill of Sale dated 3rd November 1812 when the house was sold at auction in the Fleece Inn, St Matthew's Street, Ipswich. The sale details mention a substantial red brick dwelling house containing two good parlours alongside an adjoining brick built malt office, stables, cart and cinder house, granary with hayloft over, a large coal house and yard and two enclosures containing 1.5 acres of good arable land.

The Old Maltings or 'Cliff House' at that time, was clearly a most significant building and its pleasant situation has attracted a number of noteworthy owners and tenants. Some came to work and use the house and outbuildings to earn a living, others were drawn to the house for more leisurely reasons such as sailing and holidays. For families, its size and location have made it an ideal place to raise children. This chapter will explore some of their lives in greater detail.

The Old Maltings and its Links with the Cobbolds

In 1861, Cliff House in Waldringfield was owned by Arthur Thomas Cobbold (1815-1898). Arthur Thomas Cobbold eventually became a prominent wine and spirit merchant, councillor and citizen of Colchester. It is not known when he bought the house, but he was the proprietor at the time of the 1861 census. An inventory, made in May 1863, listed his effects and properties. These included the house, malting land and premises situated at Waldringfield and six cottages at Waldringfield alongside parcels of freehold land in Brightlingsea, a house and premises in Colchester and shares in the Ipswich and Wivenhoe gaslight companies.

The Cobbold family, once farmers and maltsters, had become brewers in the early 18th century. By the early 19th century, brewing had made them rich, influential and powerful.

The Cobbold family house in Ipswich, shown here in January 2018, was also called Cliff House [90]

Cliff Brewery, Ipswich [91]

20th-century Cobbolds better known to readers today, were John Cavendish Cobbold ('Johnny') (1927-1983) and his brother Patrick Mark, (1934-1994). They were well known for their involvement in the Tolly Cobbold brewery in Ipswich formed in 1958 after a merger between 'Cobbold and Co Ltd' and 'Tollemache Brewery'. The newly enlarged company focused on beer bottling and keg production during the 1960s. The brothers were equally known for their association with Ipswich Town FC.

Arthur Thomas Cobbold, proprietor of Cliff House, Waldringfield, was the son of John Wilkinson Cobbold (1774-1860) and Harriet Temple Chevallier (1775-1851). Arthur's father (John) had inherited the family brewing and banking businesses. His mother (Harriet) was the daughter of Reverend Temple Chevallier of Aspall Hall, well known today for the family cider-making business. Between the years 1797 and 1819, Harriet gave birth to fourteen children. Arthur Thomas was the youngest son.

In the 19th century, the Cobbold family lived at Cliff House, Ipswich. This was situated next to their brewery at Cliff Quay above the River Orwell. The house can still be seen today and is an 18th-century timber-framed listed building with a tall 19th-century chimney stack.

Just round the corner from Cliff House, in Duke Street, Ipswich lived Sarah Elliston (1814-1899), daughter of a labourer and shipwright. Sarah and Arthur Thomas both came from large families but would have had very different upbringings; the Cobbolds being an influential part of the economic life of Ipswich and the Ellistons living a life of relative poverty. Sarah's father eventually died in the Union workhouse in Ipswich.

Birth certificates and baptismal records from the period show that Arthur Thomas Cobbold and Sarah Elliston eventually had ten children together.

Arthur Thomas Cobbold's parents would probably have disapproved of Sarah Elliston and social norms of the day meant that those children born to the couple out of wedlock could not be recognised. Their eldest son, Arthur James, born in 1839, initially was to have no father named on the birth certificate. It is likely that Arthur Thomas, through a sense of duty to his parents could neither marry Sarah nor could they live together as this would undoubtedly have led to scandal and Arthur Thomas possibly being disinherited.

The 1841 census shows Arthur Thomas Cobbold still living in Cliff House Ipswich with his parents, now both in their sixties. In 1841, Sarah was living as head of her own household at 13 Wykes Bishop Street, further down from Duke Street, still unmarried but now with seven children aged between 3 months and 11. Plainly money was coming from somewhere to support the growing family as on census records, her occupation is given as 'annuitant'.

Harriet Cobbold, mother of Arthur Thomas eventually died in 1851 at the age of 73 and John Cobbold died in 1860. During the next few years, Arthur Thomas and Sarah probably felt able to start living together as a family but without openly using the Cobbold name. They eventually married at St Pancras' Church, Middlesex by licence in July 1861. The witnesses came from Sarah's family. Shortly after their marriage, Arthur and Sarah took the two youngest children to be baptised in Ipswich. At this time, they had houses in Colchester, to be involved in the running of the family business there, as well as Cliff House in Waldringfield (The Old Maltings).

Cliff House, Waldringfield, was perhaps a convenient place to escape public attention and, according to an account in Sandra Berry's book, *The Cobbold Elliston Affair*, the house in Waldringfield enabled the family to change their lifestyle. Conveniently situated on the Deben, the house was used in the winter months as a base for wildfowling. Berry writes:

> *'Arthur taught his sons to use firearms intelligently and also created in them an intense interest in the wildlife found on and in the vicinity of the river'.*

A duck punt slightly up-river from Cliff House, Waldringfield, in the late 19th century passing the Cement Works [92]

Arthur and Sarah Cobbold had to sell up and leave Waldringfield in 1877 due to financial problems. Their children had to work hard for their livings but were generally successful in South America or Australia or New Zealand.

The connection to the wider Cobbold family continued through their ownership of the Maybush.

John Hill

Cliff House, Waldringfield, saw several occupants come and go throughout the 19th century but none were as industrious or longstanding as John Hill. Born in nearby Martlesham, John Hill (1827-1892) was the son of James, an agricultural labourer and Lydia Hill, née Green. At the time of the 1861 census, John, aged 34 was described as a servant and 'maltster journeyman', a journeyman being the term for a skilled worker who has completed an apprenticeship and was considered to be competent in his field. Arthur Thomas Cobbold was described as head of the house, single and a 'master maltster'.

John had married Emma Curtis from Newbourne, (1832-1892) in Woodbridge in April 1851. At the time of the 1861 census, there were three children, Sarah Ann Ellen, known as Ellen, age 8, John aged 4 and Laura age 1. Ten years later, the 1871 census records three more children, Emma, Jessie and Robert Henry. John was now head of the house and a maltster.

Thirteen-year-old John junior was an assistant maltster.

However, things were not to run smoothly for John Hill. On 2nd January 1871, Arthur Cobbold took out a mortgage on Cliff House, Waldringfield, from Henry Egerton Green and Horace Green, bankers for £2,500 to support growing problems in the family wine and spirit business. The Maltings was subsequently sold twice in 1877; George Mason of Waldringfield Cement Works being the second purchaser. Letters and correspondence written between 1877 and 1878 regarding the lease between Cobbold and Hill, infer that things did not end well between them. When the house was sold, the lease started in 1873 was not honoured and George Mason ended the agreement. The letters show that Hill felt that if he had known what Cobbold and Mason would do, he would have bought the property himself when it came up for sale.

Despite this, the Hill family were evidently able to continue to run a thriving business as tenants. In the 1881 census, John was described both as maltster and coal merchant. John junior, now age 23 was by then a maltster in his own right. The following year brought sadness for the Hills as Ellen, their eldest daughter died in April 1882, aged just 29. She left behind her husband Charles Bunn and a baby daughter, Laura Maud Bunn, born in 1879, both living in Birmingham. Ellen is buried in Waldringfield.

In 1881, Laura Hill, aged 21 was a lady's maid and Jessie was 16. Robert Henry, possibly known as Harry, aged 13 was also described as a maltster and there was a further son, Walter, aged 9, a scholar. Perhaps with more family members able to work and a growing coal and brewing business as a result of demand from the adjoining Cement Works and river trade, the

Advertisement for beer: Walter Hill [93]

tenancy was able to continue and John's business was able to flourish? John is known to have kept 'a large and productive garden well stocked with fruit trees and bushes.' He grew his own barley and brewed his own beer, selling it at a shilling a gallon. He also made use of the river trade and the extensive frontage to the navigable River Deben which enabled him to ship malt along the river to Woodbridge.

John was still living in Cliff House by the time of the 1891 census. By then, he had been living in the house for at least 30 years, a long-standing tenant indeed! John Hill died suddenly in December 1892. According to an account in *The Ipswich Journal*, dated 9 December 1892, John had been driven by his son as far as the Duke of York corner in order to walk into Woodbridge. 'It is supposed he fell down in a fit after going a short distance.' John was subsequently taken to the home of Mr Finch but later died. His death was attributed to 'apoplexy'.

From the late 14th century to the late 19th century, apoplexy referred to any sudden death that began with a sudden loss of consciousness, particularly one in which the victim died within a matter of seconds after losing consciousness.

John was evidently an esteemed member of the Waldringfield community. According to *The Ipswich Journal*:

> *'The deceased carried on business as a maltster and corn and coal merchant, and was highly respected by all who knew him.'*

The inscription on John's grave in the churchyard at All Saints, Waldringfield reads:

> *'God moves in a mysterious way,
> his wonders to perform:
> He plants his footsteps in the sea
> And rides upon the storm.'*

John had lost his eldest daughter Ellen in 1882, mother Lydia in 1884 and wife Emma earlier that year in January.

The words on his gravestone were written by the poet William Cowper (1731-1800) who, together with his friend John Henry Newton, wrote the 'Olney Hymns'. The poem is the last hymn text written by Cowper following his attempted suicide by drowning whilst living in Olney.

Although he rented Cliff House for over 30 years, John also left a group of six 'substantial brick and tile built cottages' in Waldringfield to be sold by his executors at The Bull Hotel, Woodbridge on 02 March 1893. John Hill's son, Walter, took over the coal and brewing business and was still living in The Maltings at the time of the 1901 census.

Arthur Stollery

The 1911 census shows that Arthur Stollery, builder and coal merchant, was living in Cliff House. Waldringfield History Group member, Roger Stollery, writes:

> *'Arthur, born in 1861, was the eldest of Isaac and Eliza Stollery's 11 children. Isaac was the Waldringfield ferryman and a former landlord of the Maybush, but he died in his early forties and the Parish helped Eliza by setting up the first shop in Waldringfield, initially making Arthur the main breadwinner for the family. Arthur was a very skilled sailor and had a big influence on the sailing activities of my Grandad, Alfred, usually known as AW, who was 16 years his junior and on my Dad, Cyril Stollery.'*

All Saints Churchyard, where several of
John Hill's family are buried [94]

Sir Clifford Copland Paterson [95]

In 1919 Cliff House (The Old Maltings) was sold by Mr Mason to Alfred Albert Everson (b 1862), Woodbridge boatbuilder. Everson was a joiner and carpenter by trade who came from Diss and moved to Melton. He started the Everson's boat business in 1889 from a coaling quay. The Yard burned down in 1911 and was rebuilt on the same foundations, hence the name 'Phoenix Works'.

Sir Clifford Copland Paterson

During the 1900s the house was frequently rented by Sir Clifford Paterson for holidaying and for storing sailing gear. Sir Clifford was the son of a tanner and leather merchant and had attended Mill Hill School in North London.

After leaving school, he had begun a broad training in general and electrical engineering. In 1901, he entered Faraday House as a special student assistant in the testing department. Around this time, there were rapid improvements in the manufacture of electric lamps and Paterson presented several papers on the

Florence Stollery, Arthur's eldest daughter, putting on her stockings with one of the Ogden sisters looking down from the cliff. 1895 photograph taken by Thomas Naunton Waller [96]

The engagement of Eleanor Daisy Ogden and
Clifford Copland Paterson, 1904 [97]

subject. By 1913, he was a recognised authority on
illumination. During the 1914 war, he was engaged in
investigations in fields such as ignition systems and
height-finding equipment for anti-aircraft gunnery.

He was a director of the General Electric
Company PLC, as well as founder of their Wembley
Research Laboratories. Paterson was the recipient of
several honours during his lifetime. He was elected a
Fellow of the Royal Society in 1942 and was knighted
in 1946. Paterson became the first president and then
commodore of Waldringfield Sailing Club (1921-
1930) and was a keen sailor and gardener.

In 1905, Clifford Paterson married Eleanor Daisy,
daughter of Mr WT Ogden. She introduced him to
Waldringfield where her family regularly spent their
holidays. In their younger days, practically all their
holidays were spent sailing among their much loved
Suffolk creeks. They also shared a love of gardening
and they created and built several gardens together.
In their later years, they moved to a house they built
themselves near Watford. The garden here became
one of the showpieces of the neighbourhood. They
called that house 'Waldringfield'.

During the 1914 war when the Waldringfield
area was said to be 'a hot-bed of spies', the family
still chose to spend their holidays in the village. On
one occasion, they narrowly escaped arrest when
Paterson's midnight activity aboard a boat, on the
last night of his holiday, aroused some suspicion and
their arrest was planned for the following morning.
However, Paterson left on his motorbike for work at
dawn the next day, and the rest of the family followed
on the first available train. It wasn't until a few years
later, that Paterson heard an account from the chief
constable of the escape of a spy who had been in
a boat with a green awning and had got away on a
motorbike in the nick of time!

After the war, Sir Clifford Paterson owned a
gaff-rigged cutter, *Clytie* which he had built in 1922
at Everson's Boatyard, Woodbridge. This historic
boat has been in the same family ever since and
has now been restored. She can still be seen on the
River Deben today and is owned by Sir Clifford's
great-granddaughter, who continues faithfully to
keep the logbook that Daisy started. *Clytie* is moored
near Woodbridge. Although the Patersons used
Cliff House as a base to store their sailing gear, they
were also regular visitors to both Windyridge and
Broomfield in Waldringfield.

Clytie at the 1996 WSC 75th
Anniversary celebrations [98]

The Heaths

In 1931, the ownership of 'Cliff House' changed once again when Alfred Everson sold the house to Captain C Noel Heath and his wife Dorothea. Captain Heath had been posted to RAF Martlesham from Halton. The Heaths had three children, Anne, Charles and Adrian. The family changed the name to 'The Old Maltings' and it became their family home.

Anne, a keen sailor, often sailed competitively on the Deben. Their sailing dinghy, *Frolic* was built by the Nunn brothers, and they bought her from Mr Wickman who had a shed next to the Quay for housing his yacht *Prudence*. *Frolic* was soon treated to

a new mainsail and entered for the novice race where she won a silver cup. Captain Heath was co-opted on to the sailing club committee and Dorothea made use of a rowing boat called *Judy*. Anne's brother Adrian, with Hamish Fraser's help, ran the 'Hood Club' from a hut built at the top of the garden, with local boys Jim and George Turner.

Anne attended Felixstowe Ladies College in the mid-1930s but later moved to Ipswich High School where she excelled in art and printmaking. Placed in a historical context, perhaps Anne and her friends were aware of Arthur Ransome's newly published novel *Swallows and Amazons* (1930) later to become a children's classic and set to inspire many youngsters to learn to sail and seek adventure on the water?

In an article for the River Deben Association magazine, Anne remembered sailing with her friend Margaret Reeves and getting up to mischief as a young girl in her early teens. One of the incidents she describes involved learning to smoke Woodbines from Mr Spurgeon's shop and hiding aboard Margaret's father's fishing boat to enjoy them! Anne later studied sculpture at Wolverhampton School of Art.

Anne married Geoffrey Whiting. In 1955, they established Avoncroft Pottery at Hampton Lovett, Worcestershire, one of the pioneering studio workshops established after the Second World War. Anne helped to design and develop the 'standard ware', a domestic pottery range which was fired in a coal and wood kiln and modelled on that made by Bernard Leach in St Ives.

WALDRINGFIELD SAILING CLUB

Prize Distribution

Waldringfield Sailing Club held their annual prize distribution and supper in the Hall, Waldringfield, on Saturday, when a presentation was made to the Hon. Treasurer, Capt. C. N. Heath, who is leaving the district.

The Commodore, Mr. A. W. Stollery, welcomed the visitors, and Mr. P. Upchar proposed the health of the Waldringfield Sailing Club.

The Commodore, in reply, said the success of the club was due to the self-sacrificing work of the officers and Committee, and thanked all officials for the work they had put in.

"The Ladies" was proposed by Mr. G. Arnott and Miss A. Heath replied.

After the Commodore had thanked Capt. Heath for his services to the club, Master Jim Turner presented an electric clock to Capt. Heath on behalf of the club members. Replying, Capt. Heath said he and Mrs. Heath wished to present a cup to be dedicated to the "mud crawlers." (Applause.)

The prizes were then presented by Mrs. C. N. Heath, and a bouquet was handed to Mrs. Heath by Miss Audrey Hunt.

The prizes were as follows:—

14ft. Class: 1 Mr. A. D. Spear, cup and replica; 2 Mr. C. H. Thomas, 3 Wing-Commander T. Trinder.

12ft. Dinghy Class: 1 Miss A. Heath, cup and replica; 2 Master J. Turner, 3 Master R. Garnham.

12ft. National Class: 1 Mr. K. W. N. Palmer, cup and replica.

Yachts: 1 Miss F. B. Orvis, cup and replica; 2 Mr. G. Garnham and Mr. C. Lindop.

Ladie' Race: Special prize, presented by Mr. A. T. Hunt, won by Miss F. B. Orvis.

WALDRINGFIELD SAILING CLUB.

List of Members, 1936.

Mr. F. S. R. Allen	Mr. D. M. Haig	Mr. K. W. N. Palmer
Mr. G. W. Arnott	Master A. Haig	Mr. Manning Prentice
Mr. P. C. M. Ash	Mr. D. H. Hanson	Master K. Parker
	Mr. A. W. H. Hawkes	Mr. C. C. Patterson
Mr. J. M. Barham	Mr. A. W. B. Hawkes	
Master P. M. Barham	Captain C. N. Heath	Mr. J. Quantrill
Mr. E. E. Barker	Mr. C. B. Heath	
Mr. R. Batcher	Miss A. Heath	Mr. L. M. Reeve
Mr. W. M. Blake	Master A. Heath	Miss M. Reeve
Mr. A. C. Bloomfield	Mr. N. Heatley	Miss Y. Reeve
Miss J. Bloomfield	Mr. A. Hill	Mr. G. Venmore-Rowland
Mr. E. Burlingham	Mr. A. W. Hollis	Master J. Venmore-Rowland
	Mr. A. F. Hunt	Dr. Russell
Mr. Callender	Mrs. A. F. Hunt	
Mr. Catchpole	Miss J. Hunt	Mr. D. Spear
Mr. T. C. Charlton		Mrs. D. Spear
Mr. W. B. Clarke		Dr. Cloudesley-Smith
Miss B. Coke	Mr. C. A. Jones	Mrs. Cloudesley-Smith
Mr. J. W. E. Cooper		Mr. F. Kingston Smith
Miss Cooper	Mr. D. Kennedy	Mr. A. Stollery
Mr. Creasey	Mr. J. Kennedy	Mr. A. W. Stollery
Mr. A. R. G. Curjel	Master P. Kennedy	Miss L. Stollery
		Mr. C. Stollery
Mr. G. Doughty	Mr. J. C. D. Lamb	Mr. E. Stollery
	Mr. E. C. Lindop	Mr. S. Stow
Sir E. A. Eborall	Mr. T. S. Lock	
Mr. R. Eborall		Mr. J. H. Thomas
Miss Eborall		Mr. C. H. Thomas
Miss Eborall	Sir G. Manners	Mr. J. N. Thompson
Mr. C. W. Ellerby	Mr. F. Mace	Squadron-Leader F. N. Trinder
Mr. A. Everson	Mr. R. Mace	Master J. Turner
	Mr. E. Marsh (Hon.)	Master G. Turner
Mr. B. Fisk	Mr. H. Mason	
Rev. J. Fraser	Mr. E. F. Mason	Mr. F. Upton
Mr. I. Fraser	Mr. E. Mason	
Master H. Fraser	Mr. R. Matheson	Rev. A. P. Waller
	Mr. B. E. Matthews	Mr. T. N. Waller (Hon.)
Mr. G. Garnham	Commander P. Muers	Captain N. F. Wells
Mr. W. Garnham		Mr. A. C. Wickman
Master R. Garnham		Mr. P. C. Wilson
Mr. A. A. Gibbons	Mr. T. H. Oldham	Mr. J. J. Wilson
Major B. B. M. Glossop	Master F. Olson	Mr. H. F. M. Wilson
Dr. M. W. Gonin	Master J. Olson	Mr. H. C. Wood
Mr. Gooderham	Mr. E. W. Orvis	Mrs. H. C. Wood
Mrs. Gooderham	Miss F. B. Orvis	Mr. D. Wood
	Mr. R. P. Orvis	Mr. P. B. Wooton

Anne Heath with her
dog Kepp [101]

Ian and Hamish Fraser, Adrian
Heath known as 'Copper',
George Turner [102]

The Old Maltings during World War II

In World War II, the Allies wanted Nazi Germany to believe that the invasion of Europe would land at the Pas-de-Calais, not Normandy. Consequently, in early 1943, a grand deception plan was devised, code-named Operation Fortitude. A small part of this plan was known as Operation Quicksilver. The idea was to position dummy landing craft with fake army encampments in the East Coast rivers from Yarmouth to Folkestone. These dummy craft were known as 'Bigbobs'. Many men had to be trained to build them and Waldringfield was chosen as the training centre. Courses started in February 1944. Men from two battalions of the 61st Infantry Division, the 4th Northamptonshire and the 10th Worcesters were selected to play an important part in this deception plan. Some were billeted at the Old Maltings and other properties in Waldringfield. By the third week in April, approximately 600 officers and men of each Battalion had received training. The Deben, with 66 Bigbobs was to have the largest fleet after the Orwell with 70. The Quicksilver operation may have played a vital part in holding the German army in NE France throughout the critical months of the Normandy battles.

George Jones at 21 [103]

The Old Maltings in the winter of 1947 [104]

The Jones Family

In 1946, the Old Maltings was sold by Charles Noel Heath to Mrs Edith Maud Jones, a widow. Both Mrs Jones's younger sons had served in the RNVR during the war. Both had developed a great love of Waldringfield and the River Deben in their pre-war boyhoods. Both were eager to return.

George Jones (1918-1983) had left Waldringfield after the August Bank Holiday 1939. He had been accepted into the RNVSR and invited to join other volunteers for a Baltic cruise on the small motor yacht *Naromis*. He had no idea it would be so long before he would see Waldringfield again. Three weeks on board *Naromis* turned out to involve some unofficial pre-war reconnaissance. At Kiel, for instance, they photographed the German battleship *Gneisenau*. George sent this immediately to the Naval Intelligence Department and other photos from the cruise followed later. It was September 2nd before *Naromis* arrived home and his call-up papers were waiting. He hurried to join HMS *Forth*, the depot ship for the 2nd Submarine Flotilla in Dundee and subsequently served in Canada and Sierra Leone before a final posting in Harwich. It was then that he managed slip back to Waldringfield, have a drink in the Maybush and glimpse his beloved river:

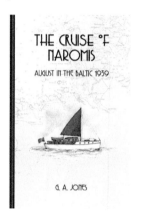

THE CRUISE °F NAROMIS
AUGUST IN THE BALTIC 1939

G. A. JONES

[105]

'I came to a reassuring conclusion when I was at Waldringfield. I've lost faith in most of the things I used to have as ideals or fancies. They've dulled and don't fire me anymore. But one thing still retains its fascination, mystery if you like, and that is the Deben. To see it as I left it at eight o'clock last night with the sun setting low in the west lighting up the fresh spring green of trees over Stonner Point and The Tips, a single sailing ship beating down the Bowships on the last of the ebb. To hear the familiar sound of a tractor putting in some overtime across the Estuary at Shottisham, the occasional call of a curlew or redstart on the saltings, then I know there is nothing I want more than to get back to this part of Suffolk.'

George Jones, *The Cruise of Naromis: August in the Baltic 1939*

In 1939, Jack Jones (1915-1990) was an industrial designer, living in Birmingham, writing for *Yachting Monthly* and encouraged by the editor, Maurice Griffiths, to publish his first designs. His was a reserved occupation so it was not until spring 1941 that he, like George, joined the RNVR. His first command was HDML *1024*, based at Sheerness. Jack was wounded in an explosion and spent four months in hospital. He had not long returned to duty when he was given command of RML *513* and ordered to Operation Jubilee the devastating Dieppe raid of 19th August 1942.

When the flotilla was attacked by Focke-Wulf 190 fighters, two fellow rescue vessels were set alight. RML *513* and another craft managed to save 47 RAF personnel and bring them home to safety. In the attack, either a bullet or shrapnel went through Jones' neck, severing and damaging his left side cranial nerves. Despite this wound, he managed to issue orders and none

Jack Jones as a wartime lieutenant in the RNVR [106]

of his men were hurt. Julia Jones remembers the former Rector of Waldringfield, John Waller, describing Jack returning, lashed to the wheel of his motor launch.

After another period of recuperation Jack was given command of a landing craft on D-Day. (Characteristically he sent a short account of this experience to *Yachting Monthly*.) Increasingly incapacitated by his injuries, he was put on shore duties then invalided out of the Navy shortly before the end of the war.

He described the Old Maltings as 'the one house he had always wanted'.

Whilst Jack had been training in Scotland in 1943 he had met Derek Niven van den Bogaerde (better known as actor Dirk Bogarde) who was then a 2nd Lt in the Queens Royal Regiment – also preparing for D-Day. Their friendship would prove lifelong, though it became more distant as their careers diverged.

Very soon after Jack had moved to the Old Maltings, Bogarde persuaded him to sit for a studio portrait and take a screen test. Jack wrote on the back of the photo that he failed 'dismally'. 'I'm not photogenic and I only wanted to design small craft.' It was probably in the autumn of 1947 that Bogarde came to stay at the Old Maltings and left this description:

Jack's portrait from the screen test [107]

'London being what it is at the moment, a great cauldron of vicious, shabby and money-grabbing people, lacking hotels, food, flats or jobs... I have cleared out to a small village on the Deben in Suffolk. This village is a huddle of cottages on the river bank with a pub called the Maybush as its centre point, and a charming red brick Church set amid Ash and Pine trees.

The river here is wide, flat and salt, the sea being but a few miles down. Riding at anchor, straining gently against the tide, float hundreds of little boats. Yachts, dinghies, sharpies, cruisers and punts, canoes and prams... the sky is raked by a hundred empty masts; booms and tillers waggle gently and weed-grown buoys bobble and bounce under the force of the running current. This village is a yachting village – a haven for the men from the City who have sailed boats in their dreams, their baths, their imaginations all their lives until they have managed, at last, to purchase a real one of their own. In the evenings, the Public of the Maybush is filled with the jargon of a yachting community. People talk of their day's work, their sails, their masts and booms, charts and caulking... if you like this sort of conversation you join in, for they are the friendliest of people; if you do not – then you sit back over the fire and enjoy your Old and Mild, which is what I do. The peace of this place, the damp smells of mud and October mist, the rust and slate colours all around, and the cronk! cronk! of the Heron wading his solitary way across the marshes, is a breath of heaven after London. I regret that I shall have to go back in a day or two.'

Dirk Bogarde (Extract from *Dirk Bogarde; The Authorised Biography*, John Coldstream)

The Old Maltings gave the brothers their opportunity to develop noteworthy careers in the postwar yachting industry.

The elder, John 'Jack' Francis Jones lived at the Old Maltings with his mother and commenced his career there as a significant postwar yacht designer and naval architect. The younger, George Aubrey Jones, initially established his successful postwar yachting agency in the building behind the house that later became Greenaway.

Jack and George had been coming to Waldringfield regularly since 1928. Their father, a farmer, had supplied them with a former chicken-hut near the sailing club steps and put them under the care of Jimmy Quantrill as they learned to sail.

George's daughter, Julia, remembers her uncle Jack's design studio on the top floor of the Old Maltings with its wonderful view across the river. Early postwar designs include *Sarcelle* (1949), *Corista* (1952), *Le Frais* (1952), *Callao* (1952) all built at Whisstock's of Woodbridge and *Louisa* (1952) built in Nunn's

View from the design studio window of the Old Maltings [108]

Looking across the flooded Boatyard on a stormy day in March 1949. *L'Atalanta*, owned by Jack's friend, local historian and auctioneer George Arnott, is moored on the right [109]

Yard in Waldringfield. The very popular Kestrel class was designed at Waldringfield and some were also built there. Jack also designed a number of distinctive motor-sailors and motor-boats such as the Inchcape, Fleur-de-Lys and Sole Bay classes. The smaller Jaunty designs came later. Many of Jack Jones's fine classic yachts are still around today and continue to bring their owners much pleasure. Among them, locally, are *Sun Cloud*, *Patient Griselda*, *Avola* and *Celandine*. Jack's nephews Nicholas and Edward Jones own a Jaunty 19 and a Kestrel respectively. Both are frequently on the Deben.

Although Jack's passion was for yacht design, his eye for colour and feeling for aesthetic quality made the Old Maltings a beautiful house where he enjoyed entertaining Friends such as George Arnott and Norman Scarfe. Julia particularly remembers him turning the downstairs rooms into a gallery to exhibit paintings by the then unknown artist Jonathan Trowell. In Jack's later years he moved to Woodbridge and a design partnership with Peter Brown. Both he and George found the 1960s-1970s transition from wooden (or steel) hulls to glass-fibre very difficult to accept, though several of Jack's designs were also built in GRP. By the end of his career, in 1972, Jack had been responsible for over 3000 yachts, dispersed around the world.

Jack died in 1990 and his ashes were scattered at sea after a memorial service in Waldringfield Church

Well-known designer and *Yachting Monthly* editor Maurice Griffiths called *Celandine*, a gaff ketch launched in 1967, Jack's 'prettiest' yacht [110]

June Jones (expecting her youngest child) in 1959 teaching the two older children to sail in *Snowdrop*, built for them by Ernie Nunn [111]

The front garden of the Old Maltings was the perfect place to begin to develop an eye for a boat [113]

conducted by Rev John Waller. Stewart Platt, owner of *Celandine*, wrote Jack's obituary for the *Times*: 'The characteristic which showed most clearly through the wide range of sailing and power craft designed by Jack Jones was their unmistakable beauty of line.' Perhaps an even greater tribute was that paid by the late Brian Hammett, owner of *Avola* who said, 'Jack Jones designed his boats to keep their owners safe'.

By the late 1950s, Jack had trained two apprentice draughtsmen who later became notable designers themselves. They were Alan P Gurney who moved to New York to design fast ocean racers and Christopher Rushmore 'Kim' Holman. Holman produced plans for countless boats such as the Holman 26 and the Stella and Twister classes. Twisters dominated the East Anglian circuit for much of the 60's. Holman was also a founder director of Suffolk Yacht Harbour.

When he left the RNVR in 1946, George Jones made use of the building (now called Greenaway) at the back of the Old Maltings to establish his East Coast Yacht Agency (known by its staff as the 'Easy Cosy') in partnership with an RNVR friend, Anthony Daniel. The business was soon successful and the office moved to Quay Street in Woodbridge. George and Jack continued to work together as often as possible: Jack responsible for designing and surveying; George for building and selling.

Avola, a 1965 gaff cutter designed by Jack Jones [112]

George Jones with Edward Heath, former PM,
at the renaming ceremony for *Lady Jean* [114]

Christmas at the Old Maltings in 1958.
Left to right: June, Nick, Julia, Edith and Jack Jones [116]

One of the East Coast Yacht Agency's early customers, in 1948, was a young woman named June Scott who came from London and bought a small, fast yacht called *Snow Goose*. She always remembered her first visit to the Old Maltings where she was immediately made welcome by Edith and Jack. George and June married in 1950 and their three children (Julia, Nicholas and Edward) were born in Woodbridge and introduced to sailing at Waldringfield, first on the Hillyard-designed *Barnacle Goose*, then, briefly, the 'Cherub' *Ceres* and from 1957, on *Peter Duck*. Items such as dinghy oars were stored at the Old Maltings and the children spent happy hours playing in the garden while George and Jack talked business and June spent time with Edith, who was increasingly an invalid.

As the yachting scene changed and mass-produced boats became the standard, George grew disenchanted with the yacht agency. He sold his business and put his energies into a range of schemes to ensure that the former working boats such as the sailing barges and light vessels were not forgotten. He was responsible for the initial collection of historic vessels in St Katherine's Haven, London and worked tirelessly as the honorary secretary for the East Coast Sail Trust dedicated to preserving the barge *Thalatta* and using her to introduce inner city children to sailing. He instituted a successful appeal to add *Lady Jean* to the Trust, renaming her in honour of writer, campaigner, and Thames barge lover, Sir Alan Herbert.

George was an enthusiastic amateur painter and was one of a group of artists who formed EAGMA, the East Anglian Group of Marine Artists, who organized annual exhibitions both locally and in London. He was a regular columnist for *Yachting Monthly* magazine and campaigned fiercely on issues such as the proposed Maplin airport and chemicals in anti-fouling paints which were damaging the river shell fish stocks. George died in 1983.

George Jones sailing *Peter Duck*. Jack was a convinced admirer of *Peter Duck* and encouraged his brother to develop this class of yachts in the 1960s [115]

George Jones on *Peter Duck* [117]

The Stinsons

In 1973, Edith and Jack sold The Old Maltings to Mrs Eleanor Judith Stinson and Judge David John Stinson and family.

David Stinson was called to the Bar in 1947 and was deputy chairman of the Herts quarter sessions from 1965-1971. He was appointed a county court judge in 1969, becoming a circuit judge in 1972. He retired from the bench in 1986. A devout Anglican, Judge Stinson was chancellor of the Diocese of Carlisle 1971-1990. He was also president of PACT (Suffolk), for many years. The family moved to Waldringfield from near Bishop's Stortford, Hertfordshire where they had lived for 20 years. They had four children, Sarah (then 21), who was already living away from home, Adam (then 19) who was doing odd jobs whilst waiting to go away to college, Emma (then 16) who was at school in Bishop's Stortford so she boarded with friends during the week and Dan (then 13) who was a member of Waldringfield Sailing Club Cadet Squadron. They chose the house because of the sailing opportunities it presented. David and Judith soon became involved with Waldringfield Sailing Club and sailed number 11 Dragonfly. Later, Judith had a

A PUNCH dinghy [119]

boat called *Punch* created for her by Roger Stollery. The two were referred to as 'Punch and Judith' by the family. Judith also became chair of Waldringfield WI, a member of the Waldringfield Wildlife Group and a governor at Waldringfield School where she gained much pleasure from hearing children read.

The Stinsons in 1976. From left to right: David, Judith, Emma, Adam, Dan and Sarah [118]

The Old Maltings, May 2020 [120]

Visitors to Waldringfield today will be interested to know that the Old Maltings is still very much a family home and that the present occupants are a family of keen sailors.

Greenaway

A short walk up Cliff Road from the Old Maltings takes the modern visitor to a house called Greenaway, formerly known as the Studio. During the Second World War, British agricultural machinery maker Ransomes, Sims and Jefferies Ltd, who produced a range of general engineering products (including traction engines, trolleybuses, ploughs, lawnmowers, combine harvesters and other tilling equipment) outsourced much of their work from Ipswich to village hubs in order to make room for war work and to mitigate the threat from bombing. The Studio became one of these workshops.

1940s: War work being undertaken in Greenaway [121]

Early 1970s: Ransome's advertisement from the front cover of a grass machinery leaflet showing a Ransome Sprite mower [123]

1946: The East Coast Yacht Agency [122]

Before conversion: View from the Old Maltings [124]

Greenaway was formerly coachhouse to the Old Maltings. After the war Jack and George Jones realized this was an ideal location for the fledgling East Coast Yacht Agency.

Then, in 1957 it was sold to Terry and Stella Vernon who renamed it Greenaway after their favourite beach near Padstow in Cornwall. Its current residents are members of the Waldringfield History Group.

THE EAST COAST YACHT AGENCY, LTD.
(Members of the Yacht Brokers' and Designers' Association)

YACHT BROKERS & MARINE INSURANCE AGENTS

WALDRINGFIELD, NR. WOODBRIDGE, SUFFOLK.

Telephone:
Waldringfield 289

Telegrams:
"Yachts, Waldringfield"

The letterhead of the East Coast Yacht Agency [125]

The Kestrel Class

Paul King and Harry Nunn outside the Old Maltings (c. early 1950s) [126]

The Kestrel class of small cruising yachts may claim to be the quintessential Waldringfield community creation. Their story began in the mid 1950s when local sailor Paul King, who had owned a Waldringfield Dragonfly, wanted a small yacht with similar characteristics. He and Harry Nunn built a model to embody their ideas, then took it to Jack Jones at the Old Maltings to finalise the design and provide the necessary technical details.

The very first Kestrel was then built at Waldringfield by Ernie Nunn for Paul King. Her name was *Flare*. She was 22' LOA gunter-rigged, with a centre-board and without an engine, though she later had one fitted. These small, inexpensive, family-friendly yachts were perfectly suited to the later 1950s-60s, when money was often short but families were keen to get on the water and enjoy their time together.

After *Flare*, however, all the later Kestrels were Bermudan-rigged. As Mike Clark, who was an apprentice at Nunn Brothers, remembers: 'most of the boats we built had Bermudian-rig as no one wanted gaff rig any more then.' With the energetic advocacy of Jack and George Jones and members of the Waldringfield Sailing Club, the class spread beyond Waldringfield to be built at boatyards across the country, including Larkman's and Robertson's at Woodbridge, King's of Pin Mill, Hall's at Walton-on-the-Naze and also in Hull. In total 150 wooden Kestrels were built: the majority 22' but others a little longer, 24', plus a sister class of Peregrines. The design was later adapted for GRP and a further 250 produced nationwide.

The classic wooden Kestrels are beautifully balanced and owners claim that they sail 'like a dinghy' – which given their origins is not entirely surprising. Their shallow keels with retractable centreplates make it possible for them to explore the smallest creeks while they are also generously canvassed so that the more competitive sailors (such as those in the WSC) were able to build up a small class for racing. *Nosama* was built by Larkman's Yard for Arthur Mason and *Sally Brown* by Nunn's Yard for Hamish Fraser. Other WSC Kestrel owners were Ken Wincer who commissioned *Crecerelle* and Roger Hansford who owned *Chaseaway*. Dr Earl, Henry Connell, Doug Humby, Geoff Hollis, Mr Cowling and the Frasers all competed in the fleet races.

Nosama being built by Larkman's on the Quay [127]

Roger Hansford, former yacht class captain and commodore of WSC, was said to be the 'young upstart' of the Kestrel fleet. It was said that he tacked when he could touch the bottom with the boat hook. Roger soon introduced a 'kicking-strap' which he reckoned was worth at least 1/2 mile on the regular 'Kingsfleet and back' course. Like one or two other yacht racers, he was usually late for the start. On one occasion, the fleet was well down river before he started in a severe northerly wind. Every sail went up – including the spinnaker. At about the end of the island it started to rain wood as *Chaseaway*'s hollow spruce mast compressed into itself.

Roger was due to defend the Pin Mill Regatta Cup the following weekend on the River Orwell, so Dick Larkman set to with gusto and glued, planed, varnished and fitted out a new mast. In the meantime *Chaseaway* was motored to Pin Mill – mastless. But if her River Orwell rivals breathed a sigh of relief, they were wrong. Just in time the new mast was rowed out from Pin Mill Hard to the mooring in an 8ft dinghy, stepped and the Pin Mill Cup was duly retained for Waldringfield.

Sadly the clinker-built Kestrels have not weathered well. Though George's son Ned Jones nurses his *Gingerbread Man* (built in Hull 1965, usually moored at Methersgate) from 'final season' to 'final season', the Fraser family's *Sally Brown* was consigned to the Waldringfield Boatyard bonfire in 2019. RIP *Sally Brown*.

Currently (2020) there are no more Kestrels moored at Waldringfield.

White Cloud, sailing at Waldringfield – used as the advertising photo for the early Kestrels [128]

Hamish Fraser's daughter Jinny watching *Sally Brown* being built at Nunn's (1965) [129]

The Sailing Barge Families of Waldringfield

'Time and tide will wait for no man, saith the adage. But all men have to wait for time and tide.'

Charles Dickens, *Martin Chuzzlewit*

Thames Sailing Barges have played a key part in facilitating trade between the East Anglian and Kent rivers as well as the Thames Estuary and by the end of the 19th century, their visits to Waldringfield were at their peak. Three main fleets operated from the 1870s until the 1930s and were concerned with the muck and straw trade, coprolite and cement trades.

Skippers and mates of the Waldringfield barges are recorded in Customs House reports and local newspapers. These men were highly skilled seamen, fit and strong. They worked all year round and in all weather conditions.

John (Jack) Wesley and Lavinia (née Clark) Stebbing in retirement at Boyton [131]

Ben and Elizabeth (née Friend) Page [130]

Inevitably, some of them married into local families and their descendants can be traced to modern day village residents.

Notable local characters were John 'Jack' Wesley Stebbing (1864-1951), Skipper of the *Kingfisher* barge which collected most of the mud needed for the Cement Works, and his mate Ben Page, who was reported to enjoy the odd brawl in the Maybush.

Ben Page [132]

John (Jack) Wesley Stebbing [134]

Jack lived in Cliff Road in 1901 and married Alice Levinia Clark

Phosia Stebbing aged about 19 [135]

(1859-1940) who gave birth to 9 children, including twin girls. The only time when the Rector Thomas Henry Waller, was said to have been really disturbed, was when he baptised the twins and there was some confusion over their names during the service. Mrs Stebbing later explained that she had formerly worked for two Italian countesses and wished her twins to be named after them, Phosia Retia and Retia Phosia Stebbing.

Entries in baptismal register for Phosia Retia and Retia Phosia Stebbing [133]

ON DECK: A recent photograph, taken at Ipswich Docks, showing (left to right), Jimmy Quantrill, Fred Strange, Arthur
Quantrill, and the present barge-master, L. Polley, on board the
"Orinoco," the only one of the former cement barge fleet which is
still sea-going.

A 1950s picture of three retired skippers who had gathered for a reunion [136]

Arthur Quantrill (1874-1946) and his brother James 'Jimmy' (1871-1953) were also well known locally. Both were master mariners who skippered barges for Masons whilst the Cement Works were in operation. Originally from Chelmondiston, Arthur was Skipper of the barge *Jumbo* and subsequently *Excelsior*. By 1911, he had married Jessie Stollery (1879-1937) and was living in Waldringfield at the village shop. Jimmy Quantrill was listed as mate on *Azariah* of Ipswich in the 1901 census and was grandfather to many of the village Nunn and Turner families. He married Edith Durrant (1872-1947) from Waldringfield. Jimmy 'came ashore' in 1904, when the tenancy of the Maybush became available. He was landlord there until 1914 when he left to take over at the Butt and Oyster at Pin Mill. He later retired back to Waldringfield and lived in 'The Moorings' until his death in 1953.

Fred Strange (b. 1890) originally from Holbrook, was related to the present day Waldringfield Quantrill family who are well known local sailors. He skippered the barges *Augusta* and *Orinoco* and was said never to have been surpassed at handling a barge. He was known as the 'Toff' as he was always very smartly dressed and had a neatly clipped beard.

Robert (Bob) Ruffles (1874-1956), another barge skipper originally from Chelmondiston, was master of the barge *Justice* in 1911 and skipper of *Orinoco* in 1914. Cyril Ruffles (1908-1977), Robert's son, married Olivia Stollery (1909-1974) – a distant cousin of Cyril Stollery – and Robert's grandson Paul, through his other son Aubrey Ruffles, eventually became commodore of Waldringfield Sailing Club in 2002.

Brothers Ernest Smith (1880-1951) and Isaac Smith (1891-1973) both became barge skippers. Ernest was born in the nearby village of Newbourne, Isaac in Waldringfield. Ernest served as mate on *Jumbo* with Arthur Quantrill before becoming master. Isaac was mate on *Grace* of Ipswich. Sadly, Ernest witnessed the drowning of George Juby, mate on *Augusta*, off the beach at Waldringfield in 1898.

Evening Star   23 Feb 1898

Ipswich Seaman
Drowned in the Deben

On Tuesday Walter Brook Eng. Coroner for the Liberty of St Etheldreda, held an inquest on George Juby, of Ipswich, mariner, aged 31 years, who was drowned at Waldringfield on Thursday last. George Brooks, of Tomline Road, St Clement's, skipper of the barge *Augusta*, stated he had known the deceased some 15 years and had been mate with him for a year and 9 months. Deceased was always a steady and quiet man, and I during the last 9 or 10 months had been a total abstainer. Last Thursday they were on board *Augusta*, which was lying off Waldringfield, in the River Deben: they got under weigh about 9.30 in the morning. Witness was at the tiller and deceased was weighing the anchor, and they had spritsail, topsail, and jib set. Witness saw deceased go to the bow to see if the anchor was clear. He did not see deceased fall overboard, but heard Ernest Smith call from the shore that he had fallen overboard. Witness looked over the starboard side and saw deceased rise near the leeboard, and threw him a wooden ladder. He made no attempt to catch it. And

sank almost immediately. The barge was hardly moving, there being only a gentle breeze blowing at the time. The jib was not flapping, the jib sheet was to windward, and witness was certain that nothing touched the deceased, causing him to fall over.

Ernest Smith, of Waldringfield, stated that he was standing on the beach at Waldringfield last Thursday morning watching the *Augusta* get under and saw deceased weighing the Anchor and fall over. No sail was flapping to knock deceased over and nobody was near him. The barge appeared to go over the deceased as he came up the starboard side. The barge was almost stem on to where witness was standing.

Harry Ward, of Waldringfield, deposed to dragging for and finding the body on the edge of the Channel, and PC Charles Green also gave evidence.

The jury returned a verdict of 'Death from accidental drowning.'

A Walk along the River in 1881

'I do not know much about gods; but I think that the river / Is a strong brown god.'

TS Eliot, *Dry Salvages*

An artist's impression of the Cement Works as it would have looked from the north westerly aspect. Copyright unknown.
In 1881 there would have been only four kilns on the left side, the last bank of four kilns being built in 1898 [137]

It may come as a surprise to many that in the second half of the 19th century Waldringfield was much more an industrial village than it was agricultural. There were many active coprolite pits in and around the village and, at the very heart of the community, there was a Cement Works with eight to twelve kilns, the last row of four being erected in 1898. Then, of course, there was all the infrastructure and paraphernalia that went with them. The distribution of homes was quite different to earlier times. Nevertheless, although the working population was large, the resident population was only about 270.

We will take our walk in 1881, the time of the second industrial or technological revolution. Queen Victoria had been on the throne of Great Britain and Ireland since 1837. Her late husband Albert, the Prince Consort, had died in 1861 and she continued to mourn his loss deeply but, despite that or perhaps because of it, she remained a popular Queen.

Once again we will start our walk close to the northern boundary of the village but this time we start on a sea defence, or river wall. This has been in place since the 17th century and, as a consequence, the shoreline of the River Deben has altered considerably. The condition of the 'wall' has deteriorated recently, mainly due to the economic depression in agriculture. However, it is still walkable.

Nearby, inland on our right as we proceed in a southerly direction, is Cross Farm; in 1674 this farm was associated with the family of John Crosse.

It is possible that the name of the farm derives from that time but an earlier, eccliastical origin has been suggested because, originally, it is possible the farm was in the Manor of Preston (priest's town).

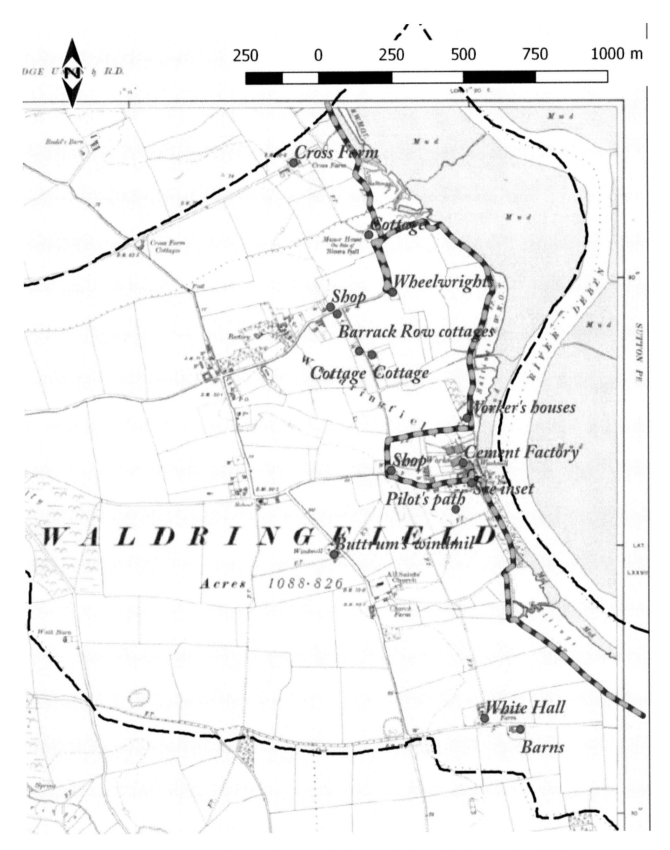

The Village in 1905, 24 years after our walk. Our route is denoted by the green line [138]

Considerable organizational changes have occurred in this area since the observations of our ancestors in the 14th century; Preston lives on only as the name of a field, the Parish of Waldringfield has been properly defined and boundaries have been set between Waldringfield and its neighbouring parishes, including Martlesham to the north and north-west.

At the time of our walk Cross Farm is included in the Parish of Martlesham but the farmhouse has always been either on or very close to the boundary between Martlesham and Waldringfield. At a later date there would be a boundary shift and it would become part of the Parish of Waldringfield. Samuel and Alice Leach live there with their seven children. The eldest, Bernard, is eighteen; he works with his father as a carter on the farm. The other children are all twelve or under. The youngest, Bessie, was born just last year. The farm shepherd, David Bye, also lives on the farm with his wife, Mary, and their three children. The eldest is sixteen; he is following in his father's footsteps as a shepherd, being listed as a shepherd's assistant. The other Bye offspring are eleven or under.

From the shoreline below the fields of Cross Farm the river wall, intact in 1881, follows the natural contour of the land and turns slightly inland into what we have called Rivershall Creek where a small stream flows, bringing water down from the heights of the Heath into a natural inlet in the saltings. At the time of our walk the Parish boundary follows this stream as it approaches the shoreline.

Across the river we can see Methersgate Quay. There are several barges on the river with their skippers and pilots taking full advantage of the flood tide and a favourable wind in order to try and reach Woodbridge. The river provides a beautiful vista but there can be a certain eeriness to it at times especially in misty weather. Just three years ago, in 1878, a young lady from Woodbridge was found drowned just down-river from here. An inquest held in Waldringfield concluded that she had taken her own life, having been sorely affected by the death of her mother a few years before.

South of Cross Farm and about 100 yards inland through a grove of ancient oaks there is a field in which it is likely that archaeological excavation would expose the ruins of the Manor of Rivershall. This is now the grounds of Manor House Cottage but there is reference on the 1881 OS map to the pre-existence of Rivershall.

From Manor House Cottage there is a track leading to The Street (later to be known as Fishpond Road). On the first bend in the track there is an old wheelwright's / blacksmith's shop, now empty but occupied until at least 1871 by George and Anne Last and the five younger members of their family. The oldest four, Georgiana, Walter, Alfred and Charlotte, had left home by 1871. There is evidence of this 'small wheelwright and blacksmith's shop' being up

A look northward upriver towards
Woodbridge and St Mary's [139]

for lease in 1846 and it seems from the 1851 census that the lease was taken by one Mr Garrod. By 1861 the shop was in the hands of Mr Last.

Looking further inland and around the bend we are able see other buildings falling into disrepair – Barrack Row (a row of four cottages) and a shop, possibly, on the corner of The Street and Long Lane (later to be known with its extension into Lower Road as Sandy Lane). Some of these buildings are now unoccupied.

NB: The reader is asked to note that there are no public footpaths in the area of Cross Farm and there is no public right of way in any of its fields or yards. In reality anybody wishing to repeat our 19th-century walk should start on the river wall footpath near Manor House Cottage.

The intention of our walk is to follow the shoreline and explore the seaward side of Waldringfield so we must retrace our steps past the wheelwright's building with its partially collapsed roof and the detritus of a derelict workshop lying all around.

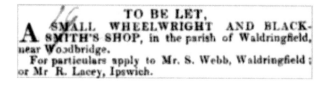

TO BE LET,
A SMALL WHEELWRIGHT AND BLACK-SMITH'S SHOP, in the parish of Waldringfield, near Woodbridge.
For particulars apply to Mr. S. Webb, Waldringfield; or Mr R. Lacey, Ipswich.

Suffolk Chronicle or *Weekly General Advertiser County Express*, 23 May 1846 [140]

We regain the shore of The Ocean, as it is described in the Glebe map, close to the site of Rivershall. Once back on the river wall we can take a northward look back up-river towards Woodbridge where the tower of St Mary the Virgin has dominated the sky-line since it was built in the 15th century. There has been a church

The Cement Works with its imposing chimneys [141]

there since Saxon times and there is mention of it in the Domesday Book. In our own 19th century St Mary's congregation has grown so large that a second church has been built and now we can also see the 138' spire of St John's which will survive until 1970 when it will be declared unsafe. In our own village of Waldringfield, the spirit of evangelical piety led to the foundation of the Baptist Church in Newbourne Road in 1823 and its building six years later. Many of the cement workers and their families worship there.

The scenery is beautiful and complemented by the sound of the curlew and the sight of geese flying in formation over the other side of the river. There have been no egrets for several years – ever since it became fashionable to include their long white feathers in ladies' hats.

Despite the natural beauty of the river there is an acrid smell emanating from the direction of Waldringfield. There are sounds of industry and we can see dirty smoke billowing from eight vast chimneys – the kilns of Masons Cement Works. The sight of these contrasts intensely with the rural view across the fields toward Lower Road. There are two buildings in close proximity on that road, one each side of the lane – to the right, a pair of agricultural cottages not yet fifty years old (later to be known as the Orchard), to the left a larger homestead in need of major re-construction (later to be known as Deben Villa and then as Novocastria).

James and Eliza Sheldrake live in one of the cottages; he is a 59 year-old agricultural labourer; she is five years younger. Eliza's mother, a widow by the name of Amelia Goodall, lives with them; she was born in Otley in 1802 and gave birth to Eliza in Bucklesham in 1827. The next decade would see great change in that small household with the deaths of James and his mother-in-law and the arrival of Eliza's older sister, Harriet, and her husband, David Jennings from Nacton.

Ahead of us, as we walk the river wall, we see the River Deben in full width, a strong brown working god, its waters reflecting the colour of the contaminated sky. To our right is Grove Field; now reclaimed arable land following the building of the river wall, this was once a sizeable watery inlet.

Then as we get nearer to the village the imposing rows of kilns come into view together with the end of the jetty, protruding from the Quay. A sailing barge tied up to the jetty is being loaded with barrels of cement. Directly to our left, in the saltmarshes, there is a small barge laden with mud which has been dug from the riverbed by specialist labourers like Ben Page and Jack Stebbing. The mud is taken to a landing stage on the Quay and then tipped into the washmill for use in the manufacture of cement. It is likely that most of the mud was obtained from downstream of Waldringfield.

A barge berthed at the wharf by the Cement Works. Note the piles of mud already deposited on the wharf [142]

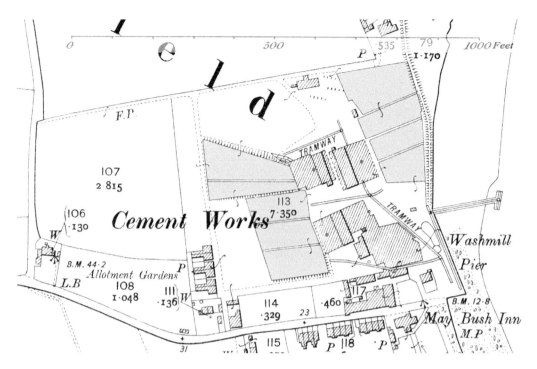

Plan of the Cement Works 1904. The plan shows all twelve 'cement' cottages and
six workers cottages along what is now called Deben Lane [143]

Some employees of the Cement Works have the benefit of living in a pair of semi-detached houses which have been built just inside the river wall a couple of hundred yards before we come to the Works. William Elliott, a cement maker from Northfleet in Kent, moved into one of the houses with his wife, Ellen and their family fairly recently. His eldest son, also William, is 18 and is employed in the works as an engine driver. The second son of the family, George, is still a scholar although he is now 14. There are two sisters, Elizabeth, 16, and Mary Ann, 4, all born in Northfleet.

Next door live Alfred and Maria Sawyer; Alfred is a labourer in the Cement Works. The benefit of living there is somewhat questionable because there is always a risk that a high tide will come over the river wall. Our Rector, the Reverend Thomas Henry Waller, has kept a perennial diary since at least 1850 and he recorded on 20th March 1874, just seven years ago, that there were very high tides over the walls. More recently, at the end of January 1877, he recorded that the high tides had flooded the marshes.

There has been some pretty awful weather earlier this year, the 19th of January 1881 to be precise; there was deep snow and there were 100 miles per hour gales which caused considerable damage. Thankfully there was no flooding in Waldringfield.

Just past the Works' housing, we have to leave the river wall and make our way inland to Lower Road in order to avoid passing through the Works'

grounds. As we walk along the footpath in a westerly direction we hear the piercing, 1-o'clock summons of the Wunnerful Whistle, a static steam engine, built in Leiston and used to power the machinery in the factory. At 1 o'clock each day it is used to notify the workers of the time.

Followed to its completion the footpath from the shore takes us to Lower Road (later to be known as Sandy Lane) but we would prefer, if we could, to turn left halfway along, just past the pond and a small building. The path would take us over to May Bush Lane (later to be known as Cliff Road). Unfortunately, that path also leads directly into the Cement Works, less than 100 yards behind the kilns, so Lower Road it has to be. The two hundred yard walk along Lower Road would be a pleasant rural experience but for the noise and the smell. At the end of the lane, on the corner with May Bush Lane is the village stores, run by Mrs Stollery. Poor Eliza was widowed only last year – just 42 years old with eight children in the family home. Her eldest daughters, Emma and Alice have left home; fortunately, the eldest son, Arthur, who is nineteen, works as a thatcher so that helps to keep the wolf from the door, so to speak. Frederick, 16, and George, 14, are agricultural labourers so they, too, help the family income but that still leaves eleven year old Harry, Isaac, 9, and Alfred, 6, as well as three year old Eliza and young Jessie who is just beginning to walk and talk. It's a hard life for Mrs Stollery. We'll pop in and buy something from her shop.

Mrs Stollery's shop [144]

Bidding good-bye to Mrs Stollery we walk down May Bush Lane in an attempt to regain the shoreline. Old widow Moles – Sarah Moles – lives in a ramshackle cottage on the left – one of two or three dwellings in a similar condition. Widow Moles is now 84 years old and she is supported by the Parish. She lives next door to widow Button who is a nurse. Mrs Button shares her house with her daughter, Sarah, and her son-in-law, James, who is a labourer in the Cement Works. Their first baby, Edith, arrived less than a year ago. Just after these cottages there is a footpath to the left which leads into the Cement Works. There is talk that they may build a row of cottages along there one day and even build a new village shop and bakery on the corner of the footpath with May Bush Lane. However, that is not going to happen any time soon. If and when it does, they may call it Deben Lane.

We cannot be absolutely certain that these two ladies occupied these two cottages because the censuses do not necessarily record occupation in strict order. A process of elimination carried out independently by two different parties within the History Group concluded that the ladies lived either in the two cottages on the left side of May Bush Lane or in the cottages which backed on to Pilots' Path. The census suggests that John and Sarah Moles, probably related to widow Moles but likely to be living in a cottage backing on to Pilot's path, had been blessed with a daughter only the day before the census. John was 24 and worked in the cement factory.

Off to the right of May Bush Lane, at the back of a terrace of three old cottages is another footpath – Pilots' Path – so called because it gives access to the top of Waldringfield cliff where the river pilots can watch for barges requiring their services. The top of the cliff affords the pilots a good view of Bowships where the barges wait for a pilot to board before advancing further upriver.

Clifftop view downriver through the trees [145]

The Cement Cottages with the Bush Inn
at the far end on the right [146]

We will not take Pilots' Path as it will cause us to miss out two of the most important buildings along the Waldringfield shoreline. They are Cliff House and The Bush Inn (Maybush). It would also cause us to miss the most recent of developments in the village – the twelve very new homes built in three blocks of four along the right-hand side of May Bush Lane, across the lane from the stable-block behind Cliff House. The new houses have been built to accommodate families of workers associated with the Cement Works and they are known collectively as 'Cement Cottages'. These cottages are so new that only the first block of four are depicted on the OS map for 1881. They have been constructed with 'no fines' concrete which is a relatively new technique involving the pouring of concrete between sheets of wooden shuttering.

The exact date(s) when these twelve cottages were completed is not known. One current owner, Roger Stollery, has records of statements made by his great grandfather which suggest a building date in the 1860s for the block nearest the inn.

I do have a rather badly photocopied eight-page legal document about various properties which my grandfather, AW Stollery (AW) had dealings with, mortgages on, purchased or sold from 1917 to 1962. They are difficult to read but:

From this information I can tell you that on 10 October 1877 the following concrete cottages existed, because this was when the 3 pieces of land with the six cottages Ryefield & Riverpoint, Ivydene & Basingstoke, Northcliffe & Ship Cottage were conveyed to George Mason from Henry Egerton Green & George Egerton Green and Arthur Thomas Cobbold. George Mason died in 1893 and these properties passed to his son Frank William Mason subject to the payment of annual rent to the successors of the late Colonel George Tomline, his heirs etc. Col George Tomline himself died in 1889, didn't marry and so didn't have any heirs; as a result there was no claim for rent made after 1891.'

However the OS map for 1881 shows only four of the cottages – those furthest from the inn. The 1881 census suggests that in this part of the village there were many more people living than could be accommodated if the twelve cottages were not there. The argument against the earlier date is the fact that George Mason did not begin to expand the business until 1873; it is possible that Frederick Last, the original owner, started a building programme, in which case that might have been the reason for the debt owed to Shadbolt, and for Last's eventual bankruptcy. However, such an explanation is purely speculative. Certainly, the technique of building relatively cheap concrete houses for workers was coming into vogue in the mid 19th century.

The Bush Inn and Cliff House with Cement Cottages in the background. The Bush and Cliff House were connected by tunnel in those days. This photograph was taken about 30 years after the 1881 Walk by which time the landlord was selling Cobbold Ales instead of the ale brewed by John Hill in Cliff House. See photo [80] for the Maybush in 1880 [147]

Roger Stollery continues:

'They should be called "CONCRETE COTTAGES". The concrete used was a mix of cement and stones for aggregate, but without any sand; this was an innovative method of construction. The walls were cast in quite large sections and the reasons for the lack of sand was so that there was no capillary path for water to travel from the outside to the inside of the wall. The voids between the stones, which were held together by the cement acted as insulation as well as preventing the water passing through from the outside. The other reason for not having a smooth finish to the outside of the concrete, was that the cement-render external skin, which is traditional on brick buildings was able to adhere well in the voids between the stones.

I have investigated a patent by either Taylor Woodrow or Wimpey who used exactly this method of construction in the late 1940s and early 1950s as a design to get round the lack of bricks after the Second World War. The description of their use of this 'no fines concrete' in large panels cast on site is exactly as our Victorian forefathers constructed the cottages. In the postwar period it was regarded as innovative. How much more innovative then was the construction of these concrete cottages 100 years before.'

The start of the tunnel from the Old Maltings (previously Cliff House) to the Maybush. The tunnel is now completely closed off so that there is no trace of it in the Maybush [148]

As we pass we bid 'Good-day' to David Smith and William Blewitt who are chatting on a doorstep – they are both steam engine drivers in the Cement Works. David and his wife, Matilda have an eleven year old daughter who was born in Ipswich but William and his wife, Sarah have a larger family with six children under the age of nine, also all born in Ipswich, except for the two month old baby, Frank, who was born in Waldringfield. A neighbour from a few doors away, Elizabeth Rands, married to Mark, a cement labourer, passes by with her four young children. They have recently moved down here from Gateshead, as the children's accents suggest. They are calling on Elizabeth Page, the wife of Ben, a mudder bargeman. Ben and Elizabeth also have four young children. Elizabeth also has an older child, Edward, who carries the surname Friend; he is fourteen years old and is away at work as an agricultural labourer.

It is time to move on and as we do, we see, at the end of the lane, on the right, the entrance to the 'Bush Inn'. The current landlords, George and Caroline Hunt, have been here since 1856. They are very busy people between coping with coproliters, cement workers and bargemen, as well as raising eleven children. For several years George Hunt ran the ferry to and from Stonner Point, conveying workers from the other side of the river; when he stopped, Isaac Stollery, Eliza's late husband, took over.

Across the lane from 'The Bush' and connected to the inn by a tunnel which passes under the lane is Cliff House. The current tenant, John Hill, runs a coal and malt business from the property. John also brews at Cliff House, growing his own barley in the plot at the back. John is now 54 so he is grateful for the help afforded by his sons, John and Harry, both of whom are learning the trade from their father. They use the tunnel to supply the Inn with beer which they sell at a shilling a gallon. We would go into the Bush to sample their wares but it is all rather rowdy, being that time when the thirsty workers come for their refreshment.

Outside the younger John and Harry are working on the jetty loading their wares on to a barge bound for Woodbridge. Alongside Cliff House, to the north, there is a brick-built storehouse recently constructed for the storage of coal.

Leaving Cliff House and making our way past the Bush we reach the beach. There are various horses, carts and tumbrils there and at the water's edge there is a barge laden with straw, destined for horses in London. Very shortly, at high water, this barge will be floated off prior to a passage to London docks.

As we pass below the cliff we are able to see the steep track which passes from the beach up to the

Buttram's Mill – a closer view than we would have from the shoreline. The Church tower is just visible to the left [149]

pilots' lookout point and then, about one hundred yards further along the beach, the end of a track which was used in the past for carting coprolite down to the shore from the region of Church Farm.

The lie of the land to the west gives on to an horizon which is dominated by the sails of Buttram's Mill. Closer scrutiny shows the very top of the Church tower, further to the left within the trees. Then we resume our walk southward across the saltmarsh which lies at the entrance to the Hilton inlet.

On the other (southerly) side of the saltmarsh there is a footpath for us to follow along the lower edges of two fields belonging to White Hall. The house, the barns and the stables do not come into sight until we are well into the second field with the saltmarsh below us to our left, and the house some three hundred yards away to the right. White Hall was the birthplace of Thomas Henry Waller who has been the Rector of Waldringfield since 1862. Although he will never know it, he started a 151-year consecutive run of Waller Rectors in Waldringfield.

His son John Henry now farms the land; the younger of twin boys, he was born in Ramsholt in 1858; currently single, he has taken over the tenancy

White Hall [150]

of both his father's farms, White Hall and Church Farm. Anna Hart, a 65 year old widow currently lives in White Hall and, at the time of the census there was a 12 year old servant girl, Annie Page from Newbourne.

We are now about half a mile from Early Creek which marks the southern limits of Waldringfield; in the distance we can see Hemley, Kirton Creek and the lower reaches of the Deben where barges ply the waters with cargoes of hay, coprolite, coal, chalk and cement.

The meadows at White Hall [151]

Working Boats

'I must go down to the seas again, to the lonely sea and the sky.
And all I ask is a tall ship and a star to steer her by;
And the wheel's kick and the wind's song and the white sail shaking,
And a grey mist on the sea's face and a grey dawn breaking.'

John Masefield

[152]

Trading schooners lying off Kyson, attributed to Thomas Churchyard 1798-1865 [153]

Working Vessels on the Deben

Who knows when the first working vessels appeared on the Deben? Britain's status as an island means that trade and transport from overseas has always been a feature of our history, as well as the arrivals and departures of people. The evidence of artefacts from the Bronze Age show that the 'Beaker people' had extensive trading networks with the continent – and they had settlements in the Waldringfield and Deben area.

Fast forward three thousand years of Iron Age, Romano-British and Anglo-Saxon periods, past the incursions of the Vikings and the Normans. Our 1348 mediaeval walk discovered a well-developed range of shipping, not only operating from the port of Goseford (near present-day Bawdsey) but up river to Waldringfield and Woodbridge, with possibly some of the smaller vessels calling at creeks and landing stages on the way. The word 'barge' came into the language around this point. Chaucer's seaman in *The Canterbury Tales* (written between 1387-1400) was master of a 'barge' called the *Maudelyne*.

Barge was, and is, quite a general word indicating a transport vessel: there are canal barges, state barges, river barges – but on the River Deben mention of a barge is most likely to conjure an image of a distinctive silhouette; tan sails, a strong, cargo-carrying hull, an aura of self-contained purposefulness. The Thames sailing barge, which gave late-19th-/early-20th-century Waldringfield families such as the Pages,

Muddies pause for a photograph. Only two photographs of muddies have been discovered
in our searches. Both originate from elsewhere, either Essex or Kent [154]

Ruffles, Quantrills and Stebbings their livelihoods, is a locally developed craft which has won an astonishing place in public affection.

John Kemp (mid-20th-century master of sb. *Thalatta*) believed that 'the distinctive character and individuality of thought' of these earlier sailor men, which had been developed by 'the hardship they continued to endure and the resourcefulness that their primitive methods demanded' was a prime factor that ensured that these sailing vessels survived long enough for their worth to be recognised -- and, in some cases, for great efforts to be made to ensure their preservation. Kemp was inspired by his predecessor Bob Ruffles (skipper of *Thalatta* for 15 years) to found the East Coast Sail Trust in 1966 and when money was needed for the ECST's survival and expansion in the 1970s George Jones worked tirelessly to help. George had been mentored by Jimmy Quantrill in his boyhood and this had included some time working on a barge aged 14. So perhaps there is something in John Kemp's theory.

Mud, Mud, Glorious Mud

Possibly no bargemen's work was harder than the Muddies. In the 19th century, the manufacture of Portland cement required a plentiful supply of good quality mud. It lay in abundance in the riverbed at Waldringfield and according to the 'muddies' who dug it 'yew c'n tell from tha' taste thass the best'.

These men knew how to work physically. It would take seven or eight hours for four men to fill the hold. The digging ground would be selected long before low water and the barge would be kedge-anchored in place or tied to poles. Chains would be passed below the hull. Then, at low water, the barge would be lying on the mud over those chains which prevented the vessel from being sucked into the very stuff the men were trying to dig. Sackcloth would be wrapped around the base of the mast and over the shrouds and gunwales on the working side; the mud would literally fly once they got going with their fly-tools. This was work for the entire crew including the skipper and his mate; those two were also experts in boatmanship, or to be precise, barging. These flat-bottomed vessels had characteristics of their very own. According to Martin Hazell, in his book *Sailing Barges*, bargemen would boast that their 'craft could go anywhere after a heavy dew and turn to windward up a drainpipe'.

One of the barges used for mud collection in Waldringfield was the *Kingfisher* and there are rare photographic records of her or a sister-vessel plying these waters or berthed at the Quay. Called 'stumpies', they were distinguishable from other barges by their shorter masts and also by their lower gunwales.

Jack Stebbing was the skipper of *Kingfisher* and Ben Page was his mate, although several years his senior. They both lived in the Cement Cottages on Cliff Road. According to Walter Tye, their favourite place for digging was off White Hall Farm. The mud there was relatively free of grit and 'dug up just like pork lard'. Walter Tye was also responsible for the information that 'Jack Stebbing, quiet on water, could be a terror on land and was well known in the local inns for his pugilistic ability.' That, despite his sharing a name with a famous Methodist, John Wesley.

Heyday of the Sailing Barges

Thames barges which are still sailing in the 21st century (such as *Thalatta*, *May* and *Orinoco*) give an impression that they have been part of the local landscape for ever. In fact, the period when sailing barges were in full commercial use lasted rather less than a century. They developed in parallel with the later stages of the Industrial Revolution, faltered in the 1920s and 30s and almost entirely ceased trading soon after the end of WW2. The last commercial cargo was carried to Ipswich by the sb. *Cambria* in 1970 but their trade had died decades earlier. Nevertheless it's a measure of the affection they inspired that they have not all been forgotten – unlike, for instance the trading brigs and schooners that had preceded them.

There were hundreds of barges by the year 1900 and most have gone – some repurposed as houseboats, some built into new wharves and quays, others abandoned on the saltings or up small creeks, their timber skeletons blackened and rotted. *Three Sisters*, for instance, built in 1865, a regular Waldringfield and Deben visitor, carrying agricultural products (including London waste) was scuttled in Kirton Creek (further down river from Waldringfield) in 1922 when there was no more work for her, and has been decaying there slowly ever since.

However, although we might like to believe that Jack Stebbings's sb. *Kingfisher* has disintegrated in the small creek that bears her name, just south of the Beach at Waldringfield, it probably isn't true. The *Kingfisher* who worked in industrial Waldingfield was built in 1899 as a 'stumpie' – usually the cheapest, roughest construction – and her work as a 'muddie' would have ended with the closure of the Cement Works. Her fate might well have been the same as *Three Sisters* except... in WW2 a barge named *Kingfisher* was one of a group irreparably damaged when a German FW bomber came down in the Medway where they were on mine-watching duties. This type of duty, which involved barges being moored, scarcely moving for the duration of the war left many of them fatally weakened by marine worm, even if they escaped more dramatic harm. But was this the Waldringfield *Kingfisher* or another? – we may never know.

Fortunately, *Kingfisher* need not be entirely forgotten as there is a photograph in the collection of Cyril Stollery, where she is identified visiting Woodbridge in the company of other spritsail barges.

Kingfisher at Woodbridge (also in the photo are two spritsail barges and a 'boomie') [155]

Cargoes

Even in their 19th-century heyday, the barge's role was not a glamourous one. The firm surface and deep water access of Waldringfield beach made it an ideal location for the unloading of 'London muck' – horse and cattle excrement that was brought to Suffolk to be used as manure, whilst the return load might, for instance, be hay or straw from the local farms to fuel the cycle when London was still a horse-drawn city. Barges with their shallow draft, generous capacity and flat bottoms were ideal for their purpose. It was not new that farms and the city should interchange in this way but the extraordinary growth of London during the 19th century increased the volume exponentially.

The materials needed to fuel 19th-century industrial development also needed transport. While the developing networks of canals and railways took some of this load, the British coastal trade was busier than it had ever been. Coal, for instance, was regularly brought to Waldringfield and Woodbridge by water. Brigs, 'billyboys' and trading schooners would still have been seen on the river at the time of our 1881 walk (though Woodbridge lost its status as a customs port soon after). The Deben, however, was beginning to silt up; the river entrance had always posed an additional problem to deeper-keeled vessels. From the 1860s the Thames barges were being developed to work outside their home river as strong sailing vessels with varied and flexible uses and were displacing many of these older designs, such as the schooners. Some of the barges used for longer distance work – such as freighting coal – were gaff-rigged with booms to their mainsails and mizzens. They required larger crews and were known as 'boomies'. Coal continued coming up the Deben until the 1930s but by that time engines had been fitted to the barges that were used.

Barges, however lovely, are essentially cargo-carrying boxes. Their basic shape is simple and their hulls could be cheaply and quite quickly built to freight the increasing range of cargoes. Fortunately for Thames barge development the 19th-century owners and the skippers were competitive in their leisure as well as their business practices. Annual barge matches began on the Medway in the 1860s and soon became established off the Suffolk and Essex coast. This made for greater interest in design and construction. Although barge-building never took root on the Deben, major centres were established on the neighbouring Orwell and Stour. Many of these Suffolk and Essex barges became known for their more attractive, less 'box-like' lines and good sailing qualities.

Unloading muck on the beach (note sail used as a cover on the barge in the background) [156]

Spritsail barge, believed to be *Una*, at Waldringfield in 1910 [157]

The main type of barge developed in the later 19th century and regarded as 'classic' today was the 'spritty' whose mainsail (and usually their mizzen) were loose-footed and therefore easier to brail (tie up) out of the way. Their topsail, being 50' above the deck, was considered especially useful to catching the first stirrings of a morning breeze and enabling them to get moving early.

The 'Spritsail' owes its name to the type of four-sided mainsail which is supported by the 'sprit', another name for a spar.

The development of this simple and rugged rig meant that no adjustment was needed from the crew when the boat was tacked. The incorporation of winches and the brailing of sails eased the demands on the crew. Such improvements meant that the Spritsail Barge could carry cargoes of up to 100 tons, and could be handled by just a skipper, mate and, if required, a 'third hand'. This made the Spritsail a very cost-efficient means of commercial transport. Whilst the Spritsail rig is recorded as far back as the Middle Ages, the hey-day of the Spritsail was the late 19th century and early 20th century. By the 1930s its commercial advantage had been eroded and its role was ultimately overtaken by road transport.

Despite its shallow draft the Spritsail sailed well, due to leeboards on each side of the hull. These could be lowered to prevent the barge being pushed sideways by the force of the wind on the sails. When the leeboards were raised the draft was limited to just the depth of the hull, meaning the Spritsail barge could sail virtually anywhere. This made it ideal for working the winding, muddy, shallow Deben.

Avocet, registered as *Adieu*, built in 1929, passing through the Stonner Channel in 2003 [158]

Owners and Their Barges

Some of the main barge operators serving 19th-century and early-20th-century Waldringfield were Hastes, Wrinches and Whitmores and Parkers of Bradwell – of whom at least Wrinches and Parkers operated 'stackies'. These were spritail barges often with the slightly wider decks on which hay, straw, wood or bricks could be stacked. *Rachel Julia* is an example, also *Bluebell* and *Victoria*. When carrying hay or straw they had special irons to hold the stack in place and the skipper had to lean out to see round it. The return trip to London was likely to have taken about a fortnight.

Packards of Ipswich ran the Coprolite Barges. At the height of the trade in 1877 10,000 tons of coprolite were dispersed all over the kingdom from the quays of the Deben and the Alde. Some of the barges loading coprolite from Waldringfield included *Ammonite*, *Fossil*, *Nautilus*, *Dewdrop*. In 1920s Packard's merged with Fisons.

From the 1870s until about 1912 Waldringfield's main industry was the Cement Works which required barges of different types – the 'muddies' (often 'stumpies' like *Kingfisher*) to deliver the locally sourced mud and then 'spritties' delivering other raw materials (such as chemicals) and taking away the finished product. Bigger barges (often 'boomies') were used for longer voyages. Eight Masons' barges operated in and out of Waldringfield. George Mason (1812-1893) and his son Frank William Mason (1848-1927) who worked alongside him and carried on following his father's death, named some of the barges after family members: *Augusta*, *Grace*, *Elsie Bertha*.

Frank Mason had married Bertha Turner (1855-1927) and their baby daughter who died in her first year (1898) was called Elsie. George Mason had both a sister and a daughter called Augusta and another daughter called Grace Eliza. Frank and his family moved to live in Northcliff in Felixstowe from which vantage point they could watch their barges on passage. Barge topsails often carried their owner's logo.

Their other barges included *Petrel*, *Excelsior*, *Orinoco*, *Jumbo*. *Kingfisher* was another one of theirs. After the Masons moved their Cement Works inland, many of their barges were taken over by the Ipswich companies of Cranfield and R&W Paul, who

The *Sir Alan Herbert* [159]

continued to employ the Waldringfield families as their skippers. Other barges not owned by Masons but which served Waldringfield Cement Works were *Ocean Queen*, *Three Sisters*, *Frederick William*, *Lady of the Wave*. The barge *Alcyone* is recorded delivering coal to the Quay in 1903.

Barges were flexible and not usually confined to a single specialist cargo. They often changed hands and sometimes changed rigs. It's usually a mistake to generalise about barges. The barge used to take away the final cargo of Mason's cement and the dismantled machinery was *Freston Tower*, owned by Haste's and the last barge regularly working the Deben (carrying loads of shingle from the Deben Bar for the construction of the Woodbridge by pass) is said, by Hervey Benham, to have been the *Tuesday*, from Kent, whose skipper was found dead in her cabin.

On a happier note many Waldringfield, Woodbridge and other Suffolk residents supported the East Coast Sail Trust in the 1970s when the Rochester-built barge *Lady Jean* was re-purposed to join John Kemp's *Thalatta* as a school ship and renamed the *Sir Alan Herbert*.

Hufflers and Pilots

Other river jobs connected with the 19th-century and early-20th-century barges and working boats included 'hufflers' such as Dick Elvin of Woodbridge who would assist vessels through the upper reaches of the river and into their berths. Hervey Benham records two pilot-hufflers based at Waldringfield, Ted Marsh and Nelson Oxborrow. Further down river the Newsom family were river-mouth pilots, assisting barges and other trading vessels in and out of the difficult entrance. They later adapted their skills to assisting some of the cruising yachtsmen who visited Waldringfield when working boats began to decline and sailing for pleasure became more popular.

Waldringfield (and the Deben generally) has not developed fishing fleets as have some other rivers. Fishing from Waldringfield has tended to be an individual enterprise conducted in a variety of ways (trawling, trammel netting, spinning). Boats are used as available. One former working boat, still seen on the beach until approximately 1950 was *Hustler*. Although to modern eyes she looks like a large old-fashioned dinghy, she was originally built – in 1881, the year of our walk – as a fast pilot cutter. She needed to be fast to be the first to reach a likely customer and offer her

Ena [160]

services. When *Hustler* was not needed for this work she was used for trawling under sail. Later she was used for pleasure cruising (sleeping on the floorboards under the stars) and even for racing. *Hustler* survived two World Wars and perhaps symbolises the way many Waldringfield working families, as well as their boats, needed to adapt as the world changed around them.

Jimmy Quantrill and George Jones's *Hustler* [161]

Never Leave Your Teeth Behind

Stories abound about Dunkirk and the evacuation, in May 1940, of just over a third of a million Allied soldiers from the beaches. There are stories of death, of desperate injury and destruction and there are stories of miraculous joy, of bravery and of heroism.

Code-named 'Operation Dynamo' the evacuation involved not only Royal Naval vessels but also approximately 850 'little ships'. British destroyers and troop ships were unable to approach the beaches; as a consequence, small boats with shallow drafts were required to ferry the soldiers to the larger ships.

Barges fitted the bill ideally and their crews, of course, were professional, brave merchant seamen. In response to a Government appeal on May 27th 1940, six of the barges owned by the grain merchants, R & W Paul, set sail down the East Coast and across the mine-ridden English Channel toward Dunkirk. Air attacks were constant. This was a highly dangerous operation.

One of these barges was *Ena*, a robust looking vessel that is known to have visited Waldringfield. She was built at the Navy Yard in Harwich in 1906, a sister ship for *Thalatta*, and very like her. Both were described as 'mulies' because of the arrangement of the rigging. They have mizzens with booms, but mainsails with sprits. *Ena* was built of wood (pitch pine on oak frames) and had a cargo capacity of about 150 tons of grain. She was purchased, new, by

Paul's in 1907 and for her entire working life she was owned by that company or its successors. In the Great War she served as an ammunition barge and carried supplies to the armies on the continent of Europe.

In May 1940 the skipper of this particular brave 'little ship' was Alfred John Page. Born in Waldringfield in 1886, he was the seventh child of Ben Page, mate of the sb. *Kingfisher*. Despite the height of his father and others in his family Alfred stood just under five feet and seven inches and he was known as 'Tich'.

On arrival off Dunkirk 'Tich' Page was ordered to beach *Ena* close to a smaller sand barge, *H.A.C.* The crews of both barges were then ordered to abandon their vessels and return to England on a minesweeper. It seems that both barges remained there for some time before they were spotted by late-arriving troops and used to make good their escape, despite constant enemy bombardment.

Alex Smith of the Duke of Wellington's Regiment recalls how he and fellow soldiers refloated *H.A.C.* whilst *Ena* was refloated by Lt Col WG McKay and men of the 19th Field Regiment, Royal Artillery. Captain Atley of the East Yorks Regiment recalls

making a raft and using shovels to access *Ena* and then helping on board thirty-six other men, some of them wounded. Few of the men had any sailing experience except, perhaps, Atley's on the Norfolk Broads but Alex Smith describes 'the most remarkable barge race of all time' as they crossed the channel successfully under continued bombardment.

Ena made her way close to the South Goodwin lightship where she was spotted at 8pm on 2nd June by the Watkins tug *Kenia* and taken in tow to Margate in Kent. However, the harbour was full so she was towed back out to sea and anchored off Deal. The soldiers were put ashore and she was left at anchor.

Days passed before there was any more news of her. Quite naturally Alfred and his employers at Paul's had assumed the barge lost, like many others. Consequently, they were somewhat amazed to learn that she was languishing off the Kent coast. Alfred was sent from Ipswich to recover her.

He found *Ena* seaworthy but stripped of all her gear. 'They had taken the sweeps, mooring lines, fenders and even my false teeth which I had left behind in a glass of water by my bunk!' he said. 'You

Paul's barge skippers (including 'Tich') during a dock strike in 1936. Left to right: Charlie Webb snr (Ipswich), 'Tich' Page (Waldringfield), Dick Finbow (Trimley), 'Scotty' (Pin Mill), Walter Hill (London), Bob Manning (Holbrook), Ernie Bloomfield (Harwich), Len Webb (Pin Mill), 'Brooky' (London), Stan Lucas (Pin Mill) [162]

can't trust these men of Kent!' He had assumed – and the myth persisted – that *Ena* had sailed her own way toward home and had been plundered on arrival by the said 'men of Kent'. The true story of the soldiers' achievement in re-floating her and sailing her back themselves, was not generally known until about thirty years later – and even now people sometimes hanker after the legend.

Alfred John 'Tich' Page sailed *Ena* back to Ipswich where she continued working until 1948 when she was converted to a motor barge. 'Tich', her skipper, born and bred in Waldringfield, died in 1950 aged 64.

Ena continued to trade as a motor barge until 1974 when the story of the soldiers' rescue from Dunkirk had become known from eye-witness accounts and letters preserved in the Imperial War Museum. She was then restored to sail and retained by the company (Paul's and Sander's) over the next 25 years for corporate hospitality. She sailed to many Dunkirk reunions and took the company's guests to barge matches as well as on trips abroad. When the company was taken over, *Ena* was deemed surplus to requirements. She now lies abandoned on the Hoo peninsula in Kent. As yet even a TV appeal has not found someone to take on the challenge of her restoration. Will *Ena* survive in fact or fiction? This is her legend, as told in AP Herbert's 1968 novel *The Singing Swan*, in which *Ena* becomes *Full Moon* and her skipper is called 'Arthur':

'In the morning, at nine, Dunkirk – and many thousand soldiers – surrendered. But 338, 226 men had been safely taken to the English coasts.

Now Full Moon *was truly alone. Nothing moved in the roads, no man moved on the silent beaches where din had reined for nine long days. She had not done much but she had done all that was demanded. Now she was not needed, she was not molested, her masters had left her to the enemy; she was uncomfortable; and one day she decided to go home.*

How exactly she went cannot be told for there was none to see [...]

One night, or midnight, on the top of the tide, she lifted her anchor and sailed away [...]

I like to think that she presented her fine broad transom to the wind and pointed her proud head the way she was going. At all event steering six hours westward and six hours north easterly, the streams canelling out, she made her stately passage home [...]

Her last leg took her to the Sandwich Flats. There at least they found her, Arthur's topsail still set.'

Ena, who rescued so many at Dunkirk, now in need of rescue herself [163]

The Waller Family

The very existence of the Waldringfield History Group is due to the discovery of a collection of photographic glass slides taken by Thomas Naunton Waller. Therefore it seems only right to include a short history of the Waller family.

One of the earliest Wallers recorded was Jeptha Waller, born about 1590. Another Jeptha Waller, baptised in 1616, married Susan Goss who was the owner of some land in Waldringfield.

In 1830 George Waller, son of Thomas Waller of Ramsholt, married Anne Edwards whose parents were tenanting Wood Hall in Sutton from Thomas. The newly-wed couple came over the river to live at White Hall. They had two children, Thomas Henry, born in 1832 and Georgiana born in 1834. Shortly after the birth of Georgiana, George died. Anne and her two small children returned to her family on the other side of the Deben.

Thomas Henry Waller studied at the College of Agriculture in Cirencester before proceeding to Clare College, Cambridge to study for a BA before being ordained to the curacy of St Matthew's in Ipswich.

In 1856 Thomas Henry Waller married Jane Pretyman of Ramsholt Lodge. In 1862 he became the Rector of Waldringfield and remained as such for 47 years during which time he kept a perennial diary. The Rectory, then, was Rivers Hall. Thomas Henry and Jane went on to have eleven children

- Mary Jane, born at Ramsholt, lived to 100 years
- George Edward – 1st twin b 1858 who worked for a bank, married – one daughter
- John Henry – 2nd twin, married and farmed White Hall. No children
- Anne Elizabeth b 1859 at Ramsholt – sadly died at 25 years old
- Agnes Vertue born 1861 at Ipswich
- Thomas Naunton b 1863 in Waldringfield. Married, had 4 children
- Alfred Whalley b 1864 in Waldringfield married and had two children.
- Georgiana b 1866 in Waldringfield
- Katherine Emma b 1869 in Waldringfield
- Eleanor Pretyman b 1871 but died at one month
- Arthur Pretyman b 1872 in Waldringfield

None of the daughters married. Georgiana was confined to a bath chair for reasons unknown. John Henry Waller was a farmer. Thomas Naunton Waller trained as an engineer. His hobby was photography.

Alfred Whalley Waller qualified as a doctor at St Thomas' Hospital. Sadly his son, Thomas, was killed at Ypres in the Great War. His sacrifice is commemorated in a window at All Saints Church, although the place of his death is incorrectly stated there as Arras.

Arthur Pretyman Waller followed in his father's footsteps, eventually becoming Rector of Waldringfield. He was married to Constance and they had four children Trevor (Kit Clark's father), Henry, Ruth and Constance (Poppy). Trevor followed in the family tradition and became the next Rector. He married Nora Morfey in 1934 and they had four children – Alfred, Katherine (Kit), John and Julia. Kit, a nurse, married Joseph Clark, a mariner who became the first chairman of the Waldringfield History Group and is now its lifelong President.

John Waller went to sea but eventually returned and became Rector of Waldringfield, Newbourne and Hemley. He died 151 years to the day that Thomas Henry Waller became Rector.

Coprolite

"My Village"

'…We'd "Pits," deep dug for raising
The coprolites they found;
In layers oft abundant,
Far down below the ground.

Then washed with river water
Twas duly put aboard
The pretty red sailed barges,
Our artists so adored.'

[164]

An extract from 'My Village' by Georgiana Waller, in *A Guide to Waldringfield and District*, edited by Walter Tye c.1950

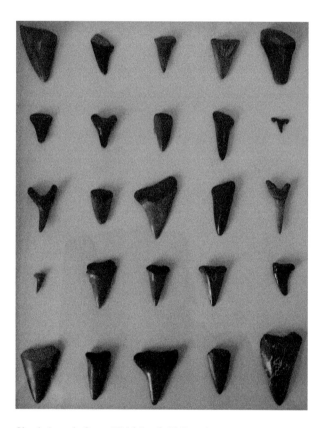

Sharks' teeth from Waldringfield Beach collected by Jackie Brinsley [165]

The finding of coprolite in and around Waldringfield represented a turning point in the history of the village. From being a quiet, agricultural environment it became a centre of open mining and of sail barging.

Coprolite, from the Greek kopros (dung) and lithos (stone), is found in seams up to 24 inches thick, lying between the London clay and the more superficial red crag, often at a depth of 30 or 40 feet but sometimes very close to the surface. Despite its name the phosphate-rich, nodular material is not simply fossilised dung; it is also derived from bones of prehistoric creatures and from whales, sharks and other creatures of the sea which covered this area so long ago. The coprolite is known colloquially as 'dinosaur dung' but its formation is likely to have been far more recent than 66 million years ago when dinosaurs disappeared from the scene.

The first recorded use of coprolite to fertilise crops was in 1717 in Levington where its benefit had been discovered fortuitously. At least a century passed before deposits were discovered in Waldringfield but the industry then flourished quickly.

Edward Packard began grinding coprolite nodules for use as fertiliser at Snape in 1843. In 1850 he set up a coprolite grinding business in Ipswich with a view to encouraging the production of super-phosphate not only in Ipswich but further up the Suffolk coast. This involved the dissolving of coprolite in sulphuric acid. In 1857 Packard set up a complete fertiliser factory in Bramford where he not only ground the coprolite but also manufactured the sulphuric acid. Joseph Fison followed soon after with his own factory. Both gentlemen owned barges with which to collect the coprolite.

Thomas Henry Waller, Rector of Waldringfield [166]

Several landowners on the east side of the Deben became involved in the digging of coprolite in the decade before 1850. One such landowner was Thomas Waller of Sutton. There were quays both at Methersgate and Stonner Point from which barges were able to transport the material to Ipswich.

The earliest reference to the industry in Waldringfield was in 1858 when Kelly's Directory reported the excavation of coprolite as a feature of the Parish. Thomas Henry Waller became the Rector of Waldringfield in 1862 and in his perennial diary he makes many references to the coprolite extraction which took place on his land. There was considerable money to be made and the good Rector used a significant amount of it to renovate All Saints Church and to build a village school.

The industry developed at a rapid pace, providing employment for hundreds of workers who might otherwise be unemployed as a consequence of agriculture being on the decline.

By 1877 ten thousand tons of coprolite were despatched annually from the Orwell and the Deben, much of it from Waldringfield where it was loaded on to beached barges at low water. The time available for loading between tides was short so it was a matter

Fertiliser advertisment from the late 19th century [167]

of 'all hands on deck' and the adoption of a one way system up and down planks with the barrows.

There were excavations on most farms and people were even digging for it in their gardens. Some were prepared to steal it, such was its value.

The Ipswich Journal   9 Jan 1858

Charge of Stealing Coprolite

Alfred Hurren, 26, Francis Lawrence, 24 and Samuel Tunmer, 23, labourers were indicted for stealing at Sutton, on the 26th of October one ton of coprolite value 40s, the property of Robert Knipe Cobbold, Esq, Bredfield.

Mr Dasent appeared for the prosecution; Mr Marriott defended the prisoners.

Prosecutor has property on the Sutton side of the Woodbridge River, and on Friday, the 23rd of October, he had two heaps of coprolite at his wharf at Wethersgate [sic] ready to be shipped; they were fenced round with elm and whitethorn faggots, bond [sic] with brier and covered over with seaweed. They were seen safe at two o clock in the afternoon of the day in question William Dammant, in Mr Cobbold's employ, who said they were got from several pits on his master's farm; there were some shells with them. A few coprolites were picked up on shore, but they 'ran bigger and clearer' than those found inland. On the morning of the 24th he found one or the heaps been disturbed, and about a ton missing. Cutts, the constable, afterwards showed witnesses a sample of coprolite which he identified as his master's; there were portions of faggot with it.

By Mr Marriott: Other persons beside Mr Cobbold have coprolite pits on the same coast.

Mr Marriott: How do people protect their coprolite?

Witness: Some let them lay naked. (Laughter) Mr Cobbold puts wood round his, but I don't know anyone else who does on that shore.

John Hill, maltster, Waldringfield, remembered on Saturday morning, the 24th October about 7 o'clock. seeing a boat lying on the mud opposite the cliff at that place, about a mile from Mr Cobbold's wharf. He then saw one man in the boat. In the afternoon between 2 and 3 o'clock, witness went and offered to help the boat off; there were then three men and some coprolite in the boat and witness remarked. 'You load deep.' He left the boat and afterwards returned when he said to Hurren 'I doubt this will be a bad job for you for yonder comes Hunt, Mr Cobbold's man, downriver.'

George Hunt said he was employed by Mr Cobbold to raise the coprolite on his farm. In consequence of what Hill had told him on the day in question witness went to the boat on the mud and found the three prisoners there. He asked permission to take a sample of the coprolite and Hurren said he might do and 'shaked like a leaf.' (Laughter)

Mr Dasent: Did you say anything to make him shake?

Witness: I 'axed' him if he could give a good account of the coprolite. He said he could. I could see directly it was Mr Cobbold's, I afterwards compared the sample with my master's heap, which had disturbed and found them correspond; there were in the sample shells, small twigs, and seaweeds, such as the heap was covered with.

Mr Dasent: Was the boat loaded with inland coprolite or coprolite found onshore?

Witness: Inland; there is a great difference. Lawrence afterwards told me he had picked up the coprolite from under Mr Pretyman's rocks, which are about a mile from where the boat was found.

Witness produced a small sample he had picked up at the latter place which was found to be quite different from that found inland.

Mr Dasent: How fast could you gather it under the rocks mentioned?

Witness: I should think you might get a bushel in a twelve month. (Laughter.)

By Mr Marriott: I have no doubt the coprolite found in the boat was Mr Cobbold's.

Re-examined: I don't know anyone who fences this coprolite in the same way as Mr Cobbold does.

James Nicholls, bailiff to prosecutor, also spoke to the correspondence of the sample from prisoner's boat with his master's heap. On evening of the 24th of October he accompanied Police Constable Cutts to Bawdsey Ferry and apprehended the three prisoners at the Victoria Inn. Witness afterwards went in search of the boat found it lashed to the smack of a man named WM Clarke: the boat and smack contained coprolite. One of the prisoners said he thought it a 'rum one' if they could swear to coprolite.

Cross examined: Could not swear to clean coprolite but he swore to it from the different things mixed with it being the same those in his masters.

Policeman Cutts: On Friday afternoon, the 23rd Oct, saw the three prisoners drinking together at the Swan Inn, Woodbridge and one o'clock the following morning he saw them at the Cock and Pie. Lawrence and Hurren are fishermen, and Tunmer a labourer.

Upon going to Bawdsey on the following day he asked Lawrence where his boat was and he said it was gone to sea; but Mr Clarke afterwards told Witness it was alongside his smack and that he had advanced 2s 3d on the coprolite. I took possession of the boat smack and coprolite. When in the cell Tunmer said. 'I should like to see a magistrate to-day for I can clear myself. I was only a hired servant to Lawrence and Hurren and I was to have 5s for the night to help them with the coprolite in the boat and out.'

Mr Marriott: Were the prisoners present during this conversation

Witness: No. Tunmer began it.

It was proved by other witnesses that Lawrence cleared out the boat at Kingston on Friday the 23rd Oct, and borrowed a skep at Woodbridge he said he going fishing; the latter was afterwards found filled with coprolite in the boat.

This being the case for the prosecution.

Mr Marriott addressed the jury for the prisoner's, remarking that the question for them to determine was whether the coprolite found in prisoner's boat and which they were found dealing with as innocent persons, had clearly proved to be Mr Cobbold's. He contended it had not—that there nothing conclusive in any of the proofs of identity which had been set up; for although it been asserted that twigs and other things mixed in the sample, none bad been pointed out. As to the statement made by Tunmer that must not prejudice the other prisoners as they were not present when it was made.

The Chairman summed up and the jury at once found all the prisoners guilty.

They were each sentenced to 6 months hard labour.

'Old' Sam Moules with his cart: A tumbrel returning from the beach or from the coprolite washing and sorting [168]

Coprolite diggers on the Orwell [169]

Coprolite pits tended to be 'V'-shaped, with tiered shelves from three to six feet wide running along the 'face' side where the extraction was taking place. The men worked in gangs of four, each gang keeping to its own shelf, or 'kench'. A gang of four was expected to move about 3½ tons a day. The topmost kenches were usually worked by the most practiced coproliters; wheeling a barrow of soil on a nine-inch plank over a pit some thirty to fifty feet deep took strength and a steady nerve.

But as Georgiana Waller concluded;

'Despite some obvious danger
The casualties were few.
As far as memory serves me,
No fatal one I knew.'

The work was hard as they were paid by the load, but the pay was good and the younger, stronger men, responsible for digging the seams and for loading the barges, could earn up to 16 shillings a week. (There were 20 shillings in a pound.)

Coprolite could be mined for 8-10 shillings a ton and sold at 24 shillings a ton. The manufactured phosphate sold at £6-£7 a ton, about half the price of the other popular fertilizer of the time, phosphate enriched guano.

Once the coprolite had been extracted from the seam it would be sifted, usually by teenage boys, then loaded on to a tumbrel and taken off to be washed.

That was usually a job for the older men. Coprolite nodules, along with a certain amount of dirt and bones, would be shovelled into sieves which, when full, were placed on a ledge in a tank, just below the surface of the water. The washer would push backwards and forwards with a long stick until the nodules were clean.

Often the washing would be carried out on or close to the shore. From photographs, it appears that washing took place very close to where Gorse Cabin is today, next to the Sailing Club. Once washed, the coprolite nodules needed sorting. Small boys, often only ten years old but no longer expected to attend school, would sort the coprolite for three shillings a week.

The washed material would be tipped on to a sorting table, from which the boys would pick out anything that would not pass as coprolite with the manure merchants. To avoid cutting their hands on sharp-edged shells, they would push the coprolite from side to side with a wooden scraper and use their remaining hands to throw the rejected material over their shoulders.

Once sorted the coprolite would be taken by tumbrel to the beach to be loaded on to a barge.

Bernard O'Connor quotes Walter Tye who said in 1950:

'In those days barges were always coming and going, bringing in manure and cattle food from London, and taking away coprolite, farm produce and cement. Old inhabitants say that hardly a week went by but what Fred Strange in his Victoria, *or Stebbing in the* Kingfisher *or Fred Ducker in the* Three Sisters *were seen making their way down the Deben.*

Then, of course, there was Jimmy Quantrill and his Azariah *then operating from Pin Mill, who was frequently seen in local waters, bringing back a load of "eye powder" from Dunkirk to grind in with artificial manures...'*

Back: Mary, Alfred, Tom & Georgie Waller and Fred Flegg. Sitting: Mrs Jane Waller, Mrs Sarah Dood, Rev TH Waller, Agnes Waller and Kate Waller. Front: Arthur P Waller. Date unknown. [170]

In the early 1890s the industry began to decline. The seams were becoming exhausted and safety regulations imposed by the Quarries Act 1893 were becoming tighter. Phosphates from abroad were proving cheaper. In the Waldringfield area all pits appear to have been closed by 1895. Some effort was made over the following few years to level areas where the pits had been, especially if they were in the middle of a field.

As for the coproliters themselves, having earned good wages, they had little desire to return to agriculture, which was then passing through acute depression. Many of the younger and fitter men left to join the army, navy or police and, of course, the Cement Works was still in full flight. Some of the older men, who had accumulated savings, invested their capital in small businesses.

So what remains? There are definite depressions in some of the fields in an around Waldringfield and there are some definite pits, none more marked than the side of the Waldringfield cliff where some of the beach huts are built on those 'kenches', or shelves, referred to earlier. However, the best, most used relic of the old industry must be the Flint Road described in the next section.

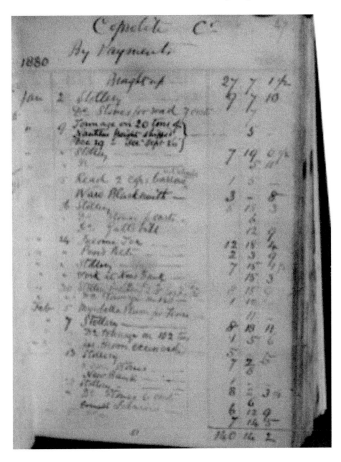

Waller accounts showing payments to diggers for coprolite digging in 1880 [171]

The Flint Road

Route of the Flint Road [172]

This story is all about access to fresh water, which in the late 1800s was about the digging of wells or access to springs etc. Waldringfield's coprolite mining industry needed to wash sand and clay off the mined material to reveal fossilised dung or coprolite, as it was known, before further transport by road or river to be ground up into phosphate fertiliser.

One such washing station, shown in the photograph, was located more or less where the Waldringfield Sailing Club stands today. The water for washing was taken from the river and the waste water from the washing operation was allowed to run down the foreshore and back into the river.

The coprolite was transported by horsedrawn tumbrels along the beach and up past the spring to the road at Church Farm. This must have been a well worn track in the late 1800s, as there was coprolite working not just into the cliff by the river, but in pits not far away at White Hall and other adjacent areas.

There was a by-product of this operation: the washed flints that were rejected. These helped to maintain the track used by the tumbrels hauled by several horses. A pile of such stones is shown in the foreground of the photograph.

Later after World War I, when sailing began to be popular, huts appeared on the shelves of land left by the coproliters and the source of water remained the spring. Roger Stollery's first memories of getting water for the huts in the 1950s was from a pump in an outbuilding at the Maybush Inn with water carried in buckets from a special wooden shoulder carrier. It was not until the 1960s that the Waldringfield Sailing Club, laid on mains water and drainage for the Clubhouse.

His father Cyril writing in 1966 about the control problems of access to the slipway at the bottom of Cliff Road recalls more of this post WW1 history:

'Going back a good way, the coprolite workings resulted in a roadway of washed flints right along the beach up the low cliff in front of the Club and along the whole front of the Seaclose Field through a gate up through the meadows to Church Farm. There is a spring in the meadows from which we fetched water for years. A right-of-way branched off this road across the White Hall fields towards Hemley. It was pleasant custom for villagers to walk along the shore and up through the meadows to Church and back.

When Everard closed the right of way at the gate on the river wall we were as annoyed as anyone else, but it was accepted by all the village as a necessary restriction to protect the cattle which were being let out on the saltings by the picnickers.'

The washing station [173]

Great Aunt Georgiana

Gt Aunt Georgiana Waller in her donkey cart. This may well have been taken around the time
of another donkey picture of Frances Waller on the beach from about 1914 [174]

Georgiana Waller was a younger sister to Thomas Naunton Waller, the engineer and photographer.
Their youngest brother was grandfather to Kit Clark. This is what she says of her Great Aunt Georgiana
and her three other great aunts:

> 'This is indeed my great Aunt Georgiana. There are many tales as to how she became bed
> bound, one was that she was crossed in love. My great grandfather certainly ruled the roost,
> and would not allow his girls to get married, so it seemed they didn't meet any suitable
> chaps. But Aunt Georgie fell for a cousin. Anyway, that was knocked on the head and with
> that she took to her bed and her three sisters, Mary, Agnes and Kate, looked after her. They
> were the most delightful great-aunts. As children we saw a lot of them as they came and
> lived in the bungalow in Mill Road. One of the card games we played with them was Old
> Maid. Anyway, that was one story but Joe (Kit's husband) said that she did go up to London
> for treatment of some sort or so he read in my great grandfather's perennial diary. She
> was always in bed with a little lace cap on and always with some very nice crochet jacket;
> and the three sisters always in black, with a velvet band round their necks and a nice little
> brooch in the front, dresses down almost to their ankles and little buckle shoes. Evidently
> one day Dad called and Aunt Mary was in the toilet. Anyway, she appeared, and as Dad was
> going out, he heard her say 'now Trevor has gone I will go and pull the plug'. They just were
> of another age and such a delight. Many, many happy days. Don't know where on earth the
> photograph was taken.'

Wildlife at Waldringfield
Tall Tales or Fascinating Facts?

'Good fishermen know that in talking about fishing, nothing is more interesting than the truth.'

Arthur Ransome

[175]

In the summer of 1893, an otter was seen by Jimmy Quantrill from his barge at the Quay. Later that day he shot it and sold it. The male otter was 4 feet long and weighed 18 lbs. Thankfully attitudes have changed and otters are now returning to these waters.

East Anglian Daily Times 16 Jun 1893

Otter Oddity

Early on Wednesday morning a man named James Quantrill, on one of Mr Mason's barges, lying in Waldringfield Dock, noticed an otter coming across the Saltings, and about mid-day he succeeded in shooting it in the river Deben, near Waldringfield. It was a fine male, measuring 4ft in length, and weighed 18lb. Mr W Hill of Waldringfield, who purchased the animal, has placed it in the hands of Mr F Aste naturalist, Woodbridge.

A European Otter [176]

Today the seals who have moved into the river are generally viewed with delight (though not necessarily by fishermen).

For Sale - Dry Dragonfly, seals intact!..-

Seals returned to the Deben in the 20th century [177]

Fishing has always taken place on the Deben, either for its challenge and interest or as an economic necessity A variety of different methods have been used from fish traps consisting of posts arranged in a V shape possibly with nets strung between them (called fish weirs or kiddles) to fishing from boats or the shore with lines. Fish weirs were outlawed by Edward III as they were an obstacle to shipping and a threat to fish stocks. This was reaffirmed by King Edward IV in 1472. Fish played a particularly important part in the diet of all classes during the Middle Ages so it is interesting to see that the government of the day may have been considering conservation measures. Other fishing methods used in the Waldringfield area in more recent times include trawling (under sail as well as with an engine) and small-scale trammel-netting across the mouths of creeks.

Whilst fishing for mullet in 1898 an angler netted a large fish, which turned out to be a Sweet William Shark. It was 5 feet long and weighed 3 st 4 lbs. The shark was exhibited and then sold to a taxidermist.

A European Eel [178]

Evening Star
24 Sep 1898

Shark Sighting

On Friday night, as one of the Woodbridge fishermen, named Henry Upson was driving for mullet in the Waldringfield Reach of the River Deben, he caught in his net a large fish, which he at first thought was a sea perch or sturgeon. On closer examination, however, he found it to be a species of shark known as 'Sweet William', which measured 5 ft long and weighed 3 stone 4 lb. The fish was exhibited in the town this (Saturday) morning, and created some amount of interest. It was purchased by Mr F Aste, taxidermist, of Woodbridge, for preservation.

A Sweet William shark [179]

Otters and sharks were not the only large creatures in the river.

An eel measuring 36 inches long was also caught at Waldringfield although, as with many fishy reports, this one seemed to get bigger in the retelling as the eel was longer and wider by the time it was reported in the south coast papers.:

The North Devon Journal
30 Jul 1908

An eel, measuring 36 ins in length and 8 ins in girth, has been caught at Waldringfield, Suffolk.

...but by the time this news reached...

The Bexhill on Sea Observer
1 Aug 1908

An eel measuring 38ins in length and 8ins in girth has been caught at Waldringfield.

Fishing has often been the source of many a tall story in Waldringfield.

According to Jim Turner, he and 'Shaver' Mills were keen fishermen in the 1930s and claimed to have caught ninety-nine bass in one haul at the Tips using nets, putting straw on the water and rowing around whilst jingling a chain to corral the fish. In World War Two soldiers sometimes used explosives to catch fish although possibly not always intentionally as the river was mined for a short time at the height of the invasion threat and these were sometimes caught by nets.

Jimmy Quantrill with young Michael Spear (founder
of Suffolk Yacht Harbour) and salmon [180]

The very large salmon above just happened to have
jumped into the boat Jimmy Quantrill had borrowed
from Andrew Haig! It only goes to show that salmon
(and sea trout) were still running the Deben until at
least the start of the Second World War.

Robert Simper recounts that in the 1930s cockles
and mussels were gathered and graded on the beach
and that Ray Lord and his successor as Harbourmaster,
Alan Davidson revived this practice between 1978
and 1986. Robert's grandson has now gone into
the business starting with oysters and mussels using
the beach at the Rocks for the grading and now
progressing to sea fishing at Felixstowe Ferry.

Scanning local papers through the 19th century
reveals frequent mention of poaching, some by
families local to Waldringfield. It was a time of
considerable rural poverty so while some might
have been motivated by the challenge of using their
clandestine skills to earn a little extra cash, others may
have needed these creatures to put some meat directly
on the family table.

Partridge and eggs [181]

The Ipswich Journal
2 Nov 1901

AN OLD Offender Charles Borrett, labourer.
was charged with having in his possession
six partridge eggs, knowing them to have
been taken, on May 8th, at Newbourne,
Defendant pleaded guilty.–Mr IT Cobbold,
who prosecuted on behalf of the Norfolk
and Suffolk Poaching Prevention Society.
said Jacob Reeder, gamekeeper at Nacton,
was talking with the tenant of the land when
defendant and another man came up but on
seeing them they turned and bolted. Whilst
running they threw a number of partridge's
eggs in the fence. They were caught and
summoned, but neither of them appeared.
The other man had since died. Defendant
had eleven previous and the Bench fined him
5s an egg, with £1.6s. 6d. making £2. 16s. 6d.
in all; in default a month's hard labour.

Robert Rix was also the Waldringfield Postmaster
at this time and lived at The Crags.

East Anglian Daily Times
21 Sep 1900

Robert Rix, and Charles Rix, his nephew
of Waldringfield, were charged with
trespassing in search of game and conies
at Sutton. Mr Charles D Girling, farmer of
Sutton, said he saw the two defendants on
the river wall which was in his occupation,
and they shot a hare. Defendants were away
from the footpath and had no right where
they were. The contention of the defendants
was they did not enter upon Mr Girling's
occupation, and Robert added that for 40
years he had used a gun along the river wall.
Defendants were fined 1s. and 19s. 8d. costs
each.

In 1833 James Drane appeared in the paper found guilty of killing game and was fined and sentenced to three months hard labour. However, it would have appeared not to deter him as he again appeared in 1834, this time with William Dammant for poaching in the Parish of Waldringfield and they were both sentenced to six months.

The Ipswich Journal

Jul 1833

James Drane, of Newbourne, labourer, in the sum of £5.12s 6d. penalty and costs for having in the first instance (in an inclosed [sic] field in Waldringfield) used a dog and gun for the of killing or taking of game and in default of payment was committed to Ipswich Gaol, to hard labour, for 3 calendar months.

It appeared to run in the family as in 1866 John Drane, a sawyer of Waldringfield was charged and convicted with killing a hare on land in the occupation of Mr Everitt of Waldringfield. The magistrate said the defendant had been convicted so often that they should inflict the full penalty of £5 and costs, in default two months hard labour. It is unlikely he would have been able to pay the fine.

The Suffolk Chronicle   **14 Jul 1866**

Game Case

John Drane, of Waldringfield, sawyer, was charged with killing a hare on land in the occupation of Mr Everitt of Waldringfield, on the 16th of January last. – Defendant pleaded not guilty. – Convicted. – The Magistrates said the defendant had been convicted so often that they should inflict the full penalty of £5, and costs, in default two months' hard labour, – Committed.

Gamekeepers had quite a busy time trying to protect their owner's property as poaching seemed rife. The newspapers show the Suffolk Game Duty payable by the Lord of the Manor and who was certified as Gamekeeper. In 1787 for Waldringfield Rivers Hall the Lord was Nathaniel Randall and the Gamekeeper was John Mayhew, in 1793 the Gamekeeper was now registered as Joseph Payne.

Framlingham Weekly News   **Sep 1878**

Charge of Killing Hares

William Garner, William Hill, and Frederick Knappett, all labourers of Waldringfleld, were charged by E Welham, gamekeeper to Colonel Tomline, with having killed three hares, on the 21st August, at Waldringfield.– Mr Jewesson for the prosecution, Mr Mills for the defence.–Several on both sides were examined, but the bench considered the case a doubtful one, and the defendants were therefore discharged.

William Cobbett's famous book *Rural Rides* offers an unforgettable picture of 19th-century starvation in the countryside. This fuelled the mass migration to cities. Waldringfield was probably fortunate that its river trade supported alternatives to field work. The development of the coprolite workings from 1858, and the increasing activity in the Cement Works, may have come as a lifeline to many local families.

PIGEON SHOOTING.

A MATCH of the above description will take place at the "CLIFF INN," WALDRINGFIELD, on SATURDAY, the 26th instant. Having a large supply of Pigeons, Rabbits, &c., the company of Sportsmen and Amateurs is respectfully requested by
                    ROBERT SALTER, Landlord.
Waldringfield, Dec. 17th, 1846.
N.B. The Birds, &c., will be on the Field at 11 o'clock precisely.

The Ipswich Journal, December 1846 [182]

John Henry Waller supervising a rabbit auction on
Garden Field, White Hall around 1880 [183]

But sometimes the landowners organised their
own pigeon and rabbit shoots and auctioned off the
catch:

Rabbits would have been pests damaging crops
and this was therefore a useful pastime in more ways
than one.

There is a vivid description of shooting and
wildfowling in *The Gifts of Frank Cobbold* by Arthur W
Upfield about the Cobbold family from Cliff House
and although the exact detail of the shooting and
wildfowling may have varied over time it remained a
popular pastime.

*'A powerful telescope set up in a top room was used
to mark the arrival and landing on the marshes
of flighting wild-fowl, and expeditions were taken
in the flat-bottom duck punts in which the boys
were trained in the craft of
stalking ducks – pushing the
punts gently and soundlessly
through the narrow water-
passages among the tall reeds,
or hugging the low bank of
a mud flat to gain position
within gun range.*

*Sometimes their father took
the boys over the surrounding
fields and sea-flats, Mr
Cobbold carrying the twin
barrelled 'Joe Manton' he
used so expertly, seldom failing
to bring down the zigzagging,
darting snipe rising from
the sedges. In those days the
custom of driving birds was*

*not practised; intelligent pointer dogs being used to
'put up' a covey of partridges, and the liver-and-
white Clumber spaniels to retrieve the wild-fowl.*

*In this way, the boys were taught not only to exercise
their mental powers in combating the cunning of
birds – especially the alert ducks – but also to
cultivate the virtues of patience and pertinacity.
Their powers of observation were trained, their
minds were widened, and tolerance and goodwill
were established in their characters.*

*If the snow lay thickly on the ground, the hunters
donned old white suits and hats, the colour
harmonising with the background and making them
difficult to be seen by the watchful and suspicious
birds. When the Joe Manton was replaced by a
more modern pin-fire action type of weapon, the
boys accepted it with admiration, and increased
their proficiency with its use.'*

Many locals would have subsidised their larder
with locally shot ducks and geese and still do today.
Modern punts, although they vary in style, have many
similar features to the traditional ones; a means of
propulsion, a combination of either sail, paddle or
pole which allows access to the shallows and a low
platform from which to fire the gun. Dogs were
usually involved in retrieving the prey although
the breed could vary too. These days Spaniels and
Labrador Retrievers are usually the breed of choice.

An example of a duck punt in front of Bawdsey Manor, taken 1889. It
shows the mast for a small sail, the long bow used to rest the gun and the
long oar/paddle/pole for manoeuvrability amongst the shallows [184]

The Coal Shed

Roger Stollery writes: This brick building built during the operation of the Cement Works was used for storing coal. Frank Mason sold it to my grandad, AW Stollery as part of the Quay in 1925. Its location is shown on both the 1881 and 1904 OS maps. The only change is that the level of the Quay itself has risen along the road in front of it, so that there is a now a ramp down to the entrance doors and the floor level beyond. This may just be seen by comparing the photograph showing the Coal Shed during operation of the Cement Works and with the photograph taken in 2003.

The Coal Shed as it is today [185]

The floor of the Coal Shed was made of rammed chalk like the main part of the Quay and is still as originally constructed. I have gone into the Coal Shed on many occasions, but never really 'looked' properly at the floor. Usually with a light covering of dust and dirt, it appeared to be concrete but recently on investigating a lighter coloured patch where water had dripped through a gap in the tiles, it was clear that this was chalk and not only that but there were fragments of coal still evident!

One other difference is a flag pole on the gable end. This was to fly the Cruising Association flag, to indicate to cruising yachtsmen where members could store their oars and other bulky gear whilst they returned home by train. This arrangement was popular in the period between the two World Wars, because then there were lots of railway lines linking yachting centres around the country and you could cruise between such places, leave your yacht there and later come back to continue your cruise. The Cruising Association, via a local boatman, would organise local storage like the Coal Shed during the summer season so that you could rejoin your boat and carry on. This arrangement continued into the 1950s but could not thereafter because Dr Beeching's 1961 Axe cut all these small local railway lines.

During Harry and Ernie Nunn's Boatyard operation on the Quay, this building was used for their winter storage of wooden masts. These were hung from the roof structure and from time to time Ernie had to strengthen the roofing timbers. The building continued to be used for storage, until it lay empty for several years when it was no longer needed for the Boatyard operation.

However in 2015 John Palmer and John Fish made arrangements with me for the WSC Dragonfly Class to store their Dragonflies there over winter. *Stinger*, no 17, is currently stored there, waiting for an enthusiast to restore her. She was the first Dragonfly to be launched in 1949 and it was in her that my father, Cyril, taught me to sail.

The Coal Shed, mid picture, beside the conglomeration of the Cement Works [186]

The Cement Works

'Concrete is, essentially, the colour of bad weather.'
William Hamilton, Scottish Statesman

[187]

'The kilns dominated the skyline' [188]

Visitors to Waldringfield (and indeed current residents of the village) might be forgiven for not knowing that it was once the site of a large Cement Works. All that now remains of the industry is the Quay, which passers-by would assume to have always been part of the boating business, the works' manager's house which may be seen behind the river wall to the north of the village and, on Quay Lane, a 3-ft thick wall, ending in a private garden as the part-ruined base of a kiln.

Photographs of the village, taken from the River Deben at the start of the 20th century, show that there were three rows of such kilns, each row sporting four chimneys, one chimney for each kiln.

In the mid 1860s, there was in Waldringfield a small Cement Works; probably, in the first instance, this was just one kiln, producing Roman cement. The identity of the owner at that time cannot be certain; one Frederick George Last has been suggested as he was described as a 'Cement Manufacturer of Waldringfield, Suffolk' when an Order of Discharge was granted to him by the County Court of Suffolk on 21st August 1875 following adjudication of bankruptcy on 24th March 1875. However, it is known that from 1870 the owner was a London based cement producer trading under the name of Coles, Shadbolt and Co. A leading authority on the history of cement manufacture, suggests that the company sent Percy Shadbolt to run the Waldringfield operation which they had acquired as a result of some debt owing to them. It is possible, of course, that this all ties up with the eventual bankruptcy of Frederick George Last. Dylan Moore, an authority on cement manufacturing, states that by 1870 there was a row of four bottle kilns in place. As these would have been used to produce 'clinker' which is a constituent of Portland cement it is possible that Mr Last had decided to modernise his Works by transferring to the production of Portland cement in line with Mr Lockwood, of Woodbridge. This latter gentleman was a builder by trade who is known to have started production of Portland cement, alongside Roman cement, as early as 1823, in Woodbridge, although not on a grand scale.

Perhaps the building of four kilns was the straw that broke the camel's back for Frederick George Last. We cannot be certain as, to date, the only other information linking him to the Cement Works is an appearance in 'mud and water accounts' kept by Thomas Henry Waller; there, Last's name is seen, somewhat mysteriously in view of the date, in an entry made in January 1875, followed closely by Shadbolt in June 1875 and Mason in October of the same year. We have found no further information about him; he does not appear to be related to the Last family who lived at the wheelwright's in Waldringfield in the mid 1800s.

Coles, Shadbolt & Co were the owners of the cement Works for no more than three years and even that short period was clouded by litigation; they were accused of failing to pay a local builder, Mr Frost, for an estimate. In 1872 the works were sold to one George Mason who, according to an interview with his grandson, Kenneth, in 1950, started production of Portland cement in Waldringfield in 1872 'on the site of an 1865 works for making Roman cement'.

On the balance of probabilities it was George Mason who committed to the production of Portland cement at Waldringfield. His obituary, written in 1893, states that 'he established Portland Cement Works at Waldringfield and these developed greatly under his guidance'. George Mason was primarily a slate and timber merchant from Ipswich whose expressed intention was to manufacture Portland cement. He was a much respected local politician and business man, born in Ipswich in 1812. He owned sailing barges and, until the start of his enterprise in Waldringfield, he had manufactured Roman cement in the Ipswich area from cement-stone (septaria) dredged from the River Orwell.

There had been no real advances in cement making between the days of the Romans and the 1820s. The initial history of the development of Portland cement was somewhat chequered by the seeking of patents, by variation in product purity and even by industrial espionage but the industry had become properly established by the middle of the nineteenth century.

The logo of Masons Cement Works [190]

The large-scale manufacture of Portland cement, which is two parts chalk to one part clay, was established in earnest by 1851 in the Medway where there were plentiful supplies of both chalk and clay. Demand had increased out of all proportion with the expansion of the London metropolis and the exportation of this 'British' cement abroad; more production sites were sought.

The River Deben, of course, would provide a good supply of clay and there was, already, an established barge route between the Deben and the Thames, with some of the barges being owned by George Mason himself. The barges would be readily available to bring chalk and coal or coke from the Medway and to take cement back to the Thames either for use in London or for export.

Kenneth Mason recalled that in the days of the Cement Works when the wind was from the north clouds of dirty brown smoke would envelop the beach, thus making it 'totally untenable'. It is very difficult now to imagine such a scene, even without the smoke.

Masons Cement Works functioned for only 35 years and closed in 1907. Profound technological changes in the 1890s had led to the relatively early decommissioning of the Waldringfield plant. There was need to upgrade to a new ball-and-roller grinding mechanism and to rotary kilns.

By 1912, the Works had gone, all but a few remnants. It had taken five years to dismantle.

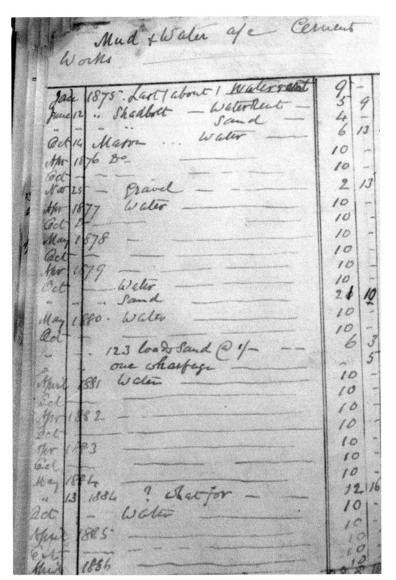

Thomas Henry Waller b 1832 was a great keeper of records. These included 'Mud and Water accounts' and his Perennial Diary. This image is taken from the Accounts [189]

Cement Works 1880 OS map. Showing the site plan for the Cement Works in 1881. The Works manager's house is shown to the north (close to the number '76'. A block of four 'cement' cottages is shown (two further blocks of four have yet to be built and/or indicated on the map – on the area labelled '118'). Just further to the west along Cliff Road and at right angles to the road there is a row of three cottages. Slightly further west and on the north side of the Cliff Road there are two or three cottages. There is no evidence of a path or a track where Deben Lane is now. River View cottages, the village shop and the bakery have yet to be built. There are only two banks of kilns. The third has yet to be built [191]

One has to ask why such an industry was ever started in Waldringfield which was, essentially, a small village in a mainly agricultural environment. Apart from the fact that there was already a small Cement Works in the village there appear to be four main reasons:

1. There was an active coprolite industry so that the village was well used to barge traffic, the necessary loading and unloading on the shore and the coming and going of horses and carts.

2. The ready availability of one of the raw materials – mud.

3. The availability of ready labour. Work was becoming scarce on the South Suffolk peninsula; farming was in recession and the large private estates were beginning to feel the financial pinch.

4. Then, finally, there was spare land.

The area on which the Cement Works were built included land belonging to Cliff House (now The Maltings) and an area behind this which had been acquired by Colonel Tomline of Orwell Park, Nacton from one Robert Lacey whose ownership of the said land was shown on the 1839 tithe map.

One family in Waldringfield has deeds which show that in 1871 George Mason bought from Arthur Thomas Cobbold, then owner of Cliff House, land adjoining the Maybush Inn together with 'the Quay or dock lying next to the river Deben and also all the land with a maltings office and other erections, including 6 cottages, the 2 parcels of land known as the office piece and the Bush piece', (probably either side of the main road) 'together with 1 acre & 23 perches of land' where, later, the Masons built cottages for the workers.

Cement Cottages. So named as they were built for workers at the Masons Cement Works. They are actually built of concrete. There is uncertainty about the date/dates of their construction. The four nearest to the photographer are shown on the 1881 OS map. The remaining eight followed on with new simpler designs but retained similar front elevations [192]

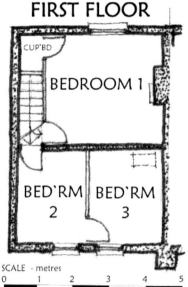

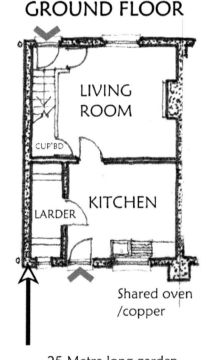

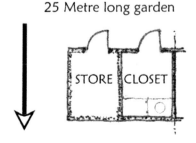

Whilst walking down the lower stretches of Maybush Lane (now Cliff Road) before 1872 one would have passed, on the left and just before what is now Deben Lane, some allotments and two, possibly three, cottages. To the right, and opposite to where Deben Lane is now, there was a row of cottages at right angles to the road – long since demolished and replaced in the 1960s by a single dwelling, White Lodge. It is not certain what else would have been seen before reaching, on the left, the coach house to Cliff House and, on the right, the Maybush – known then as Bush Inn.

The purchased land lay behind the allotments on the left, behind the left hand side of Cliff Road and behind Mr Cobbold's land. It stretched to the edge of the fields to the north of the village and down to the water's edge. In addition there was some land to the right of Cliff Road where there is now a row of twelve cottages – three groups of four. These were built for some of the cement workers. Today they are known collectively as Cement Cottages but should really be called Concrete Cottages in view of their innovative construction using shuttered 'no fines'

concrete. No fines concrete is a mixture of pebbles and cement with no sand added; it is waterproof and provides good insulation.

The cottages were simple in design and each benefited from a 25 metre long garden – space enough for vegetables and chickens.

This method of construction had been used on Queen Victoria's estate on the Isle of Wight in 1854 for building just the external walls of a pair of semi-detached cottages. However, it was in Waldringfield in the late 1870s that this otherwise new and untried method was first used for both external and internal walls. The fact that all twelve cottages are still standing proud, and loved by their owners, is testimony to the brilliant foresight of the designer/ builders of Waldringfield in the late 19th century. The only thing universally hated about working in these cottages is that the walls are incredibly hard, thus requiring several drill bits to make one sizeable hole.

Plan of a Concrete Cottage [193]

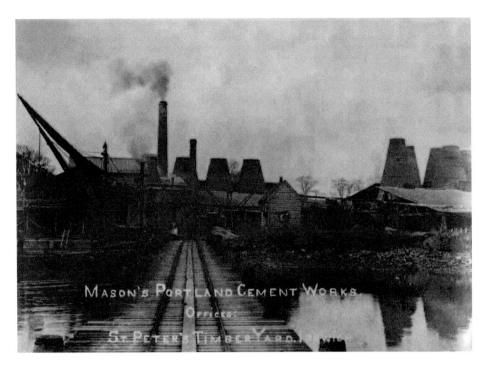

The landing stage. This is shown on the 1905 OS map but not on the 1881 OS map. The wash mill Quay is to the left. This picture must have been taken after 1898 because there are three banks of kilns [194]

By 1880 there was a second row or bank of kilns in the Works. Each bank consisted of four kilns. They were built of special heat resistant bricks known as firebricks. Those in the first bank were each 13 feet in diameter, those in the second bank were slightly greater at 17 feet. There is no question that they dominated the skyline. In 1898 a third bank was added.

A tramway was constructed across the site although much of the fetching and carrying was said to have been done with wheelbarrows. The tramway engine was probably driven by George Frost who lived in Woodbridge Road, Waldringfield (now a 'By-Road' to Martlesham).

The machines and the 12.50 lunchtime siren were powered by a large steam engine bought from Garrett & Sons at Leiston; this was known as the Wunnerful Wissel and could be heard all down the Deben. It seems there were complaints from Ramsholt one day when the Wunnerful Wissel was late, thus throwing working schedules into disarray.

It has been suggested, anecdotally, that as many as 100 barge-loads a month of chalk, coal or coke would arrive from the Medway. The usual number was probably a little less than that. In the later years these materials were off-loaded via the landing stage although that does not appear to have been present from the outset.

The mud required for the process was extracted from the Waldringfield saltings probably from shallow draft mud barges in narrow channels.

First the marsh peat would be removed by means of a shovel, then wooden 'flytools' would be used by skilled labourers known as 'muddies' to flick blocks of clay into the barge. It is said that a really good muddie, like Mr Stebbing of *Kingfisher*, could have one block in the air whilst the first block was landing in the barge and the third block was being dug. It is likely that Kingfisher Creek was named after Mr Stebbing's barge. One has to wonder what might have become of these narrow, shallow draft barges and whether any of their hulls lie covered in mud in the saltings.

A flytool [195]

The Wunnerful Wissel steam engine [196]

The mud and the chalk were off-loaded from the barges and tipped into a wash-mill on the Quay where they were mixed with water into slurry; this then flowed via wooden troughs into slurry reservoirs. The water would rise to the top of the slurry in the reservoir; it was then let off via sluice gates to be returned to the river. The remaining mixture was then wheel-barrowed to an oven heated floor, spread about nine inches thick and left until dry enough for barrowing to the kilns.

At the height of operations there were twelve kilns with a total production capacity of 200 tonnes per week. The four kilns in the third bank were smaller than the others, being only 11 feet in diameter. The base of one kiln remains today at the bottom of a private garden in Deben Lane. It is about 20 feet across on the inside. The back walls of the remaining three in that row of four are also to be seen in another private garden.

The kilns were prepared for firing by placing faggots of wood in an arched duct beneath the floor of the kiln. Then alternate layers of coke and cement slurry were placed in the kiln. The kiln was bricked up, set alight and left to burn for five days.

Once the process was finished and the kiln had cooled down the cement clinker would be removed, loaded into wheelbarrows and taken to the grinding machine to be ground into fine cement.

The last remaining kiln base [197]

117

Initially clinker was ground in a Big Ball Mill, a German invention installed in Waldringfield by German engineers. It seems there was considerable friction between the Germans and the local workforce, not helped by the Germans bragging that each one of them was worth three of the locals both in strength and in work done. There is a story, courtesy of the late Walter Tye, that one day there was a large slab of concrete to be moved. One of the wry locals stood at one of the four corners of this great large slab and said to a passing German. 'We'll soon get this shifted. 'oi'll lift this corner and yew can take the other three.'

The grindings from the Big Ball Mill were transferred by conveyor belt to the Griffin Mill for finer grinding and then barrowed or conveyed to storage sheds. Filling sacks and loading barges with the finished product was said to be the dirtiest and hardest job of all, although the clay digging sounds pretty hard going.

George Mason died in 1893 and it was one of his three sons, Frank, who continued the business. Arrangements had been made in 1892 for the land to be inherited by Frank Mason from his father, 'subject to the payment by the said FW Mason of rent to the successor of the late Colonel George Tomline' (the Pretyman Estate).

Mr Frank W Mason lived in a house called Northcliff, overlooking the sea at Felixstowe. There he was able to watch the Mason barges making home to the Deben on the London to Waldringfield run.

George and Frank Mason are said to have been truly philanthropic employers who provided well for their workers who numbered approximately 200 at the height of production. Some of the workers came over by ferry from the other side of the river, some of them walked from places like Kirton. However, the 1901 census shows that 33 employees from the Cement Works actually lived in the village and very close to the Works. Many were married with young families; between them they had 39 children, aged between 5 and 12, in the elementary school, 39 out of a total of fifty scholars recorded in that census. Cottages were rented for 2 shillings and sixpence a week and coal was to be had from the Works for a shilling (equivalent to 5p) a bag. There was a reading room (now The Old School House, on the corner of Fishpond Road and Woodbridge Road) which cost one penny a week. (There were 240 pennies in a pound.)

Mason's Cement Works, Waldringfield. This photograph now shows the wear and tear of age but it shows the Cement Works at the height of its activity prior to 1907 and it includes the Works managers house, seen just before the row of young trees at the right-hand end of the picture and behind the landing stage or jetty. There appears to be a two-storey extension to the rear of the house. It is possible that the building comprised two dwelling places (see 1881 walk) [198]

The Cement Works even boasted a staff health facility with one Dr Hollis who is said to have attributed most of the illnesses he encountered to an excess of beer, or not enough of it, depending on the drinking habits of the patient.

There was a Works cricket team which was so good in the 1890s that its players, including the likes of Alfred Stollery and Charley and Porky Nunn, were known as 'The Invincibles'.

A house was built for the manager, Mr Bare, to the north of the Works. It is likely that it was known as 'Works cottage'. It is now known as 'Swan's Nest'; it has a commanding view of the River Deben from behind the river wall.

The trades at the Works, or those associated with it, were varied – from the aforementioned Mr Bare, to the youngest of the labourers, Herbert Porter who, at 14, was still living at home with his mother, Sarah, his two younger siblings and his father, James, who was also a labourer at the Works.

George Frost was an engine driver, probably responsible for driving the track steam-engine within the Works. Another Frost, Ernest, was a young crane driver living with his wife in Cliff Road, whilst George Bloomfield, who lived in the Street, was a kiln loader.

Thomas Bloomfield, of Woodbridge Road, was a bricklayer; John Brown was a fireman.

Another young labourer, nineteen year old Jesse Clark, lived in Cliff Road with his mother, Alice, four young half siblings and his step-father Jack Stebbings, a bargeman.

Despite the apparent well-being of the cement industry in the late 19th century there were threats. The technology was changing and human resource issues were becoming more complicated. Associated Portland Cement Manufacturers (APCM – a consortium of 26 cement factories based on the Medway plus three others further afield) was expanding and casting its eyes around with a view to eliminating the competition.

The Cement Works cricket team. Known as 'The Invincibles', they won every match one season. Front: Jim Brown, Tommy Tomkins. Middle: 'Porky' Nunn, Ernie Frost, Charley Nunn, William Bare, Alfred Stollery, Tom Smith. Back: Jim Smith, unidentified, Ted Cook, Tom Bloomfield, Bill Wardley [199]

Frank Mason will have been well aware of these increasing threats. There is no definitive evidence of the precise time that a decision was taken to close down the Waldringfield operation in favour of setting up again in Claydon where geologists had found a mud/chalk mix exactly right for the making of Portland cement. Such a move would negate the need for transport of chalk from the Medway.

Six new staff cottages in Deben Lane (as it is now – although then it was a track through the cement Works site) were completed, as far as we can tell, in 1902, suggesting thoughts at that time of a long-standing future for the Waldringfield Works.

However, by 1906 Mr Bare had decided (at the age of 50) to relinquish his employment as Works manager and to return to his native Thames Estuary. It seems likely, then, that the writing-on-the-wall began between 1902 and 1906 and that a positive decision to relocate was made, probably, during that four year period.

Mr Bare's retirement 'do' was reported in the local newspaper with mention of 'a depressed cement industry' but no mention of a possible Works closure so that, if the decision had been taken by then, it was still 'under wraps'.

The Works closed in 1907. The pier was taken down; the kilns were either demolished or filled in by Arthur Quantrill and his Territorials between 1907 and 1912. It is said that one of the houses in School Road was constructed using 30,000 of the heat resistant bricks from the kilns. The demolition process proved exciting on occasions with some hair-raising exploits of The East Anglian Royal Engineers being reported in some detail in the press.

When the works closed Mr Mason gave the occupants of the cottages the opportunity to purchase them, paying as and when they could. The manager of the works at that time was Arthur Stollery who went with the Masons to manage their new works at Claydon. With the close of the Works at Waldringfield the village was seemingly left in peace to develop the pastimes it supports today but, of course, the first of two shattering World Wars was about to affect most people's lives.

Six staff 'Riverview' cottages in Deben Lane. The bakery and the chimneys of the village shop are seen on the left [200]

Bedfordshire Times and Independent   26 Aug 1912

The training of the East Anglian Royal Engineers rapidly drawing to a close. Until early this week the weather was fairly favourable for life under canvass (sic). For a day or so rain has pelted down from morning to night, but the silver lining appeared again, and the gaiety of the camp was resumed. The health of the men has been excellent.

Some very useful work has been performed during the training, and we believe that those in authority are well pleased with the progress made. Various phases of engineering have been gone through, and...

DEMOLITION

The Non-commissioned Officers had a thoroughly instructive and enjoyable half-day's outing on Saturday. Forty years ago there were erected at Waldringfield some large Cement Works, but for the past four or five years they have not been worked. The proprietor, Mr FW Mason, who now carries on the business at Ipswich, gave permission for experiments in demolition to be carried out at the disused works, and accordingly the officers of the Corps, with about 40 NCOs set out for Waldringfield on their mission of destruction. The journey, which was made in wagons, was much liked, especially as a detour amid fine scenery was made before reaching the destination. En route the harvesters hailed with delight the appearance of the civilian soldiers, who were not slow to respond to the greetings.

The Cement Works are situated in the heart of the little village Waldringfield, and on the banks of a broad tidal river. They consisted of a number of kilns, three chimney stacks and out-buildings. It was decided to demolish first a chimney stack, about 6 feet square, and from 65ft to 70ft high. The NCOs were instructed in the the use of explosives, and the work of demolition was begun. About fourteen slabs of gun cotton, each weighing one pound, and

resembling white fire-bricks were used. Equal parts of the charge were tied to two boards and wedged in position on two sides of the chimney. The primers and detonators were then inserted by Lieutenant Preston and connecting these was a wire through which the electric current would pass and fire the charge. When all had retired to a safe distance, the bugle sounded and a whistle was blown twice. Immediately after the second whistle Major Steinmetz, under whose direction the demolitions were carried out pressed down a handle, the current passed through the detonator, and instantly there was a terrific report, which shook the ground.

The chimney appeared to burst in the centre, bricks and mortar came hurtling through the air then huge masses of fiery smoke enveloped the scene. The lofty stack, which had taken weeks to build, was completely shattered and scattered in seconds, and those who witnessed the demolition are not likely to forget it. Previous to the explosion the villagers were advised to open all their windows and we heard of only one being broken but a wash-house was damaged. A hole of about four feet in width was made in the wall and bricks and dust littered the place. Pots and pans were strewn about and a bicycle a few yards from the gap in the wall had a narrow escape.

The NCOs had the foresight to bring with them some cook's materials and utensils for tea, and very soon khaki clad groups were doing justice to a decent meal. ...

The officers present were Lieutenant Colonel GH Wells, Major AB Steinmetz, Major Hartley, Captain Mowatt, Lieutenant Preston, and Captain and Adjutant Stokes.

The Impact of the Great War

Charles Rix [201]

The closure of the Cement Works in 1907 could have been an economic and social crisis for the village. Workers' wages had been unusually high for the area and the most obvious alternative, agricultural work, was notoriously poorly paid. As a consequence, many families left the village and individuals sought out other forms of more lucrative employment such as the brewing trade in Burton-on-Trent, the Constabularies and the Services. But all was not doom and gloom because, quite apart from the improvement in air quality around the village, some manual labour must have been required to help Arthur Quantrill and his Territorials in the gargantuan task of dismantling the Works over the next five years.

Fast approaching was another more ominous, but evidently exciting, employment opportunity for young men and that was the outbreak of the First World War in 1914. Some, like Arthur Wardley and Alfred Scarlett, were ahead of the game, having joined the Army well before the war, but many others were to join them, particularly in the initial patriotic rush to join up from August onwards. Arthur's younger brothers, Henry and Jack, joined the Gunners too, as did Walter Canham, Sidney Howard, Walter Hill, Charles Rix and Harry Button, who was to lose his life on the Western Front in April 1917.

Both Charles' and Harry's brothers, Fred and Bob, served in the Royal Navy and, as befits a riverine village, they were joined by many more, including Edwin and Walter Bloomfield, Frank Fulcher, Fred Glanfield, and Tom Lillingstone. Bob Button had joined the Royal Navy in 1895 and by the outbreak of war, when he was serving in the pre-dreadnought battleship HMS *Africa*, he was a Chief Petty Officer. Bob retired from the Navy straight after the war in early 1919 when he and his wife Lil settled in Cliff Road for the rest of their lives.

Another career sailor contemporary of Bob's was Henry Hill who grew up at Oak Tree Farm, Martlesham. Henry was the uncle of Albert Hill who ran the Maybush during and after the Second World War and a cousin of Walter Hill who closed what was originally his father John's brewing business in the Old Maltings and Greenaway after the Cement Works closed. Just to show how closely connected these families often were, in 1903, he married John Hill's granddaughter, Laura Maud Bunn, and later

Henry Hill [202]

Grave of Sidney Scoggins [203]

Ernie Nunn married Henry's daughter Jessie. Henry enlisted in the Royal Navy on 8 Jan 1893 and was already well decorated for services on the Nile and in South Africa before the war. By the Great War he was a Chief Torpedo Coxswain and was already in his late 30s. On 25 April 1915, whilst at the wheel of a ship and under heavy fire during landing operations at Anzac Cove, Gallipoli, he was struck in the mouth by a bullet, which removed all his front teeth. He was taken below but, after washing out his mouth, he insisted on returning to his duty at the wheel, where he remained for the rest of the landings on 25 and 26 April, both days under fire. For these courageous actions he was awarded the Conspicuous Gallantry Medal, second only to the Victoria Cross, on 15 May 1916 and he followed this up with the Medaille Militaire for his actions during the Ostend Raid of 27 Aug 1918.

But what is also interesting about Henry's story is that a Newbourne lad (who had been born in Waldringfield) called Robert Prentice, was landed on the beach at Gallipoli on 25 April, and therefore possibly in the very vessel being steered by Henry, and moreover after the war Henry came to settle in Newbourne as the publican of the Fox (a very typical Hill occupation, and one perpetuated also by his son Harry who took over from him at the Fox when he retired).

William Bear, Foster and George Brett, Isaac Dickerson, George and William Thompson, Edward Moules, Arthur Tuckwell, Sidney and William Scoggins, and Stanley and William Bloomfield all joined their local infantry regiment – the Suffolks. Both Sidney Scoggins and William Bloomfield were also to lose their lives on the Western Front; Sidney near St Omer in August 1918 and William at the Battle of Passchendaele in October 1917. Sidney Aldis and Thomas Farrow meanwhile joined the Suffolk Yeomanry, and by 1915 found themselves also at Gallipoli, followed by a spell guarding the Suez Canal in Egypt during 1916, before taking part in General Allenby's 1917 Palestine campaign. Another serving son of a Waldringfield girl, Alice Stollery, was Robert Kemp who, after emigrating to Australia in 1913, found himself back in Europe with the Australian Imperial Force and won the Distinguished Conduct Medal in August 1918 for showing conspicuous gallantry in capturing a German machine-gun position on foot after his tank was disabled. He was granted leave in 1919 to help his parents at Dairy Farm, before returning to Australia.

Pte William Bloomfield in the newspaper [204]

WILLIAM LAWRENCE
BRAGG
KT C·H F·R·S NOBEL LAUREATE
1890-1971
AND HIS WIFE
ALICE GRACE JENNY
C·B·E 1899~1989

Lawrence Bragg's memorial in Waldringfield Church [205]

Charles Prentice died a year earlier in November 1916 whilst serving with the Royal Fusiliers on the Somme. His two brothers, Robert and Henry, also died – Robert at Gallipoli in 1915 and Henry as a result of contracting TB in 1917 – leaving the Prentice parents and their four daughters numbed to the core. Later in the war others, such as Erich Mill, Ernie Rowe, Walter Scarlett, Edward Stevens and Edgar Woolnough, joined the fledgling Royal Flying Corps, and many more sons of the village, too numerous to mention them all but numbering well over 40, served during the conflict.

Many later residents of the village also served with distinction, perhaps none more so than Sir Lawrence Bragg, who served as a young officer in the Royal Engineers, winning both an MC for gallantry and an OBE for his development of an innovative artillery locating system. Extraordinarily he was already the youngest Nobel Laureate in 1915 at the age of only 25, and went on to teach physics at Cambridge, become a Companion of Honour and Fellow of the Royal Society, before retiring with Lady Bragg to Quietways. Vincent Gilbey and Bill Ogden also won MCs on the Western Front, whilst Douglas Kennedy was awarded an MBE for his services in the Royal Defence Corps. Future married couples also played their part, with Don and Dorothy Haig meeting in Yarmouth whilst both serving in the Royal Navy, whilst Glyn and Gwen Venmore-Rowland served in the Royal Artillery and Queen Mary's Army Auxiliary Corps respectively. The Rev TH Waller tragically lost his first grandson, Tommy, in the Ypres Salient in 1917, and commemorated him with a stained-glass window at the back of the church.

THIS TABLET WAS ERECTED
BY THE PEOPLE OF THIS PARISH
TO PERPETUATE THE MEMORY OF
CHARLES PRENTICE, R.F. HARRY BUTTON, RGA
WILLIAM GEORGE BLOOMFIELD, SUFFOLK REG
SIDNEY SCOGGINS, SUFFOLK R
WHO FELL DURING THE

The Roll of Honour plaque in the church [206]

Another wartime resident of Waldringfield was William Walden Hammond, who grew up in Cambridge. He was passionate about photography and began his working life as an apprentice to a photographic chemist, immediately joining the local photographic club. Shortly before the outbreak of World War One, Walden tried several times to enlist but was turned down on health grounds. He was eventually interviewed by The Royal Flying Corps (RFC) who concluded that he had all the qualifications required for a fledgling aerial photography and research unit.

Walden was subsequently posted to Orford Ness, an experimental station for the RFC, in March 1917. Here he excelled in pioneering aerial photography initially using a hand held wooden camera with glass plates. As activities expanded, Orford Ness became the technical centre, with Martlesham Heath becoming the focus for aeroplane testing. It was whilst stationed at Martlesham Heath that Walden Hammond and his wife stayed in one of a pair of cottages in Lower Road, now known as Sandy Lane, home of Miss Lankester, a dress-maker.

Walden's pioneering photos of significant events and installations were far in advance of anything previously attempted. He took some astonishing reconnaissance photographs which are still celebrated for their immediacy and precision today.

Whilst this tumultuous conflict left a scar across the nation and some local families, the village appears to have escaped the worst ravages of the war, at least physically. Presumably because, unlike 25 years later, the threat of invasion was considered negligible, no significant beach or river defences were positioned inland from the coast, and therefore none, as far as we know, in the vicinity of the village. Thus, when the Armistice came in 1918, it was able to revert quickly to its peacetime activities, be they work or play. The next stage in Waldringfield's development was beckoning – the day of the leisure and racing yachtsman.

Shot down by aircraft from Orfordness, sixteen members of Zeppelin L48's crew died when it crashed in a field at Theberton on June 17th 1917. Amazingly three survived the flames, though one died later from his injuries. This is William Walden Hammond's photograph of the event (from the Hammond collection) [207]

Waldringfield's Links with HMY 'Britannia' (Royal Cutter Yacht)

Captain Jack Carter [208]

As yachting became a more fashionable sport, many men in riverside villages found alternative employment in the summer months crewing on the 'super-yachts' of their day. Waldringfield had particular links to the Prince of Wales (later Edward VII)'s famous HMY *Britannia*, a gaff-rigged cutter built for him in 1893.

Former WSC Commodore Tony Carter's great uncle, John Carter, (1850-1910) took over her command in 1893 and between 1893 and 1897, he sailed her in 219 races, winning 122. He was awarded the Royal Victorian Order.

His son, John Richard (Charles) Carter also captained *Britannia* between 1910 and 1921 after serving under his father from 1897 as an able seaman. Both Carters would have been in a good position to witness the increasingly rapid deterioration in relationships between Edward VIII and his nephew Kaiser Wilhelm as their rivalry in the regattas mirrored the Naval arms race that would eventually lead to WW1.

In 1922 *Britannia* was refitted for King George V. The Turner family, who still have descendants in the village today, were also linked to the yacht. George Turner (1862-1940) and his two sons, George T Turner (1888-1975) and Edward Cecil Turner (1894-1929) often crewed for King George V. In the winter months, they would return to their work on sailing barges and piloting vessels on the Orwell. George T Turner was landlord of The Maybush for a while in the 1920s and he and his wife Grace eventually retired to Deben House in Cliff Road to run a guest house.

George's brother, Edward Cecil Turner, known as Cecil, married Hilda May Quantrill daughter of Jimmy who also ran the Maybush and the Butt and Oyster at Pin Mill for a while before moving back to Waldringfield. Cecil and Hilda had three children, James, George and Barbara. Sadly, Cecil died in 1929 but Hilda married again, this time to Albert Henry Nunn, known as Harry Nunn. With Harry, Hilda had three more children Margaret, Michael and John and some still live in Waldringfield today. It was Albert Henry (Harry) Nunn who, with his brother Ernie, ran the Boatyard at Waldringfield for many years.

HMY *Britannia* [209, 210]

WSC member James Palmer tells of the day his great grandfather sailed down to Harwich to look at *Britannia* when she was racing from there:

> 'As they approached, the King appeared on deck. Great grandfather didn't know whether to salute or raise his hat. In his confusion he tried to do both simultaneously, embarrassing himself and amusing the rest of the family greatly. A different time altogether.'

The Waldringfield Anchorage, 1900-1939

Ratty by the reservoir, 2006 [211]

'Believe me, my young friend, there is nothing — absolutely nothing — half so much worth doing as simply messing about in boats. Simply messing… about in boats — or with boats. In or out of 'em, it doesn't matter. Nothing seems really to matter, that's the charm of it. Whether you get away, or whether you don't; whether you arrive at your destination or whether you reach somewhere else, or whether you never get anywhere at all, you're always busy, and you never do anything in particular; and when you've done it there's always something else to do, and you can do it if you like, but you'd much better not.'

[212]

Ratty, *The Wind in the Willows* by Kenneth Grahame

Prior to the 20th century, boats at Waldringfield were primarily functional, the overwhelming majority being used for transport, for fishing and for pilotage. Yachts designed simply for pleasure and racing were certainly not unknown on the Deben in the 19th century, the poet Edward Fitzgerald's *Scandal* being amongst the more famous of them. Waldringfield, being in its industrial phase from the 1850s, was probably not very appealing as a centre for leisure sailing at that time. However this does not mean that the various functional sailing craft were not used competitively when time allowed.

Regatta at Waldringfield in 1909 [214]

WALDRINGFIELD
AND
WOODBRIDGE REGATTA,
Wednesday, September 3rd, 1873.
THIS REGATTA will take place at Waldringfield, three miles down the river, on the above day, commencing 11.30 a.m.

JNO. DALLENGER,
Secretary.

Announcement of the 1873 Regatta [213]

By 1906, such competition and associated fun and games had developed into an annual Waldringfield

Village Regatta. This activity would increase with the start of the 1920s, the establishment of the Boatyard and the development of the Sailing Club.

Meanwhile, some local men had found alternative employment crewing on superyachts of the day such as HMY *Britannia*.

So, from those early days of leisure boating through to the Second World War, how many non-working boats were to be seen from the shore at Waldringfield? A few survive, most are only memories.

The oldest inhabitant of the Waldringfield anchorage today, the yacht *Kestrel*, is even a little older than HMY *Britannia* herself.

Kestrel, sailed by James Palmer at Felixstowe Ferry [215]

Oldest Inhabitants

Kestrel was built in Cowes in 1891 by the well-known John White Yard and one can imagine that she might have been one of the fleet of small pleasure yachts which gathered to watch the racing of the princes, emperors and millionaires.

Kestrel is a 27'7" gaff cutter, thought to be one of the oldest boats on the Deben. She has been lovingly restored by her current owner, James Palmer, boat builder of Larkman's Boatyard, Woodbridge, and WSC member. James bought her for £1 (donation to the RNLI) in 1996. He carried out the restoration work pretty much singlehandedly. Only two-thirds of the original boat, planking, tiller, mast and boom remain. Such is her reputation, she has frequently been referred to as 'the flagship of the Deben'. At a recent 50th year celebration of the 'Old Gaffers' in Cowes, she won the 'Concours D'Elegance' award for the best looking yacht.

Kestrel's previous owners include three nautical authors: Hervey Benham (1910-1987), W George Arnott, and Richard Woodman (born 1944) who retired in 1997 from a 37-year career, mainly working for Trinity House, where he is now an Elder Brother. Woodman owned *Kestrel* from 1976 and sailed her as a family boat until he came ashore after commanding THV *Patricia*. He gave her a 100th birthday party in 1991 but laid her up soon after as he was aware of her increasing fragility and he wanted to cruise more widely. He bought the John Leather-designed *Andromeda* (1966) also from Waldringfield. Woodman describes *Kestrel* as 'very fast' and with a hull 'to die for'. After a long period of uncertainty he sold her to James Palmer who had the skills to restore her to her former glory.

James Palmer has kept *Kestrel* moored at Waldringfield since 2001. She was also in Waldringfield when she was owned by George Arnott. James remembers his late grandfather talking of hearing gramophone records being played on board. He also understands that there was a paid hand who lived in the foc'sle, a tiny space, where he cooked 'plum duff'.

Local historian and auctioneer George Arnott, one time owner of *Kestrel*, is more usually associated with the yacht *L'Atalanta* which he kept on the Deben from the late 1930s to 1967, often moored at Waldringfield. *L'Atalanta* has had 12 owners and 7 names! She was built as a Swedish pilot cutter in 1906 and converted to a yacht in 1919, arriving in England in 1934. Arnott bought her in 1937 and based her in Waldringfield. In August 1939, he and friends were cruising in Holland. In May 1940, he was among those who responded to the call for help with the Dunkirk evacuation. Woodbridge shipwright Frank Knights accompanied him, but *L'Atalanta* proved too deep to get close to the beaches so remained in Ramsgate as an accommodation vessel. She then spent the rest of the war in Ferry Dock, Woodbridge before returning to her mooring off Waldringfield Quay in 1945.

Kit Clark, who grew up in Waldringfield, remembers as a young girl noticing George Arnott's yellow socks. Her mother told her to look away when observing George and his chums swimming 'as nature intended' from *L'Atalanta* down at 'The Rocks'. Arnott sold the vessel in 1968 and she eventually passed into the care of Robert Simper who cruised the Thames Estuary in her with his wife and family.

L'Atalanta today is owned by Martin Wenyon, great grandson of Frank Mason. An arrangement for her restoration by the International Boat-building Training College at Lowestoft having fallen through, she is currently stored at Parham airfield and Martin is open to ideas for her future.

L'Atalanta off the Quay [216]

Houseboats

Adelante by David Ruffle [217]

Although, historically, houseboats have not been a feature of Waldringfield as they have been elsewhere on the Deben, a few have appeared at times and some of these, having been built pre-WW1, have been among the oldest vessels on the river. Some were converted from former working vessels, such as barges.

An unusual Dutch Barge called *Adelante of Heerenven* belonged to Mr Chris Thompson, one time Commodore (1967-1968) and then President (1976-1985) of WSC. The Thompsons lived in Wickham Market and also owned the yacht *Deben Tango*. *Adelante* was 87ft long, 16ft and drew 3'6". She was built of iron in 1902 and was a sailing vessel until 1922 when an engine was installed. Mr and Mrs Thompson bought her in 1967 and ran her under engine, to the Deben from Heerenven via Lemmer, where 20 tons of sand ballast were taken on. After stopping at Lemmer, they continued to Amsterdam, Ostend, Harwich and finally Waldringfield. On a brilliant summer's day, 40 members of WSC unloaded *Adelante*'s cargo of sand ballast with 20 shovels and 20 buckets on ropes. The sand was placed between the two slipways and the whole operation took just 45 minutes. *Adelante* took part in a sail past for the official reopening of the Sailing Club in 1982. Following this, she was converted internally and Mr and Mrs Thompson made her their home whilst they travelled through Europe.

One of the deckhouses shown being delivered in 1936 [219]

Only a fragment of the former thames sailing barge *G.A.M.C.* has made its way to Waldringfield where it became part of the home of a Waldringfield resident and WHG member. It offers an example of what happened to some of the working boats when their industrial purpose had been lost. *Golden Hope* was the converted sailing barge on which the Haig family lived in Essex before they moved to Waldringfield in 1936 and built their house 'Broomstubbs'. The deckhouses of *Golden Hope* were brought by lorry and re-erected in the field where the Haigs were building. The Haigs eventually gave the deckhouses to Douglas Kennedy, and he included them in another wooden property on the same field.

A previous owner, Cyril Ionides, who lived aboard with his family in the early years of the 20th century, wrote a book, published in 1918, about their way of life afloat. The watercolour illustrations in the book were the work of novelist and Essex yachtsman, Arnold Bennett. The book, *A Floating Home* was acknowledged as one of the first on the subject of Thames Sailing Barges. *Golden Hope* had originally been converted from a working barge known as *G.A.M.C.* In the book however, she is given two fictional names. Prior to conversion she was called *Will Arding* and beyond conversion she is referred to as *Ark Royal*. Andrew Haig was born in the deckhouse of *Golden Hope*. He continued the story of the houseboat and his own family in a later edition of the Cyril Ionides book, published in 2003, entitled *A Floating Home and Born Afloat*.

Adelante of Heereven, owned by Mr and Mrs Chris Thompson [218]

Dreadnought [222]

Cornelia about 1935 [220]

Donald Haig, father of Andrew, appears to have had an individual and imaginative taste in yachts as well as houseboats. He owned *Cornelia*, another unusual yacht found in Waldringfield in the thirties. She was built in Holland, almost 50' long, 35 tons, steel-hulled and with an oil engine (most were petrol, paraffin or diesel). Donald Haig was sailing in the Baltic in August 1939 and his son Andrew believed that he was also taking the opportunity to carry out some reconnaissance into German preparations.

After the war, Donald Haig owned a motor boat, *Barbara Pelly*, a converted lifeboat, formerly the *Charles Dibdin* (built 1910).

Dreadnought can be spotted in many photographs from the mid 1920s. She was a houseboat moored at Waldringfield from at least 1924. She was converted from the hull of a barge but the name of the original barge is not known. Names were usually changed on conversion and it was almost certainly not the barge *Dreadnought*. For a while, *Dreadnought* belonged to yachtsman Sir Arthur Eborall who also owned *Cormorant* and *Mary* (designed by Albert Strange). *Dreadnought* eventually went to rest on the marshes just upriver from the Boatyard.

Waldringfield Regatta 1924 with *Dreadnought* in the background and a bowsprit used as a greasy pole in the foreground [221]

Enigma when she was owned by the Orvis family [223]

Some of the large, 19th-century, gentleman's yachts also ended their days as houseboats. *Enigma*, 53 feet long with an 11'6" beam, was originally called *Alpha Beta* but was renamed in 1904. She was designed by Dixon Kemp and built by Alfred Payne and Sons of Southampton in 1881. Between the wars she was owned by EW Orvis, a shipbuilder at St Clements Shipyard, Ipswich. It is believed that she may have been acquired as payment for a debt. *Enigma*'s interior fittings included cut glass door handles and on three of the cabin doors were oil paintings of large yachts. Orvis eventually removed the rig and used *Enigma* as a houseboat moored at Pin Mill. This enabled his family to spend their weekends there during the summer months. Occasionally she was towed round to Waldringfield for the Regatta, where Miss Poppy Orvis successfully raced her yacht *Rainbow*, much to the annoyance of some of the 'old salts'. Readers of E Arnot Robertson's novel *Ordinary Families*, published in 1933 and set in Pin Mill, will recall what a big local event a regatta was in those days. They might even wonder whether the keen racing family in that novel was not a little like the Orvis family.

Surviving logs from *Enigma* date from 1917 to 1925 and one in 1937 when she was on the Deben. Whilst the family stayed on board, Orvis would return to Ipswich, often by water, to run the Yard. The Orvis family were always very active, making trips, swimming, sailing dinghies, racing *Rainbow* and rowing. They also used a family motor boat. This is an extract from 1937 when *Enigma* was moored at Waldringfield.

'Saturday July 30th: father, Poppy and Roy left Woodbridge in the launch at 10.45 and arrived aboard Enigma *at 11.20 and unloaded stores, then prepared* Rainbow *for racing. Mother arrived with Teddy and Henry Barber and skipper in the car with more stores at 12.30. Father took launch*

(Flying Cloud) *to gather them up and left Henry aboard* Rainbow, *which immediately got underway well reefed for Woodbridge to race at 1.30. On the way up three people shared a lunch for two. Only one other starter* Rohaise, *so had a good flying start, had a ding dong down to Cross Reach then* Rainbow *went ahead increasing her lead slowly down to Waldringfield and still further on the run home, finishing 6 minutes before* Rohaise *but not enough to save time. Rolled up the jib and Henry sailed us back to Waldringfield for tea on HB. After tea, ashore for stores and water. John Cooper arrived in time for supper. Ships company now complete, plenty of talking, turning in on Teddy's command of 'To Bed!', Poppy in the deck house, Roy and John in the fo'c'sle.'*

NB: We believe Rohaise, *mentioned as* Rainbow's *competitor here, is Cherub no. 5, built by Everson's of Woodbridge in 1931 for Mr RW Shipman. She is now owned by his son, WSC member Mr David Shipman.*

Rainbow being sailed by Miss Orvis
(later to become Mrs Nicholls Palmer) [224]

Waldringfield Regatta 1924 [225]

During WW2, *Enigma* ended up in Woodbridge and continued there as a house boat. Lance Cooper, former Bosun WSC, remembers:

'My early years were spent on the river at Woodbridge including quite a lot of time playing truant. I recall pumping out Enigma, *who lay alongside the Tide Mill as a houseboat for the owner Commander Challis. She had a large round pump with a curved handle bolted to the deck and on a fairly regular basis I earned 6d. working this device, a futile operation. She did not float or sink but was permanently on the mud. Commander Challis lived in the wheelhouse that had been added at some point. I recall looking down the saloon skylight to a completely flooded interior with a Seagull outboard on top of the saloon table only just dry. My pumping job started in about 1957 and lasted for several years.'*

Enigma was eventually bought from Frank Knights in the late 60s and was to be towed round to Walton. However, during the trip down the Deben she veered about wildly, broke the tow at Felixstowe Ferry and ended up on the mud. After a particularly high tide, she finally settled on a mud bank. Later in another gale, she fell onto her side, damaged her frames and there she remained to fade away.

Believed to be *Enigma* in her racing days [226]

Whilst the hulk of *Enigma* decays at Felixstowe Ferry, her sister ship *Samphire* (previously owned by Frank Mason of Waldringfield Cement Works) has been more fortunate. Described as 'a rare survivor from the late Victorian days of gentleman's yacht racing' she has been professionally restored and remains in sailing condition.

The success of Miss Orvis and the competitiveness of lady owners like Miss Winn and the well-known Miss Muriel Wiles, who came to Woodbridge in the later 1930s, make it clear that sailing was not a male-only sport – at least in lighter craft like *Rainbow*. Gear was undoubtedly heavy in those days and women who owned cruising yachts often took a paid 'hand' to cope with mainsails and anchors.

Racing

Waldringfield Regatta 1924 [227]

Racing at Waldringfield was fiercely competitive. In the early days, slim, fast yachts were imported from other racing centres – later they were built at home.

Jim Turner remembered that his grandfather, Jimmy Quantrill, brought from the Thames to Waldringfield a boat which was an unusual design. She was later identified as a 'Thames Rater'. *Adlam* was built rather like an oval saucer with a heavy steel centre board which, when raised, showed more of the gunwale rather like the neck of a black swan. Raters were conceived in the late 19th century as the pinnacle of small boat design of that era. During that period, wealthy gentlemen competed in ever-changing yachts that lasted only a few seasons before being overtaken by faster craft. At 27' LOA (8.30m approx) with a 46' (14.15m approx) mast and 350 sq ft sail area, the Raters made a spectacular sight. The oldest Raters date from 1898 but developed quickly. One built in 1907, *Vagabond*, was the first to carry a Trapeze which is now a standard feature of many performance sailboats. Some also had sliding seats like racing canoes.

Jimmy Quantrill's boat *Adlam* won a good many races for him. In due course an offer was made, and *Adlam* was sold, to be renamed *Clio* – but thereafter, *Clio* never did as well.

By 1952, she was a mere hulk and was on the beach causing an obstruction.

Adlam sailed by Jimmy Quantrill – quite a contrast to the Thames barges [228]

Adlam at a later stage after she was renamed *Clio*, looking a little sad on the beach [229]

Prudence was one of the most eye-catching yachts in the anchorage. She was designed by GL Watson & Co who also more famously designed HMY *Britannia*. She was built by the well-known William Fife Yard of Fairlie in Scotland. At 22' and only 3 tons she was smaller than she appears in photographs. Mr Axel Wickham of Woodbridge, her owner, kept her at Nunns' Boatyard where he had a shed specially built to protect her from the weather.

Three other Fife-designed yachts are recorded at Waldringfield in this period. They are the Saint class of yachts (a centre-board sloop), all registered in 1919. There were four built altogether and around 1930 three moved to the Deben. *St Patrick*, owned and sailed by Cyril Stollery and Ken Palmer, *St David*, owned by Miss Constance Winn of Aldeburgh and *St George* owned by Mr George and Bob Garnham. They were open boats, half decked. Apparently *St Patrick* was painted green, *St George* white and *St David* might have been red. The Saints were a good match for *Prudence* as they were all designed to the 18 foot BRA rule which helped to make the sailing of small yachts very popular after the First World War. This may well be the first picture of Cyril and Ken as a team and the photograph shows

Glad Tidings at Waldringfield [231]

them dressed in white and defined their identity as a team. It was taken in 1929 when Cyril was about 24 and Ken 16. Sailing together in *St Patrick* honed their sailing skills, which led to their success in the National 12 class in 1936. It is thought they sold *St Patrick* to CW Woodall of London in order to pay for their National 12 *Terror* in 1935/6.

St Patrick has recently been lovingly restored by Fairlie Restorations under the supervision of GL Watson & Co, with some help from Roger Stollery and John Palmer. She was re-launched on 30 June 2011.

The Fife Yard did not survive in the same form beyond the end of WW2. William Fife III produced his last designs in 1938 and died in 1944. Nevertheless this Scottish dynasty made a lasting impact on the yachting scene. Their boats were built to high standards and a number of centenarians survive. Today you can see *Glad Times AH213* leaning against the Waldringfield Boatyard Quay where she is being restored by shipwright John Archer.

St Patrick on the left and probably *St David* on the right, about 1929 [230]

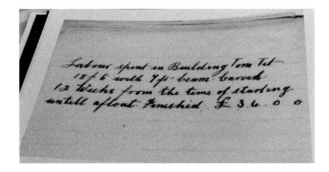

Bill for the building of a Tom Tit by Nunn's Yard [234]

Locally Built Yachts

It was not long before Harry and Ernie Nunn at Waldringfield Boatyard were building some fast, high-quality yachts. Among their pre-WW2 successes were *Onemore* and *Twomore*. These were half-decked 18' day boats, usually known as Bombay Tom Tits. They were adapted from a design by Linton Hope and built initially on the Clyde, where Harry Nunn had worked during WW1. Today they survive at Orford.

Checkoa was 28ft long and built by WH Orvis in 1912. She would have been very similar to James Palmer's yacht *Kestrel*.

Checkoa was owned by Ernest Palmer from 1931-1933 and was his first yacht bought from his good friend Jack Fisk's uncle when he was just 18. It had a 26' long wooden boom and there is a wonderful story of the boom being moved from the Palmer family home in Lower Brook St by Ernest on the front end on his Triumph motorcycle with Jack Fisk (who also lived on Lower Brook St) on a push bike holding the other end, all the way from Ipswich to Waldringfield, about 9 miles.

When *Checkoa* first sailed round from the Orwell to the Deben she leaked around the stem, where they had stuffed a bar of soap to stem the flow.

Onemore owned and sailed by Fred Upson [232]

Twomore sailed by Ernie Nunn [233]

Checkoa in 1931 [235]

'Third River Deben Regatta in a Week' (!)
The competitors in the race for the Cherub class passing the Clubhouse for the first round [236]

Cherubs

The 21' Cherub class, built by Everson's Boatyard at Woodbridge, was the first 'series production' yacht to be built on the East Coast.

Links and rivalries between Woodbridge and Waldringfield were strong. Alfred Rhys Groveham Curjel, a solicitor who owned *Cherub* (the first in the class after the prototypes), was one of the earliest members of Waldringfield Sailing Club and the class soon became popular for racing in Waldringfield as well as Woodbridge. *Cherub* is still on the Deben and in good sailing condition. Her current owner is Sebastian Watt.

Dr Harald Ernest Brucksham Curjel, Alfred's brother and a career Naval Surgeon, also owned a Cherub class yacht called *Seapig* (Cherub no. 4, built 1930) which had a port hole in the bow. He is said to have lived on board her at Kyson, though it is not known for how long.

A few years ago, *Seapig* was in Oakhampton, Devon undergoing restoration.

Cherub sailing at Methersgate [237]

Rev John Waller, who was Rector of Waldringfield from 1977 to 2013, is remembered for the wonderful eulogies he gave at the funerals of sailing people. When he officiated at Harald Curjel's funeral he also spoke beautifully of the joys of sailing a wooden yacht like a Cherub on the River Deben:

'24 May 1991, Waldringfield, Captain Surgeon Harald Ernest Bruckshaw CURJEL. (83 YRS.) Brethren, we are gathered here today to pay tribute and honour to the memory of Harald Ernest Bruckshaw Curjel. Harald's life long interest has been the sea right from his days as a young man. His joy was complete whether he was serving on Her Majesty's ships or sailing his cherub Seapig *on the Deben. He … was a colleague of my father Canon Trevor and my uncle Rev Henry. It is very fitting that my father should be taking part in this service for him. Both of them were constantly meeting as they sailed up and down the Deben, they were like yachts that passed in the day. The river was the nearest one could get to heaven – it afforded a glimpse of what is to come when we leave this earth. I gather* Seapig *is now round at Maldon – I believe that* Seapig *was the 2nd cherub that Everson's of Woodbridge built. A fascinating design for a river boat which sadly will be built no more – everything is plastic now. Wood remains alive whatever it is shaped to become. Wood lives and breathes in its yacht form. On leaving Woodbridge School, Harald naturally applied to join the RN but was turned down because of some speech impediment. Not to be daunted by such disappointment he took up medicine and trained at St Thomas' Hospital. Once qualified, he re-applied to the RN and was accepted this time as a naval surgeon … – he rose to Surgeon Captain and was appointed an Honorary Physician to Her Majesty the Queen. He was also appointed President of the Central Air Medical Board and Specialist in Aviation Medicine. … We say farewell to a very lovable sailor and commend his dear salty Soul to Our Lord's safe keeping.'*

If John Waller were still alive in 2020, he would undoubtedly be glad to know that Everson's (now the Woodbridge Boatyard) have collected a small fleet of five wooden Cherubs and intend soon to revive the race for the Cherub Cup, not sailed since 1950. The Cherub *Ariel* won *Classic Boat*'s 'Small Yacht Restoration of the Year' award in 2020.

Canon Waller in *Nora* [238]

The Racing Rectors

Many members of the Waller family have loved to spend time on the river. In the years between the two World Wars, the Rev AP Waller and his brother TN Waller were among the founding members of the WSC and keen competitors.

For the Wallers, as for many Waldringfield residents, sailing was not only about racing but about the enjoyment of the river and the development of friendships.

Past president of WSC Reverend Trevor Waller had *Nora*, his Deben 4-Tonner, moored by the island starting posts for many years. *Classic Boat* magazine recently described these as 'one of the nicest small British cabin cruisers of the 1930s'. Many such smaller yachts were popular during this period of financial depression. The Deben 4-Tonner was first offered in 1933 by the Woodbridge boatbuilder Claude Whisstock, then relatively unknown. The design was by William Maxwell Blake (1874-1939) and an instant hit, with 66 built in 22 years.

Theo belonged to the Rev AP Waller but passed to his son Canon Trevor Waller after his death. He took part in some of the first races at WSC and finished well in the 1926 Paterson Cup. Rev James Fraser and his family used to frequently visit from London to holiday and to learn to sail. They used to stay in one the cottages along Pilots' Path and take their turn sailing with many of their boat owning friends. They were also friendly with Jim Turner and the Heath family from the Old Maltings. This began an association with the village that has lasted to this day, four generations later.

AP Waller sailing *Theo* with Rev James Fraser [239]

Theo, *Cherub* and *Rainbow* racing at Woodbridge [240]

Visiting Owners

The 39', 14-ton ketch *Marietta* was built by Robertson's of Woodbridge and had a 'Handy Billy' petrol motor installed in 1928. When at Waldringfield during the 1930s and 1940s she was owned by Dr Edward Gimson, a GP from Witham in Essex.

Dr 'Ted' was one of a family of doctors (and a nurse) who looked after the health of Witham residents for over 80 years. In fact when their father (Dr William Gimson) died of a heart attack while operating, his two sons Dr Ted and Dr Karl carried on to complete the operation. The Gimson brothers, both bachelors had planned to retire together but this was frustrated by Dr Karl's death in 1926. Sailing seems to have been a very private hobby for Dr Gimson as Seona Ford, whose father took over his practice and also the house 'Gimsons', had no knowledge of this. 'I am intrigued about the *Marietta*,' she writes, 'as I know nothing of any interest in boats. I am surprised because he and my father were so close, very much like father and son.' *Marietta* was professionally skippered by 'Shaver' Mills.

Jim Turner remembered:

'Marietta was professionally skippered by "Shaver" Mills who was probably one of the most dedicated of fishermen on the river and he fished from the Marietta. *Shaver originated from Tollesbury and had fished practically all his life. If you asked him when to fish, he would say "while they are feeding", and that would always be either just before you started or just after you packed up! Shaver was said to have caught 99 bass in one haul at the Tips, using trammel nets and jingling or bumping. He would set his nets at the top of the tide, put cut straw on the water, row round and jingle chain in the water or pump with a special tool to frighten the fish toward the net. The straw prevented the fish from jumping over the net.'*

The 32' Bermudan sloop *Genesta* was built in Burnham-on-Crouch, Essex by William King & Sons in 1926. She was owned by the Gilbey family between 1932 and 1954 and Captain Vincent Gilbey employed Arthur Hunt as the last professional skipper on the River Deben.

In December 1914, Gilbey had been gazetted to 3rd Highland (Howitzer) Brigade of the Territorial Force as a Captain and Adjutant in the Royal Field Artillery. He was awarded the Military Cross on 1 Jan 1919 whilst serving in the 175th Brigade Ammunition column in France and Flanders.

Captain Gilbey originally lived at Bracken House, Kesgrave but came to live in Waldringfield with his second wife, Olive, after the Second World War. They lived in Cedar Bungalow, now redeveloped, which had a really beautiful garden at the end of Riverside Lane, now Quay Lane, from at least 1948 until his death in 1968, aged 91.

Marietta in the winter of 1947 when the river froze [241]

Genesta after restoration [242]

Chequers [243]

'Chequers', 'Janora', and 'Check'

WHG member Liz Kennedy, who was born Elizabeth Ogden in Mill Hill, relates the tale of *Chequers*. In her childhood her family used to holiday in Waldringfield every year. The children all grew up sailing on the river at every opportunity. Liz eventually married Douglas Kennedy of whom she says:

> *'My late husband, Douglas Kennedy, used to visit Waldringfield in the 1930s.* Chequers *was a 45' barge yacht bought from Woodbridge and kept on a mooring here until 1939. When the war came, he left her on the mud. He had a dinghy called* Check Mate. *I think* Check Mate *survived the war, but* Chequers *had a slow death on the mud which was rather sad.'*

Many yachts had to be left in great haste in September 1939 and many, like *Chequers*, did not survive their owner's absence. *Chequers* was laid up just upriver from the Quay. When the present landing stage was being put in the builders came across the keel. Liz continues:

> *'When Douglas retired, he was given, as a retirement present, the yacht* Janora, *a 30' wooden sloop. Soon after he got this yacht, he realised he hadn't got a dinghy to go with it and when he visited the American Folk Music Society, they gave him a present of a cheque to buy a dinghy. Ernie Nunn built it at Waldringfield and it was called* Check *because that was the American way of spelling cheque.'*

Douglas Neil Kennedy OBE (1893-1988) had been a Director of the English Folk Dance and Song Society. He retired in 1961 and it is thought that *Janora* was commissioned from Robertson's in Woodbridge and chosen by fellow dancer, Hamish Fraser.

Janora [244]

Earlier in his career, Douglas had compared the sensations experienced in sailing and dancing:

> *'There is no more exhilarating dance sensation than the motion of a small sailing dinghy leaping from wave to wave. Much of the exhilaration of sailing comes from that lift from crest to crest and the sense that you are in the grip of a tremendous and slightly irresponsible natural force. You have a feeling not so much of doing as of something done to you. The dancer is boat as well as crew. His feet like the helm, only need a touch every now and then.'*
>
> Douglas Kennedy, 1938 (from *A tribute to Douglas Neil Kennedy 1893-1988*, compiled and edited by Roy Judge and Derek Schofield)

Liz was still sailing *Check* at the age of 88. In 1999 the first of a yearly race of little boats was held. Initially, there were just three contestants including Liz but gradually a few more have taken part. There's a restriction of only one sail and now recently 'plastic' boats have been permitted.

Liz Kennedy sailing *Check* [245]

Two Weddings and a Funeral

In the years between the two World Wars the anchorage began to fill with moorings, so a Fairway Committee was established in 1938.

Friendships were made and romance blossomed. Civil servant Sir Ernest Arthur Eborall brought his gaff yawl *Cormorant* to Waldringfield, where she was kept on the village moorings. *Cormorant* was originally built on the Hamble in 1911 by Luke & Co. His daughter Katherine married the Rev AH Waller (artist brother of Canon Trevor Waller).

Racing helmswoman Poppy Orvis married future WSC Commodore Kenneth Nicholls Palmer – later they would own *Cormorant*. Ken's father, Ernest Palmer, enjoyed the river from his handsome motor cruiser *The Morn*. There was to be deep sadness when Ernest's younger son Jack, who often sailed with Master Mariner George Turner on *Doris*, drowned in 1935 when sailing with a friend at West Mersea.

Doris sailed by 'Uncle' George Turner (senior) and Jack Palmer in about 1920 [247]

The 35' Thorneycroft motor cruiser on the left is *The Morn*, built in 1919 in Chiswick and owned by Ernest Palmer in 1925. The yacht with someone on deck is probably *Nora* [246]

A Carpet-slippered Cruise

Nancy Blackett at Waldringfield [248]

On August 14th 1937 Arthur and Evgenia Ransome arrived in Waldringfield on their yacht, *Nancy Blackett*. Most people would have seen a neat, nicely maintained 28' cutter, designed and built by David Hillyard in Littlehampton (Sussex) in 1931. Ransome had renamed her after one of his own most popular characters saying 'But for Nancy, I should never have been able to buy her.' In the 1936 sailing season he had taken her on a brief cruise to Holland, which had given him the experience he needed for his most famous novel *We Didn't Mean to go to Sea*. When he picked up a mooring in Waldringfield, worrying about 'a horrid rumbling' somewhere around her propeller shaft, the novel had not yet been published. No one knew that this was *Goblin* the stalwart, starring character that would take the four 'Swallows' safely through the North Sea storm – and who keeps a special place in many readers' hearts to this day.

The following day AR climbed overboard to investigate the rumbling propellor. He discovered a loose nut and made arrangements with Ernie Nunn at the Boatyard to put it right. Evgenia often found *Nancy* a bit cramped so he took her back to their home in Levington and returned to Waldringfield for another night on *Nancy*. Early next morning he helped moor her against the Quay so the Yard could replace the nut and undertake some other minor maintenance jobs. 'Total bill 16/6 plus 2/6 for a week's moorings.'

On the 21st Arthur and Evgenia returned but it was blowing hard and 'Nunn said bar would be beast'. So they enjoyed a quiet day in the anchorage and entertained Captain Michael Barne and his wife to tea. The Barnes were from a big engineless Dutch yacht, *Black Fox*, built in Flushing in 1906. Perhaps they exchanged North Sea anecdotes. The Ransomes left the following morning, *Nancy* having a tough time pushing her way out of the river against the sluicing tide and AR almost knocked overboard by an accidental gybe. It would be fifteen years before they returned to Waldringfield.

A page of the *Barnacle Goose* logbook from 1951 [249]   *Barnacle Goose* on the scrubbing posts [250]

Their return took place in 1951. Ransome's novel-writing career was over; *Nancy Blackett* had been sold, *Selina King* and *Peter Duck* built and sold: there had been house moves, health problems. On September 1st they arrived once again in Waldringfield to take over another Hillyard-designed yacht, *Barnacle Goose* whose owners, George and June Jones had recently returned from a cruise to Holland.

This was a commercial arrangement: the Ransomes were chartering *Barnacle Goose* from George Jones's East Coast Yacht Agency. June, relatively newly married, remembers rowing out to lend Mrs Ransome one of the saucepans she'd been given as a wedding present. It was a mistake. Evgenia, protective of Arthur's health, recognised the saucepan as aluminium and gave poor June a fierce lecture in her heavily accented Russian English. It was raining, *Barnacle Goose*'s cabin was leaking; Ransome described the chart table as 'a swimming pool'.

The next morning they were away. The Deben mouth had changed dramatically since Ransome's last exit and he was glad he'd been cautious and taken a pilot. The halyards were wet, the sails were wet, the compass seemed to have stuck, then when they arrived at Pin Mill they could find no mooring. For the next ten days they pottered between the Orwell and the Walton Backwaters, catching up with old friends and local gossip. 'A very lazy, carpet-slippered cruise,' as Arthur described it. It was raining again when they returned to Waldringfield and the car battery had gone flat.

Perhaps, though, this cruise from Waldringfield had some good effects. As early as possible the following year Ransome dealt directly with David Hillyard and bought another small, neat yacht – which Evgenia named *Lottie Blossom* after a favourite PG Wodehouse character. And after her there was another...

Arthur Ransome died in 1967 but several of his yachts have outlived him. *Barnacle Goose* was last seen on the Deben in 2007 but *Lottie Blossom* (now *Ragged Robin III*), *Nancy Blackett* and *Peter Duck* are very much in evidence.

A Focus on the Foreshore

'They all went out together into sunshine that seemed extraordinarily friendly. A light breeze was stirring the river and they could see the water sparkling through the trees.'
Arthur Ransome, *The Big Six*

[251]

The beach at Waldringfield is unique on the River Deben because it offers a firm landing at all states of the tide. Technically the word 'foreshore' refers to the section between the high and low water marks and, at Waldringfield, the slope of the foreshore is such that a barge, for instance, timing her arrival quite close to high water, would be able to take the ground and dry out for the following 6-8 hours until the tide returns, thus enabling loading or unloading to take place. A yacht with a keel can float up against the scrubbing posts and dry out in a similar way. Beyond the low water mark the river becomes deep very quickly, further enabling close access.

Prior to the 20th century the foreshore was of

Waldringfield Beach 1888 [253]

great practical use, allowing Waldringfield to become a centre, first for agricultural cargoes, and later for industrial consignments. In the 20th century – and especially in the years between the two World Wars - many people discovered the fun to be had along the foreshore. It was firm enough to walk along even with long skirts and leather footwear, yet easy access to the water made it an ideal place to learn to swim, sail or row. After the closure of the Cement Works, it was not only villagers who began discovering the pleasures of the beach, but visitors also.

The Parish Council and the Fairway Committee and Trustees have done their best to ensure wise use of the foreshore but there have been times when individual fun and freedoms, bureaucratic control, and commercial interests have found coexistence difficult.

Unloading muck on the beach [252]

Access by Land and Water

Before the Boatyard became established, the Quay was used for various things, including as a pick-up point for the 'Tally Ho'. This coach service was owned by Mr IW Everett of Felixstowe and run from his stables in Victoria Mews. Tally Ho coaches covered a variety of routes. The Waldringfield service also called at Kirton and Falkenham.

The bridleway along the beach may originally have been to allow access for horses and carts to the barges that beached to offload their cargoes. These frequent visitors to Waldringfield carried cargoes of straw and hay to London where much of the transport network in the 19th century was dependent on horse-drawn vehicles. Horse muck or manure was then transported back to Suffolk to fertilise the fields. Some of these barges, such as the *Rachel Julia*, would have a wide deck enabling the bales to be stacked on top and held in place with irons.

The slipway near the Maybush has often been subject to challenge. There was always a right to a barge width for loading and unloading alongside the Quay and Ernie Nunn reinforced this by installing rails, which Nunn's Boatyard used for winter storage of boats. The concrete slipway beside that at times belonged to the Church Commissioners and was also claimed by the Maybush. The Sailing Club actually bought it twice, first from the Maybush and

The 'Tally Ho' coach on the Quay photo about 1912 [255]

Primrose, a stackie at Woodbridge showing how high the straw was stacked [256]

Rachel Julia loading straw, April 5th 1900 [254]

The Tally Ho coach on Waldringfield Quay in 1912 [257]

subsequently from the Church Commissioners when they were selling off their assets in the village. There was a dispute over who owned it and WSC, not unreasonably for them, wanted to ensure they could not be denied access.

In 2003/4 the Secretary of the Sailing Club had to write to various organisations to correct information regarding the slipway at the Quay that had erroneously stated it was a public slipway. It was pointed out that 'the Slipway at Waldringfield, near to the Maybush, is not a public Slipway and is for the use of Club Members, Village Residents & mooring holders only.'

In September 1932, there was concern about cycling on the right of way on the shore and a notice stating 'Cycling not allowed' was proposed; also the erection of a stile or foot gate to prevent cycling. (AW Stollery might have had something to do with this as he was worried about safety and did not like cycling on the path.) At the Parish Council Meeting of 20th

April 1933, the Chairman reported that the Rector intended to erect a notice on the shore prohibiting cars. But in July 1934 it is noted in the minutes that: 'It seems little can be done to prevent cycling on the shore path as the Rector's tenants use it as a roadway for motors to their huts'.

On 4th Dec 1934, a letter was received from the Rector: 'I have now received permission to lease the foreshore rights to the Parish Council.' It was suggested that the revenues accruing may allow some simple accommodation for bathers on a small piece of wasteland which will go with the foreshore. Mr Stow suggested fixing beach chains as shore moorings so as to avoid having to use anchors.

In 1935 the clerk reported the Rector's agreement to let sites for up to 15 seats adjoining the shore footpath at 1/= per annum payable 1st Oct each year.

There were more problems with traffic in 1935. Frequent obstruction by cars parked on the Maybush

Cycling on the beach and cars parked at the far end, February 1932 [258]

The beach at Waldringfield, with plenty of boats, in the 1930s [259]

Motor car on the beach, about 1930. Two of the men by the car look like they could be Ernie and Harry Nunn [260]

lawn was discussed. It was resolved to write to Messrs Cobbold's (the freehold owners of the Maybush) asking that notice 'No Parking Here' be fixed to their frontage. This is the first evidence of a reference to the Maybush lawn.

Congestion at the point where the Suffolk County Council's Cliff Road finished at the current drain grids was a continuing problem, which neither Albert Hill nor Ernie Nunn could solve. They tried to take action to restrict access with a lockable chain, but had opposing views, which came to a head with the opening of the Moon and Sixpence caravan site in the 1960s when the owners advertised free launching of

The Boatyard in 1966. Note the barrier, closed to prevent illicit launching. 'Thou shalt not launch illicitly' – Ernie Nunn's law [261]

speedboats to the river and Albert Hill offered to give them every assistance.

In 1934, Mr T Waller complained of the havoc caused at times by visitors and proposed that police authorities be requested to give more adequate supervision. The Parish Council evidently had great confidence in the ability of the Police.

Obviously, this all came to an end for the duration of World War Two when access to the beach was heavily restricted and the river mined.

Cyril Stollery recalls:

'From the end of World War I we drove cars and motocycles along to our huts and had a proper garage there on the site now occupied by the Club. Others did the same and because of danger to children we stopped it in 1938 and a post was put in to keep cars off the beach.

After WW2 Albert Hill or the Brewers decided to reduce the road to the bridleway status marked on the map and the posts and chains were put in… I have written … to endevour to show that a very considerable degree of restriction has taken place since the days when Burlingham drove backwards and forwards several times a day from his hut to the pub in an Austin 7 or when the tumbrels were in everyday use along the beach.'

Frances Waller riding a donkey on the beach about 1914 [262]

Yacht laid up in the hard winter of 1963 [264]

The Pleasures and Uses of the Foreshore

Local people have long used the beach for recreation and sport. On regatta days they were joined by many visitors from further afield. Between the wars – particularly as the beach huts were extended – families began to spend their holidays beside the river. A significant number never left!

Donkey rides have taken place on the beach, though it is unclear whether these were an organised

Horses on the beach in the 1950s [263]

Gunter-rigged dinghy *Lizzie*, and a duck punt. One of a set of 4 photos by Thomas Waller 1895 [265]

attraction, or whether the donkey was owned by a local family and the beach just used for exercise purposes.

There were also horses on the beach. The bridleway runs along the foreshore from the Maybush but it only goes as far as the steps, where the cliff path used to be. In the 19th century there would have been alternative access via the Flint Road.

In 1895, Arthur Stollery took time out from his work at the Cement Factory to take the Ogden family for a sail in their boat *Lizzie*. From left to right: Arthur Stollery, one of the Ogden daughters, Elizabeth Ogden, William 'WT' Ogden. WT Ogden is shown in the rowing punt although the dress code was somewhat more formal than today.

Lizzie was owned by the Ogden family in the 1890s but was subsequently sold to TN Waller who raced her as a member of WSC in the 1920s. He is listed in the entries for the 1926 Paterson Cup but did not appear amongst the prizes.

The Ogdens rented White Hall from the Wallers as a country retreat from about 1890-1905. Most of their household staff in London were Waldringfield girls, like Annie Bloomfield and Eliza Stollery. After her husband's death, Elizabeth Ogden moved permanently to Broomfield until she died in the late 30s. Edith 'Beaky' Ogden built and lived in Quietways, just behind Broomfield, near the school.`

Early beach activities Edith and Bill Ogden about 1910 [266]

149

Swimming

Swimming from the beach has long been popular, even more so since the closure of the Cement Works.

In 1932, Mr T Bloomfield, at a Parish Council meeting, suggested a range of 5 cubicle shelters for men and boys, and 5 cubicles for women and girls. Mr AW Stollery said he was preparing a model which he would submit as soon as he could finish. In the discussions, the suggestion of an experimental temporary building or canvas erection for next season was considerably favoured. The position proposed by Mr AW Stollery and Mr Button at high water mark near the Whin Stubs was thought most suitable.

Mr Booth undertook to call the swimmers together for their views on the suggested arrangements. A letter from Capt Heath was read out to the meeting by the Chairman, Mr Haig. He wished to preserve the pleasant freedom on the shore and not to oblige all bathers to use the provided shelters. Any objectionable behaviour would be dealt with by the police.

The Quay was often used as a swimming platform and during the festivities of Deben Week the greasy pole could be seen in operation here.

School swimming lessons (John Waller far right) [268]

School swimming lessons in the river before 1914 [267]

Between the 1930s and 1950s, except for wartime when the beach was closed, the village school held weekly swimming lessons in the river. Mrs Williams was initially in charge and later on the Reverend Wontnor, who was the vicar of Newbourne before it was combined with Waldringfield and Hemley. Jimmy Quantrill (and later George Turner) used to row up and down in his rowing boat as 'safety patrol'. You could only swim when the tide was coming in for 2 reasons, the strength of current being less and of course the dreaded effluent!

The Open Water swimmers [270]

'Nineteen of us did a beautiful swim for the Deben Macmillan Challenge this morning: thirteen arrived at Waldringfield after 9.4km. The remaining six didn't stop until Woodbridge Pier, swimming a total of 13.4 km. Perfect conditions, and great RIB/kayak support from Suffolk Lowland Rescue. An amazing morning's swimming for a great cause.'

The cubicles never did come about, but evidently swimming was more prevalent than today although it is gaining in popularity with the revival of 'Open Water' swimming and many villagers use the river, on hot days in the summer, to cool down.

A group of open water swimmers meets regularly each week, using one of the beach huts as a changing facility. They usually set off against the tide so as to swim back with it and they swim all year round.

A separate group, Felixstowe Swimscapes, has also made several swims between Felixstowe and the village, usually early in the morning. On 1st September 2019, they arrived 'en masse':

Peter Duck and two of her ducklings in 1958 [269]

Statue in the Open Water swimmers hut garden [271]

Learning to row, 1950s [272]

Learning to row, 2000s [275]

Lila and Hamish Fraser keeping fit [273]

Rowing

Generations of children have learned to row off Waldringfield beach and generations of adults continue to enjoy the experience. You may notice a semi circular notch cut out of the stern of Frasers' varnished dinghy and also the pale green dinghy (*Karl Marx*). This is to enable the dinghy to be sculled. In dinghies like these, sculling is done with a single oar placed in the notch and rotated in a rough figure eight movement to drive the boat along.

Madge Fraser rows her parents circa 1930 [274]

Stand-Up Paddleboards have become more popular [276]

Kit Clark née Waller being taken to catch
the train to school from Woodbridge Station
by boat, in the early 1950s [278]

Crabbing

Crabbing is an activity enjoyed by all ages and has been popular for years at Waldringfield. Many generations remember crabbing as children and the crab population seems to have grown with all the extra food provided. There are crabbing competitions throughout the summer months, but the peak time is towards the end of the school summer term when organised parties of children descend onto the beach around low tide. Not only humans, but seagulls swoop, squawk and compete for their portions of bacon!

Crabbing as the tide is coming in [279]

Crab racing at the end of the day before rain ends the game [277]

Ian Fraser on the greasy pole and George Arnott on the ladder in about 1930 [280]

Holiday Fun

Yachtsman Archie White gives his impression of a Waldringfield Regatta:

'A figure in slips appears rubbing his hands. Gingerly he puts one foot over the bulwarks onto the pole. Then the other. Standing poised for a moment he bends at the knees, straightens up, arches his back, crouches, pirouettes and wobbles, toppling backwards amid thunderous applause to fall, with a mighty splash into the river below. The greasy pole brings out a variety of technique. Some cautiously advance along, inch by inch, swaying as they go; others crouch their way along like tigers. Some attempt to slide the length of the pole gracefully, while a few, making no pretence at finesse, march boldly forward or even run in a vain endeavour to clutch the Union Jack (and the leg of ham which its capture entails) before they too plunge into the river.

There is the diverting "pull devil, pull baker" when parties of men, stripped to the waist, serve to board and upset each other's dinghies amid a terrific paper bag bombardment of flour from one boat and soot from the other. Single- and paired-oared craft are driven at incredible speeds through the water, and "crabs" are caught by old hands for the edification of the hilarious spectators. It is a pleasure to watch graceful young ladies dive from the Quay and swim a few hundred yards with the tide and be hauled aboard waiting dinghies by longshoremen specially deputed for the task by reason of their great age.

The scene is gay. From the trees flags of all kinds wave, and yachts are 'dressed' in honour of the occasion. Periodically during the afternoon music fills the air. The local band making full use of brass and percussion instruments, regales the assembly with such well-tried works as "Zampa" and "Annie Laurie" until, nearing teatime and with a final clearing of saliva from mouthpieces, they bring the proceedings to a perspiring but triumphant close with "God Save the King". In the evening comes the presentation of prizes, votes of thanks to all concerned, fireworks perhaps and certainly dancing and merry making of all kinds goes on far into the summer's night.'

A busy beach in the 1930s also showing a Punch and Judy stall (this may have been on August bank holiday) [281]

Three men on a boat: Charles Rix and companions, 1909 [282]

May 2020. For many people the beach at Waldringfield is simply a peaceful place to sit [283]

The Boatyard and Boatbuilding

'I feel there is something almost sacred about building a boat… It is almost like creating a living being, a boat seems to have a soul and character all her own.'
John Guzzwell, circumnavigator, in Trekka Round the World

[284]

The Boatyard by David Ruffle [285]

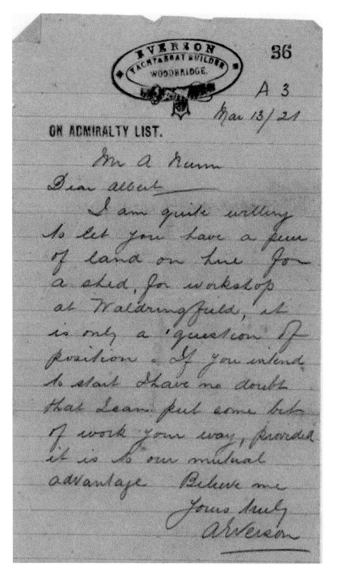

This chapter has been developed from an original account by Mike Nunn.

The River Deben at Waldringfield was devoid of boats during World War I, many of them having been laid up for the duration in mud berths on the saltings.

Although Mason's Cement Works had been completely decommissioned by 1912, the actual Quay was not sold by Frank Mason until 1925 when it was purchased by Mr AW Stollery (who we'll refer to as AW). It was then that Albert Henry Nunn, known as 'Harry', was given the opportunity to rent the Quay in order to continue his business as a boat-builder.

Harry was born in 1894. He was the eldest child of Albert (aka Alfred) and Alice Nunn. Alfred was a shepherd who lived with his family at Church Farm House in Waldringfield. Harry attended school in the 'Old School House' which stands at the corner of Fishpond Lane and Woodbridge Road; there he was taught by Mr Sutton. On leaving the school, he served his time as an apprentice at Everson's Boatyard in Woodbridge.

At the outbreak of war in 1914, Harry volunteered for the armed services but, because of his boat-building experience, he was dispatched by the authorities to Clydeside to help in the building of lifeboats. At some point, he was transferred to Weybridge and Chertsey doing more lifeboat building, but importantly he stayed with AW Stollery in his house in nearby West Byfleet; a comradeship developed which made AW intent on acquiring the Quay and using it for

Everson – Yacht & Boat Builder
ON ADMIRALTY LIST Mar 13 1921
I am quite willing to let you have a piece of land on hire for a shed, for workshop at Waldringfield, it is only a 'question' of position. If you intend to start I have no doubt that I can put some bits of work your way, provided it is to our mutual advantage. Believe me
Yours truly
A Everson [286]

The Quay at Waldringfield – before the workshop moved in [287]

boatbuilding. In 1919, Harry became unemployed and decided to return to Waldringfield to start his own business under the name of 'H Nunn Boat Builder.'

Harry's old boss, Mr Everson, owned a plot of land next to the old coal house across Quay Lane from the Quay, a plot on which there was a workshop. It was from this workshop, in 1921, that Harry launched his new venture, having arranged to rent the plot from Mr Everson who thought he would be able to 'put some bits of work' his way, provided that it was to their 'mutual advantage'.

When AW purchased the Quay, he put his boat-building intentions to the fore and resisted pressure to resell it for more lucrative purposes such as a hotel. A lease on the Quay was offered to Harry. In 1928, it became necessary to move the business from the coal house plot. Farm implement wheels were borrowed from Church Farm and, with Albert Hill from the Maybush as a project engineer, local lads helped to jack up the workshop and push it across the road on to the Quay.

It was about this time that Harry's younger brother Ernie, about 9 years his junior, joined the Yard and served his apprenticeship under Harry. They joined forces in 1932 and became 'Nunn Brothers'.

Nunn Brothers' main occupation was the construction of day boats and dinghies and boat repairs in general.

There were certainly an increasing number of boats requiring maintenance and repairs.

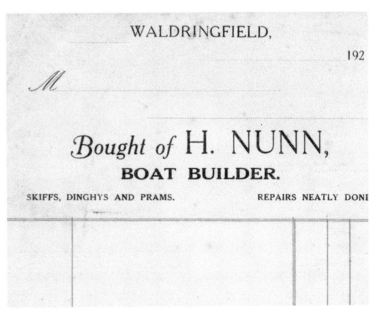

WALDRINGFIELD,

192

M

Bought of H. NUNN,
BOAT BUILDER.

SKIFFS, DINGHYS AND PRAMS.   REPAIRS NEATLY DONE

Harry Nunn's first letterhead [288]

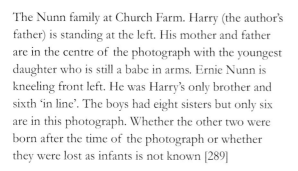

The Nunn family at Church Farm. Harry (the author's father) is standing at the left. His mother and father are in the centre of the photograph with the youngest daughter who is still a babe in arms. Ernie Nunn is kneeling front left. He was Harry's only brother and sixth 'in line'. The boys had eight sisters but only six are in this photograph. Whether the other two were born after the time of the photograph or whether they were lost as infants is not known [289]

The Nunn Family four decades on. Harry (centre) with Hilda, his wife, to his left side and Ernie to his right. Also in the photograph are three of their sisters, their parents (Albert and Alice Nunn) and, at the back, a brother-in-law. It is likely that the little girl at the front is Barbara Turner, later to become Barbara Kaznica [290]

The dinghies and yachts built at the Yard over the years included a number of 12ft restricted class dinghies. These dinghies which were sailed on both the Orwell and Deben became the forerunners of the 12ft National Class which were also built at the Waldringfield Boatyard.

In 1936, a National named *Itch*, built by Nunn Brothers, won the first-ever 12ft National championships, sailed by Cyril Stollery and crewed by Dr Kenneth Nicholls Palmer. It won again in 1948, sailed by Robin Steavenson.

Many Waldringfield One Design Dragonfly dinghies were built, along with Aldeburgh Lapwings and a couple of Bombay Tom Tits.

Also on the Quay, to the north of the Nunn's workshop, was 'Wickman's shed' which covered a launching ramp, with railway lines and bogey which brought yachts up the slipway from the river. It was built especially for the drysailing of Mr Wickman's

Boat repairs on the Quay [291]

The Restricted Class, forerunner of
12 foot National Dinghy [292]

Wickman's shed visible centre-picture to
the right of the workshop [294]

racing yacht, *Prudence*. On the postcard, it is the
dark building to the right of the Nunns' workshop.
Needless to say, Mr Wickman was blessed with some
wealth. The building just visible on the left was known
as the Paint Shop.

Records show that in 1935 the wage for a boat
builder for a 46 hour week was £2.14.3d less 1 shilling
and 7 pence national insurance.

In 1938, a Fairway Committee was formed and
a lease was subsequently obtained from the Crown

Mr Wickman's Racing Yacht *Prudence* [293]

Estate whereby it was possible to control the channel and the moorings between the Rocks, down-river, and the Tips, up-river. The Fairway Committee has functioned ever since, ensuring the maintenance of a clear channel, allocating moorings and regulating the beach below the high water mark. In 1948 the old willow withies were replaced by channel beacons. Some of the new markers were named, the 'Horse' being one of them; this is now Port Buoy No 6, marking the shallows down-river from the island.

Life on the river had been disrupted again with the advent of World War II. Nunn Brothers were instructed by the government to build lifeboats – long hours for very little reward, all part of the war effort – 66 hours a week was normal. Yachts were laid up on the saltings under the care of the author's maternal grandfather, Jimmy Quantrill. He was one of the few people who were allowed beyond the end of Cliff Road. The foreshore was closed; there was a lifting barrier, guarded by the military, close to where the telephone kiosk is now, against the wall of the Maybush.

Jimmy Quantrill – the author's
maternal grandfather [296]

In 1946, Ernie Nunn bought out Harry for £500, becoming the sole owner of the business. Harry, with a family of three of his own children as well as three Turner step-children obviously had plenty on his plate and welcomed this very substantial sum.

How or why this happened is not known but the brothers continued to work together. Harry was a perfectionist for whom things had to be just right. He would not go home if some wood needed glueing in order for him to get on with the job the next day. He would often arrive home with a wood fabrication that needed a bit of heat to make the glue dry; he would joke with the village folk that he took it to bed with his wife Hilda to keep it warm.

After the war, the building of pleasure and fishing boats restarted, including a number of yachts. A petrol pump was installed on the Quay and a derrick was used for stepping masts and fitting engines.

In the 1950s, a Tripod static crane was installed on the Quay. This enabled yachts to be lifted onto the Quay for work or storage. Winding the handle was hard work; later it was fitted with an electric motor.

Harry Nunn (left) with Corky Edmunds [295]

The usual Boatyard melée with the
Tripod crane clearly visible [297]

Ernie ran the business. He was responsible at the end of WW2 for overseeing the laying of new moorings in the anchorage. He was very strict on the positioning and also on how they were to be laid – anchors only, one at either end of a ground chain – then, in the middle, a riding chain and rope to a tin can buoy. He would inspect the position after it was laid and 'look out!' if you'd got it wrong!

The Yard became best known for building the International Dragon class. The first, *Harkaway*, was built in 1948 for Richard Pershouse who raced her very successfully.

Soon there were more orders so that, at one time, there were twelve on the order book. *Vana* won the Edinburgh Cup and *Viking* the Gold Cup, these being two of the most prestigious cups in the yachting calendar.

Other boats included the first Kestrel yacht, built for Paul King, then the 32ft *Barleycorn*, built for the Courage brewing family, and two 30' sloops *Green Dragon* and *Sea Rhapsody*. The latter was built by Nunn Bros, Waldringfield in 1956 for Kenneth Nicholls Palmer. She was sold in 1978. There is a photograph of *Sea Rhapsody* in the Maybush; it was taken in 1988 before she set sail for Rudkobing in Denmark, with a new owner. She was last heard of for sale in 2012 with a Hamburg Yacht Broker.

The largest vessel ever built at the Yard was the 42' motor cruiser *Fortuna*, now plying the South coast as *Fortuna II* and in fine fettle following a refit.

One and a half Pram dinghies were made for Carl Giles, the renowned cartoonist and local sailor. One was for rowing; the half dinghy was for a bar in his house in Witnesham!

To Harry,
With best wishes,
from Giles
67

Two-thirds of Giles' order for pram dinghies! [298]

W-itch after winning the N12 Nationals with C Stollery and K Palmer [299]

Employees over the years include names familiar to the village such as Ted Smart, Cliff Cordy, George Turner senior, Trevor and Ronnie Moore, Dick Larkman, Mike Clark, Jimmy Wicks and myself, Mike Nunn, son of Harry and Hilda, grandson to Jimmy Quantrill.

We had many laughs; one day we were helping Ernie to lay up a yacht in a creek on the saltings, 'Put that rope over that post' said Ernie. 'You must be joking,' said Mike Clark, 'the water's deep over there'. 'No!! No!!' said Ernie, 'I know every inch of these saltings'. He proceeded to jump over the side himself, completely submerging himself with his trilby hat floating above him. He did not think it was as funny as we found it.

Despite usually running a 'tight ship', servicing moorings, mast making etc. Ernie was not very good at sending out the bills; customers might be lucky to get one once a year. He and his wife Jessie had no children, but he took great delight working into the

night to repair a youngster's dinghy so that it would be ready to race the next day. 'How much do we owe you Mr Nunn?' they would say. 'Just make sure you win, that's all I want' was his reply.

That aside, he had a reputation for being grumpy, especially if a yacht dropped anchor and hooked one of his moorings. A telephone cable across the river directly opposite the Maybush was always a source of trouble for Ernie; yachtsmen would foul their anchors on it and then they would have to wait for low water to be released. The iron cross marking the point where the cable entered the water is still to be seen on the grass bank in front of the Maybush.

Ernie, it was said, once refused to take an order for a Dragon from an American Officer from Bentwaters Air Base because he said 'they made too much noise' with their aircraft. I think it was his excuse, as he had a full order book.

It was usually impossible to make Ernie do anything he didn't want to. Mike Clark remembers:

> *'I was working in the Yard with Ernie one day when a shiny new Jaguar came round the corner and pulled up. Behind it, on a trailer, was a small plywood pocket cruiser. The driver jumped out, saw Ernie, and shouted: "I say, Boatyard chappie! Could you take my boat somewhere and put it on a mooring somewhere?" I watched with amusement. If there was one thing Ernie Nunn disliked more than rude customers, it was plywood or GRP boats and their tin masts. Ernie slowly approached the man. "You come down here, and use our roads! You can take that bloody box up to the caravan site where it belongs!" He said, and walked away.'*

The Dragonfly fleet [300]

Aldeburgh Lapwings on starboard tack [301]

International Dragon Class [302]

Sea Rhapsody under construction at Nunn Brothers [304]

The brothers never made a fortune but took great pride and satisfaction in their work, watching the boats they had built being launched and, better still, winning races. Such was the pride that on one occasion when Harry was bending a plank around a yacht, part of it was across the doorway when a customer walked in hitting his head on the edge; blood was oozing from his forehead but Harry ran up the workshop floor, straight past the poor fellow, to check that he hadn't knocked the edge off his plank. He took great pride in his work!

In 1976 Harry died, just four years before Ernie. During those four years, in 1978 to be precise, Reg Brown bought the business which was then renamed 'Waldringfield Boatyard'. In 1984 Mr Brown introduced the pleasure boat, MV *Jahan* which still runs today during the summer months.

The *East Anglian Daily Times* (*EADT*) reported the official naming of *Jahan* by Robert Dougall, former

Sea Rhapsody off the Quay, awaiting her mast following the launching [305]

The Dragon fleet [303]

Harry Nunn with his grandson, David Clarke
Note that *Sea Rhapsody* (behind) is now properly equipped with a mast [306]

A tight fit for *Fortuna* [307]   *Fortuna* in her prime [310]   The wheelhouse on *Fortuna* [311]

BBC newsreader and by Barbara McDowell, an MS sufferer. The reporter described the vessel as part of an overall project including the construction of a 120'

Iron Cross [308]

jetty and a new reception and refreshment complex. The 38-foot cruiser was named after Mr Brown's two boxer dogs, Jason and Hannah. The *EADT* reporter said that 'Disabled people [were] being given the chance to cruise along the River Deben' as the vessel was 'fitted with a hydraulic wheelchair hoist and other adaptations for the disabled'. The report quoted Robert Dougall as saying: 'Here now is a matchless stretch of water with a matchless cruiser to sail it.'

Jahan has been used for river cruises from the Boatyard since her launch. Over the years she has had an orange, yellow, then orange and now light blue hull colour.

In 1998 Andrew Brown took over the Boatyard from his father and continued to run the business although, by then, the boatbuilding had ceased. In 2011 the business was sold to Mark and Emma Barton who build, repair and service boats as busily as ever. The Quay is still owned by the Stollery family who ensures that it continues to serve its true purpose.

MV *Jahan* at the time of her naming ceremony.
Note the lack of glass in the windows and, astern, the dinghy on davits [309]

High water at the Quay – a good time for fitting out. Seen in the picture are Pop Hawkes, confectioner, Joe Venmore-Rowland on the quayside and Ray Page, a tailor from Bury St Edmunds [312]

Looking across the river from the Quay [313]

165

Ernie Nunn

Taken from *The Deben* 1997, the observations of John Adams:

'1944 and a posting to Suffolk was received with an overwhelming lack of enthusiasm for surely it was part of East Anglia where there were marshlands, drains, windmills and probably numerous natives with their digits in the dykes. One of the first of these natives was a Mr. Nunn, proprietor of The Boatyard at Waldringfield to whom I explained that the Army was grateful for the use of his petrol pump and would like to return it into his safekeeping. I couldn't entirely understand what he was saying but I formed the impression he did not like strangers in general and authority in particular and as for the pump I could make my own arrangements. It was during this encounter that I had my first glimpse of the Deben and in spite of the dummy invasion barges, Nissen huts, scaffold poles and barbed wire, I thought it beautiful. Fifty-three years on and I still think it beautiful. Ernie Nunn may not have been a thing of beauty but he was not what he seemed, for in the course of time I found he was a man of many talents and indeed a kindly soul.'

Mike Clark, who was an apprentice at the Boatyard from 1953-1958 remembers being interviewed by Ernie, who was in bed with a broken ankle at the time:

'Ernie asked a few questions and seemed to think I'd do.

"How much will I be paid?" I asked.

"Oh, don't worry about that, we'll see you're alright," said Ernie. And that was it, he never did tell me. I had to wait until my first Friday paypacket, a little brown envelope. I couldn't wait to open the envelope and see how much was in it, so when no one was looking I rushed to the toilet, opened my envelope and counted my money: £1.17s.

'A tight ship' as Ernie might have said. Ernie Nunn, distinctive in his trilby, is manoeuvering Quinton Parker's boat around the Maybush corner in the late 50s / early 60s. Mr Parker is looking on. The tractor, of course, continues to do this job to this very day, now in the expert engineering hands of Mark Barton [314]

I was always in trouble with Ernie. As he said, "You're only the boy, it's your job to take the blame for everything!" I was only ever trying to do the right thing. Like the time I was told to answer the phone when no-one else was free. On the line was a client who had commissioned a racing day boat – a Dragon I think it was – and was calling to see how it was going. I was a truthful lad. "What Dragon? There's no Dragon in the shed at the moment," I told him. Ernie was furious. I should have said it was well under way – as it should have been. Well how was I to know?'

The Dragon Class

In 1928 the brilliant Norwegian called Johann Anker had designed a 2 man cruiser-racer named the Dragon. Originally with a small jib, two cot berths and doors to the cuddy, it proved to be a very popular design. In 1932 the Clyde YC on the west coast of Scotland adopted it as a class. After the 1939-45 war, the class grew significantly and with growth came some design changes. With these changes, the Dragon became a three-man racing keelboat with its own start at Cowes and many other regattas.

Ted Sudell and George Turner racing Dragons [315]

The Nunn Brothers started to build the boats at Waldringfield and were reputed, at one time, to have had a waiting list of 12! WSC decided to start a class in the early fifties and, by 1958, Cyril Stollery, Mike Spear, Arthur Mason and Eric Wright had all bought boats and the fleet would sometimes combine with the Aldeburgh Dragons. At Waldringfield, Cyril Stollery was particularly keen, starting with an old Dragon *Tai Yen*. *Tai Yen* was one of the first Dragon class boats to be moored in the anchorage. This was the oldest UK registered Dragons with the number 'D1' and had previously been a wreck in a mud berth on the Medway. She was restored before Cyril bought her in 1956. He enjoyed considerable success with *Tai Yen*, as did George Turner who helmed Arthur Mason's boat *Jarn*, a vintage 1930s Dragon with the original bunks still in place. Expensive new innovations, however, led to a steady decline in the local fleet.

The introduction of GRP hulls with metal masts, bigger spinnakers and generally more equipment once again increased the expenses. With increased popularity, moorings became harder to come by and the remaining boats gradually migrated to Aldeburgh to race.

The Beach Huts

'…this happy place where almost everybody wore sea-boots, and land, in comparison with water, seemed hardly to matter at all.'
Arthur Ransome, *We Didn't Mean To Go To Sea* (ch. 1)

[316]

View towards Waldringfield from downriver [317]

View downriver from the Look Out in 2020
– one can see it is aptly named [318]

The opposing view looking upriver in 2020. The lack of boats is due to the COVID-19 pandemic restrictions [319]

Approaching from downriver to Waldringfield, the distinctive Waldringfield Huts are the first buildings one sees. Next, Waldringfield Sailing Club, the red brick façade of The Maybush, landscaped by its terrace and the bush-clipped hawthorn trees and, beyond that, the Quay with its unmistakeable tripod crane. High at the top of the cliff by the steps leading up but hidden away, is the hut known as 'The Look Out'. To the right-hand side, you can just make out the new sculpture that was erected in 2019 to mark the 70th Anniversary of the Dragonfly Class at WSC.

The First Huts: The Waller Family

The foreshore has changed dramatically over the years from the site of the industrious coprolite fertiliser workings until 1893 and further along the Quay, the dominating Cement Works and the lime kiln chimneys which were demolished between 1907 and 1912. In the late eighteen hundreds coprolite or fossilised dung was extracted from the Waldringfield cliffs for grinding into superphosphate fertiliser. The digging created flat shelving areas close to the beach that after this industry disappeared were no longer of any use for agriculture but later proved to be nicely sited locations for a hut especially when sailing became more popular and increased leisure became possible.

No one is really certain when the first huts were put up on what was Glebe-owned land on Waldringfield beach. The late Reverend John Waller claimed that the first hut was built around 1895 for the Reverend Arthur Pretyman Waller who was the Vicar of Hemley, on a levelled site, now No 7. When it was still standing some 100 years later, it seemed to be only held up by the ivy that encased much of it!

Dragonfly Class sculpture erected Summer 2019 [321]

Early huts at Waldringfield. Note no steps in the distance [322]

This hut in the foreground is probably the very earliest beach hut, built for AP Waller around 1895 [320]

The John Waller hut about 2016, since replaced [323]

The Waller family hut in situ circa the 1960s [324]

It was a storage shed, rather than a residential type hut, although it was used as a changing room by the Waller ladies when swimming in the river, but this has now been replaced by a new pristine hut with a veranda.

Thomas Naunton Waller was a prominent person in the village. He was an engineer and designed his own self-timing camera. He took the earliest photographs of the village on this glass plate camera. Thomas was the sixth out of eleven children born into this large family. He was born in Waldringfield although several of his siblings were born in Ramsholt and Ipswich. Thomas returned to the village of his birth after retiring from the Hawthorn Leslie Shipyard in Newcastle. He built the house 'Novocastria' – hence the name (New Castle – a native of Newcastle is a Novocastrian) and had his own hut built.

His hut was built on an angle and would have been where the latest extension to Waldringfield Sailing Club (WSC) was built in 2013. Around 1990, Mike and Rani Pert successfully tendered for the hut site from the Glebe, although when they saw the state of the hut that was on it they declined to purchase that from the previous owners and promptly burned it. They then replaced it with their newer one. After the new extension was completed, the Pert family put a smart, even newer log cabin on the front part of the site and electricity was provided by WSC.

From Nissen Huts to the Millenium Building: The Stollery Family

After World War One, Waldringfield showed definite signs of development as it was gradually being discovered as a potential sailing centre and a place to visit for the weekend. New houses sprung up alongside the road leading down to the river and near the Quay and each successive year saw an increase in boats and yachts on the river. During the 1920s, other prefabricated buildings and timber huts were built on Glebe land, so starting a tradition of hut structures that have remained very similar right up to today, with timber cladding, metal or felt roofs and reused parts etc. All these materials were portable on temporary foundations and in many cases were built by family members. The more recently built, however, could be more appropriately described as wooden cabins

New Pert hut built next to WSC and in front of the extension [325]

Waldringfield beach, showing 2 Nissen huts – Stollery hut and WSC [326]

Gorse Cabin in June 1970 before being renovated [327]

Gorse Cabin belonging to the Stollery family in 2019 [329]

or lodges rather than as huts. One of them has been designed by an architect and although many huts remain without services this hut has a wood burner and solar panels fitted.

Isaac Stollery was the ferryman across the Deben at Waldringfield in the 1870s. However, he died young in 1889, leaving his wife Eliza to bring up their 11 children. She ran the local village shop which was set up for her by the Waller family. Alfred was the tenth child and from the age of 14, he was an apprentice cabinet-maker, walking to Woodbridge every day along the river wall. He moved to Surrey to set up his own business, but loved Waldringfield and wanted to return at every opportunity. He rented, from the Church, part of the old coprolite workings next to the beach, putting a gipsy caravan on the site where the round hut now stands. This was a First World War Nissen hut designed to sleep around 20 men and was erected in 1919. This was the second hut on the beach. If one looks closely at a photograph taken from the beach, one will see the two prefabricated army surplus huts at Gorse Cabin.

During the War, the round hut was taken over as a gun emplacement. (Alfred always thought that it had the best view of the river both ways.) The description

Ammunition writing in the Stollery Beach hut [328]

of the ammunition is still chalked on the shed walls.

In 1953 the round hut was re-roofed with felt tiles. Roger, Cyril's son took over the hut, after his father's death in 1969. His sister Annie moved into Ryefield, one of the Cement Cottages and used part of the land behind Gorse Cabin to grow vegetables. She used to spend a lot of the summer at Gorse Cabin tending the garden until the family moved away in 1992. In the 1980s the rusting corrugated iron walls of the round hut were replaced by columns turning it into a shelter. After he retired, Roger replaced the felt tiles with a standing seam metal roof, using waste green roofing from the Millennium Building at the All England Lawn Tennis Club at Wimbledon, where he was the architect leading the design teams.

A historic photograph shows another First World War round hut erected by Arthur, Alfred's elder brother. This subsequently became the first Waldringfield Sailing Club Clubhouse. The sailing Club was founded in 1921. Alfred and Arthur were founder members of the WSC and Alfred was the Flag Officer in 1933.

Down from London: The Ogden Family

Alfred's brother Arthur, built a series of huts adjacent to Gorse Cabin in the 1920s and the long hut behind the round hut was erected on the Gorse Cabin site in 1928.

The Ogden family also had one of the earliest huts at No 18 Waldringfield Beach, south of the coprolite workings where WSC and Gorse Cabin are sited. The family lived in North London and were one of the earliest DFL's – 'Down from London'. They have been holidaying in Waldringfield for six generations.

The original Ogden hut was built around the turn of the century. The early settlers had the prime positions and very large plots. In fact, the original plot was much larger, as a part was later given over to the Haig family to build their hut (no. 17). The hut was divided by a wooden partition. The larger section was the ladies changing room and the smaller one was for the men. This also contained oars, rowlocks,

The Ogden hut before it was replaced in 2019 [330]

The Ogden family. The tall lad at the back is Bill Ogden, the father of Jill Atkins and Liz Kennedy [331]

Mr Jordan was the coachman to the Ogden family who rented White Hall [332]

anchors and fishing gear. A second hut on their site was erected shortly before or after WW2. At some time during the War, the row of huts beyond no. 18 was removed. The grassy bank was built up to provide a ramp from which to launch 'Bigbobs'. The green and pond were never fully restored after the War. The pond was just beyond where the Wayfarer and Cadet dinghy park is currently. The children used to make matchbox boats with little square paper sails and race them across the pond. Trophies were presented to the winners made of silver paper from the inside of cigarette packets. The family never slept in the hut as they rented various houses in and around the village.

They rented White Hall from 1890 to 1905 Mr Jordan collected them from Woodbridge Station by a pony and trap. He lived at Church Farm which was divided into two residences. The Nunn family occupied a part at one time. The Ogdens eventually bought Broomfield and built Windyridge and Quietways in School Lane, just past the Village Hall. Before the last War, this was known as Nightingale Lane, because you could hear the birds sing, but it has also been called Sandy Lane, or the Folly.

The Look Out Hut

The Wallers, Ogdens and Stollerys had the first pick of sites on the foreshore, but maybe one late runner at the top of the steps had the best position. This hut was owned by Nora Waller (Hut 3) and was used as a lookout for the Home Guard during the War and before them by the pilots for barges.

It was unusual in that it rotated, although apparently after a small family disagreement the locking mechanism was broken or disabled and it remained permanently in one place from then on. The hut was subsequently sold to John Rogers of

The Look Out at the top of the cliff around 1950 [333]

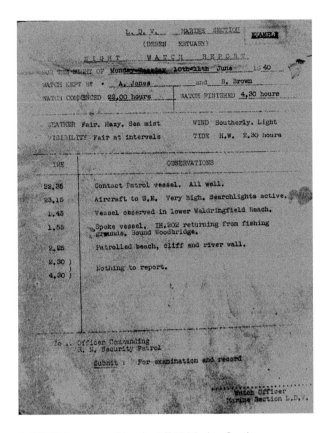

In WW2 it was used by the LDV Marine Section in 1940. Here is a sample watch report [334]

Nora Waller's hut at Rendlesham [335]

The Look Out 2019 from the steps [336]

Rendlesham and removed to their home. It has since been replaced and is now called the Look Out. It is owned by Martin and Sylvia McBeal and is often bedecked in flags to welcome visiting yachtsmen. Sylvia's family have owned a beach hut here for a couple of generations and now regularly entertain their grandchildren during the summer holidays with all sorts of adventures which remind one of *Swallows and Amazons*. They can also sometimes be seen playing on their bagpipes to welcome visitors and travellers.

The site opposite (Hut 1) at the top of the steps, was owned by Mrs Sparks of Hope Haven and subsequently Christianne Bowles who said:

> *'I bought the beach hut from an old lady when in (I think), 1980, we were looking for a beach hut for a while and one day I was following two ladies up the steps, one telling the other that she wanted to sell her beach hut and nobody wanted it, so I offered to buy it, told Ian and we had bought it. We used it a great deal thereafter until 1990, it then stood empty for a while and we removed it as no one wanted it in about 1995, not sure of the exact date.'*

They planted the Russian Vine that grows beside the path.

Huts on Glebe Land

Many of the hut users are still sailing families who have inherited them from past generations. The Nunn family own the hut on plot no 6 (blue hut below). Its use has changed over time, together with its appearance. Starting as a gear hut, it caters for five generations of the Turner/Nunn family and during warmer weather it is conspicuously enjoyed by several generations of family members.

Same beach huts in 2020 with the Nunn family hut now replaced [337]

173

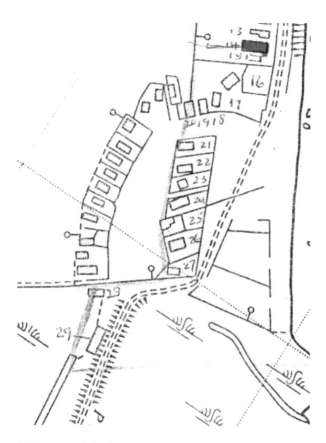

1950s map of the beach huts [338]

The Jones Family Beach Hut

The original hut on this site was probably that put up by Jimmy Quantrill in association with Hugh Jones, whose two sons, Jack and George, had begun their sailing careers off the beach at Felixstowe where their aunts ran a school. Hugh Jones was a farmer, but his younger sons had little interest in farming – boats were their passion. In 1928, when Jack was 13 and George 10, their father bowed to the inevitable. He identified Waldringfield as a safe place for two adventurous lads learning to sail, supplied them with a former chicken hut which was placed at the bottom of the sailing club steps, then put them under the care of Jimmy Quantrill. It was a long cycle ride from the farm at Witnesham, but they were able to camp at the hut, which they later named 'Bowships'.

It was a moment of revelation for Julia Jones when she was reading WG Arnott's *The Place Names of the Deben Valley Parishes* (1946) during the compilation of this book. Arnott was explaining the name 'Bowships' which Julia already knew as a former river hard, further down on the Sutton shore of the Deben where barges would sometimes wait to meet their pilots for the upper reaches. 'Bowships', wrote Arnott, was first recorded at Walton in 1541 and 'is extremely interesting as a record of an actual community of free peasants or

geburs'. It was also the name that Julia's uncle and father, friends of Arnott from the later 1930s, had given to their beach hut. She'd never understood why, but suddenly this made sense – given that Jack and George Jones were farmer's sons who had lost their direct connection with the land and socially they were perhaps a little insecure, a bit prickly. 'Bowships – a community of free peasants' – what a perfect name for their hut!

Hugh died in 1933 in an accident. Times were hard, the farm was given up, the family scattered. The hut at Waldringfield remained a blessed constant, even when both Jack and George were working in Birmingham in the years immediately before the Second World War.

George spent the weekend of August 5th 1939 in the hut with friends. His diary records that they all 'got tight in the Bush' and there was singing on the Quay. The next day (Sunday 6th) they sailed to Woodbridge to look at King Raedwald's newly discovered grave at Sutton Hoo. Monday was less enjoyable. It was a bank holiday. 'Too many boats, people, noises, bicycles and ice-cream carts at Waldringfield,' he wrote. He came last in a race, resigned from the Sailing Club after a row, and spent ten hours driving back to Birmingham. He didn't know then that it would be another six years before he returned to Waldringfield.

During the War, when access to the foreshore was restricted, Jimmy Quantrill was still permitted to take care of the boats, including George's beloved *Hustler*. Although the huts were all out of bounds, the Joneses were happy for the Quantrills and Nunns to keep boat tackle in 'Bowships'.

After the War, when Jack and their mother Edith moved into the Old Maltings, the hut was no longer needed except in 1950, when George Jones married June Scott and the young couple had temporarily nowhere to live. The first months of their married life were therefore spent in the hut.

Bowships 1928-1951 [339]

Today the plot is divided into two. Set back at the bottom of the steps is a hut which is jointly owned by two families, the Marriotts and the Whites. Over the picket fence is a recently refurbished hut belonging to the Nunn and Turner families who are descendants of Jimmy Quantrill, the Jones boys' sailing instructor.

Further Development on Glebe Land

Alfred Stollery's brother Arthur built a series of huts adjacent to Gorse Cabin in the 1920s including the long hut in 1928. Some of these can still be seen today stretched along the footpath towards the WSC dinghy park. Others appeared suddenly; as with one that appeared in the 1950s/1960s, seemingly overnight, built by Mrs Stevens. When Canon Trevor Waller found out, he was most displeased and told her to remove it quickly.

Ernest Palmer rented a 'Stollery' hut from the late 1920s. In those days one could park a car outside the hut to unload. Ernest owned a motor cruiser called *Aloma* (which was later owned by Mr Goodwin and Bob Garnham). His son Kenneth owned a succession of racing dinghies and yachts, one of which, *Sea Rhapsody*, was built by Nunn Bros in 1955. Dr Kenneth Nicholls Palmer was Commodore and later President of Waldringfield Sailing Club. The family still sails regularly and owns the hut and are now into the fifth generation to use it.

The last beach hut downriver owned by the Spear family which was originally made of packing cases

The original Spear hut when it was for sale [340]

Replacement hut on Spear site after the 2013 floods [341]

became dilapidated over the years but this did not stop it being sold for a relatively large sum of money in 2002.

This was probably due to its prime location rather than the décor. It has since been rebuilt and now belongs to two families who share it.

During the tidal surge of December 2013 quite a few of the huts flooded. Of course, the huts were designed to be flood-resistant, but the replacement hut built on the Spear site was one of the worst affected.

1950s: The 'Arab Quarter'

The remaining huts form part of what is nicknamed the 'Arab Quarter'. These huts were probably among the last plots to be allocated. It is thought that in the 1950s Bob Garnham nicknamed them because the owners used to spend the seven-week summer holiday living in these shacks and tents. They were perhaps rather tanned from the sun and Deben mud, so the name stuck. They were a temporary home to many families during this period and great fun was had by all.

Front row of beach huts 2020 [342]

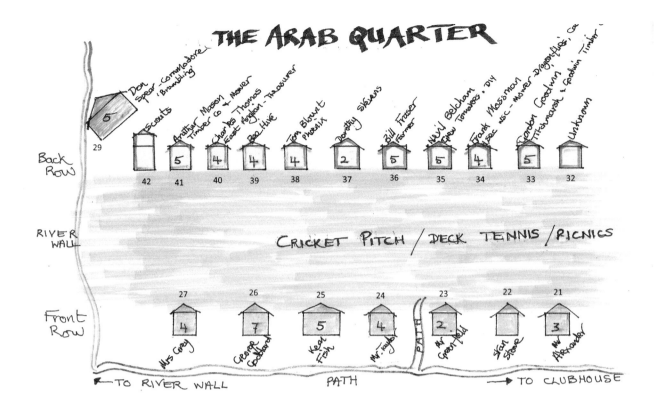

Map of the Arab Quarter showing which families owned which hut (the numbers inside represent the family sizes) [343]

The Arab Quarter was surrounded by bushes, with a neat little path hidden between the huts, which kept it very secluded and sheltered from the easterly winds. Cricket matches were hotly contested most evenings, after spending the day messing about on the river. They got water from the Maybush pump, about 5 minutes' walk away, cooked on primuses and later calor gas stoves and the lighting was mainly candles or Tilley lamps. Davey's shop was fine for all the groceries, Mrs Frost had the Post Office and Bertie Bell from the Cement Cottages grew wonderful fruit and veg in his allotment at the top of the sailing club car park; so they were very well catered for.

The first hut erected in the Arab Quarter had been used as a Guard Hut during World War II during Operation Quicksilver and was owned by the Taylor family (hut 24). They didn't come for the sailing however as they were keen golfers and members of Woodbridge Golf Club. The two huts to the left of the Taylors hut, (huts 25 & 26) were owned by the Goddard and Fish families. They were erected in 1946, and constructed out of wood from old Army huts at Felixstowe that were being demolished. Each one came by lorry and cost 10s each. The Goddard one was built in the traditional beach hut style facing towards the river and the Fish family built theirs

The back row of the 'Arab Quarter' circa 2015 [344]

The huts being re-erected after World War II [345]

The Biscuit Tin with Jeremy Belcham [346]

sideways on just to be different. Both the Goddard and Fish families took an active part in sailing activities and the children all learned to sail here, especially during the long summer holidays when many decamped to Waldringfield.

One of the huts belonging to the Belcham family (hut 35) was made in sections in the piggery of their smallholding at Newbourne and erected in Waldringfield in 1950. It was clad in new aluminium sheet of the kind used in aircraft construction and the roof was of corrugated aluminium. It was nicknamed 'The Biscuit Tin', purportedly as it was quite noisy trying to sleep on wet and rainy nights! When Chris Mason replaced it with his own greatly superior structure in 2018, he named it 'Ship's Biscuit' in recognition of the fact.

George Goddard (hut 26) had a gramophone and organised wonderful 'Hops' in the sailing club on Saturday nights. In those days circular taffeta skirts were very fashionable, they had to stick out, so mothers had to patiently thread hoops into the skirts, or if not starch masses of net petticoats just before it, so that there was no time for the salt river air to make them go all limp again. All this sophisticated preparation went on in a beach hut, just 12' x 8', amongst the cotton sails hanging from the ceiling, that were probably dripping wet. Mr Mossman (hut 34) had a drawer full of rather rusty old tools that all the hut residents used to use. The mothers had to provide clean white starched detachable collars for their husbands to go to work in, whilst staying in the huts.

The Belcham hut (Biscuit Tin) just before it was replaced by the 'Ship's Biscuit' [347]

They worked mainly in Ipswich and they had to look smart! Mrs Mossman (hut 34) had 2 flat irons that she lent to other mums, and Mrs Mason (hut 41) had a potato scrubbing machine that was passed between most of the huts.

Early morning shave [348]

1950s: Family Fun

Before swimming many of the children liked bouncing on a tractor inner tyre. The girls used to take it in turns to get into the middle of the tyre and then the boys used to bowl it down the beach into the water.

The Belcham, Mossman, Goddard and Thomas families with Stan Stow rowing, swimming in the river [349]

Thomas, Mason and Mossman families picnicing with the Kroes family [352]

Picnics on the lawn [353]

Judy Haken, Sylvia Gray, Ann Mossman playing on a tyre [350]

Deck Quoits (Tennis) on the lawn. Jill White and Doreen Belcham playing against Peter Goodwin and Jeremy Goddard with Charles Haken keeping score [351]

Jem Goddard, Michael Belcham and John Palmer with towels for sails! [354]

Ice creams at the Ramsholt Arms. Back left: Joan Mossman, Joan Mason, Sue Mason, Judy Haken, Michael Belcham, Anthony Mason, Hilda Thomas, Richard Thomas, Tim Thomas, Ann Mossman, Richard Mason, Sally White, Jeremy Belcham. Middle left: Frank Mossman [355]

Sundays were very special days. Some walked across the field to communion before breakfast. There was no racing as Reverend Trevor Waller didn't allow it; so they just went sailing and rowing and exploring the creeks at high tide. They would row one way against the wind and drift back on their little square sail with the wind the other way. Very reminiscent of Ransome's *Swallows and Amazons*!

There were frequent campfires and picnics at the Rocks and ice cream eating parties to the Ramsholt Arms. In the 1950s, the interclub racing took place here. Deben Yacht Club raced Kingfishers, Felixstowe Ferry Sailing Club had Felixstowe Ferry One Designs and Waldringfield sailed their Dragonflies and they were very hotly contested. Mrs Nunn (the landlady of the Ramsholt Arms pub), helped by the mums, prepared tea for those racing and their families. Picnics were also sometimes allowed on the pub lawn.

In the fifties, there was a very good Dragon fleet, so perhaps on Sundays, the Dads might sail around the Cork Lightship and back. The Cork was replaced in the seventies by a Lamby buoy and Radio Caroline was anchored nearby or in the same area and sometimes they would be mentioned on the radio.

'BBQ' campfire at the Rocks, Frank Mossman and Nevil Belcham [356]

179

On the Sunday prior to Cadet Week, the Cadet dinghies would all have their bottoms polished with 'Go-fast' graphite ready for the weeks racing.

The Arab Quarter lawn wasn't only a cricket pitch. Mid-way through the holiday, Charles Haken organised a very serious deck tennis tournament. He used to sit on a chair on a table umpiring a Wimbledon style championship. All the ages mixed up, with children playing grown-ups, and the children used to really spin the tenniquoits, which often broke your fingernails trying to catch it. Again trophies of little silver cups for this prestigious event were made out of the silver paper from the inside of cigarette packets.

The arrival of the Kroes family from Holland sailing their red yacht *Jupiter*, a Dutch Folk Boat, was very exciting. Not many yachts from anywhere, never mind Holland, came to the Deben, but every summer they turned up and joined in with the picnicing in the Arab Quarter. The family, who were boat builders in Holland, remained WSC members for many years.

The Huts in the 21st Century

This is the view of beach huts in 2019 and one can see how intertwined they are with the dinghy park and boats of all sorts. Things get more crowded in Cadet Week and at open meetings when the visiting dinghies swell the numbers.

Church Commissioners Sale

There was a change of ownership from what was Glebe land to the Club and Hut owners in 2002. Rent for the hut sites was £5 per annum payable to the Rector Trevor Waller until the Church Commissioners took control, when the rents were rapidly increased to around £200 per annum. In 2001 the Church Commissioners decided to sell some assets to raise finance. The front 26 hut sites on the Glebe, from the steps to beyond the dinghy park were offered to the owners individually, initially by auction. The Hut Owners formed an association and a small committee spent 6 hard-working months, led by John Fish and Roger Stollery, negotiating with the agent to buy all of the hut land as a single purchase. The hut owners formed Waldringfield Hut Owners Ltd for the purchase and this suited both parties, as the Church Commissioners got their money quickly and the hut owners sorted out the value of the sites themselves.

Aerial view of the beach huts in 2019 [357]

Every year, the Company meets to keep the finances in order, have a short AGM and a barbecue to follow. WHO Ltd has been very successful providing a control on development allowing older huts to be replaced without upsetting the neighbours. In 2020 a total of 12 huts have been replaced, with the Company design guide providing the control, but still allowing freedom and variety of appearance.

1950s OS map with hut numbers

Plan of WHO Ltd huts based on Clarke & Simpson's accurate survey on 2002-01-24

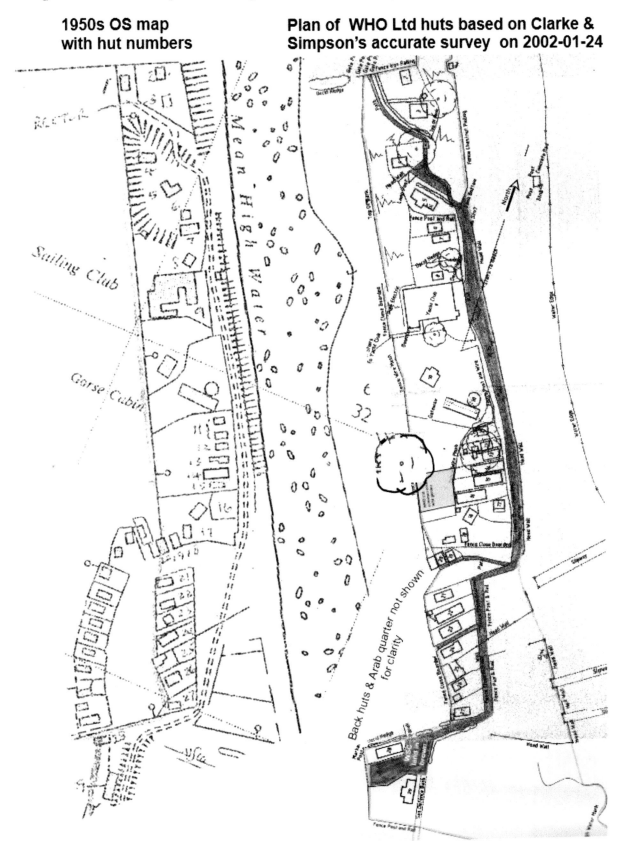

The beach hut maps from the 1950s and 2002 for comparison – it is interesting to see how the accurate 2002 survey compares with the apparently less accurate Ordnance Survey report from the 1950s [358]

Waldringfield Sailing Club (WSC) Pre-WW2

'The klop, klop of water under the bows of a small boat will cure most troubles in this world.'

Arthur Ransome, *Coot Club* (ch. 11)

[359]

The Clubhouse by David Ruffle [360]

Waldringfield Sailing Club has offered a centre for sailing activity in Waldringfield ever since its foundation almost one hundred years ago. Its focus on racing has made it widely known both locally and internationally and it has been highly successful. It has also provided welcome social and sailing activities for families within the village and further afield. In addition many non-members enjoy watching the Sailing Club activities – particularly on special occasions such as the Regatta.

Although nothing appears to have been recorded in Waldringfield until later, racing and leisure sailing had long been established in Woodbridge, with races up and down the river reported in the local press from the 1860s which also involved residents of Waldringfield. By the late 19th century, the dust and dirt from the Cement Works probably made the area unattractive for leisure.

This is an early picture of leisure sailing and shows boats in front of the Maybush. When the Cement Works closed down, yachts large and small began to take the place of the barges and there was more time and money for leisure sailing.

Boats by the Maybush [361]

Regatta programme from 1906 [363]

We have a record of Regattas being held at Waldringfield in 1906, 1907, 1908 & 1909, including a surviving programme usually organised by a Regatta committee of interested locals including Mr W Bare, the manager of the Cement Works, Mr Sutton the school teacher and Rev AP Waller. One of the events was 'men of the district grinning for a pound of tobacco' and the Mudsplashers race is often mentioned in cuttings of the early Regattas. Apparently in this race competitors wore a square of wood about 12" x 15", strapped to their shoes and raced through the mud. It appears that many of the Shore events are very similar today.

In the Spring of 1921, the first Minute Book of the Sailing Club records the meeting held at Gorse Cabin to form a Sailing Club for the Village. Sir Clifford Paterson was appointed the first President, with Mr Harry Nunn from the Boatyard as Secretary and Mr Thomas Naunton Waller, (the photographer), the Treasurer. Mr Alfred William Stollery of Gorse Cabin, became the Chairman and Arthur Quantrill, R (Bob) Button Jnr and C Rix were on the Committee: and so the 'Waldringfield and Hemley Sailing Club' was born.

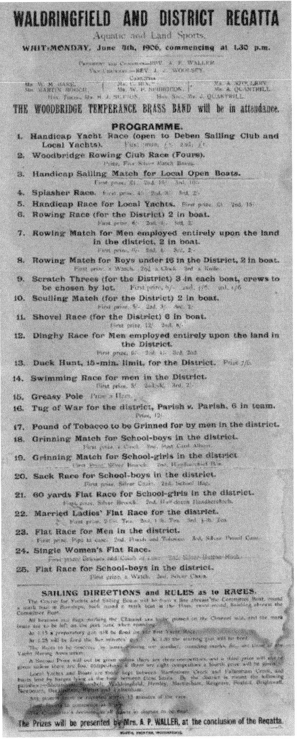

Lizzie (pictured here) had been owned by the Ogden family in the 1890s, but was subsequently sold to TN Waller who raced her as a member of WSC in the 1920s. He is listed in the entries for the 1926 Paterson Cup, but did not appear amongst the prizes [362]

The Regatta 'Mudsplashers' (boards tied to the feet with rope) race for men and boys [364]

Try Me skippered by Arthur Quantrill [365]

The regular boats sailed at the club in the following year were a gig *Try Me* which had belonged to the famous racing yacht *Brynhild*, a 14' half-decked yacht called *Wild Rose*, *Ruth* a 14' barge dinghy and *Lizzie* a 14' rowing boat which was later given a keel and sails, previously owned by the Ogden Family. The first President awarded the Paterson Cup which was won by Mr A Quantrill in *Try Me* in 1922. The cup is still presented to this day.

After the War, the government decided to dispose of surplus Army Nissan huts so AW Stollery bought the one that became Gorse Cabin in 1919. Some years later, but evidently before 1924, the newly formed WSC bought another cabin. This is the one on the right in the photo below.

By 1924, membership of the club was 19. In 1928 the Officers of the Club were altered to include 3 vice presidents and 2 secretaries and a racing committee comprising of TN Waller, C Rix and EA Nunn. It would seem that most members held important positions! A donation list for the proposed Regatta raised £26.16 6d.

The Circular 'Gorse Cabin' roof can be seen in the middle of the picture under the tree [366]

By 1929, it was decided that the title of President be dropped, and Sir Clifford Paterson was elected Commodore with Mr AW Stollery and Mr AC Wickman as Vice Commodores. Sir Clifford's professional life was gradually becoming more onerous from 1931 onwards and he was travelling a lot more, so he resigned as Commodore and Mr Stollery took over the role. A dozen blue and yellow rosettes were purchased and were to be worn by the officers at the Regatta. The story goes that there was a piece of yellow and blue bunting lying around and this was the origin of the first club burgee. This was amended to Mr TR Page's design in 1959 by the incorporation of the St Edmund's Crown to become the burgee as it is today.

TN Waller – Secretary, Treasurer and then Patron [368]

The Paterson Cup presented in 1922
(the first Club Cup) [367]

Harry Nunn as Secretary [369]

Waldringfield Sailing Club circa 1932 [370]

a clubhouse. Canon Arthur Pretyman Waller agreed a proposed site for the building and fundraising began in order to raise the £90 required. A concert in the Village Hall raised £7.7s.11d and a competition raised £20. In 1932 the new Clubhouse was opened. Two slits, with a box at the back of each, were cut into the wall on each side of the entrance doors, one for donations to fund improvements and the other for Clubhouse funds. Mr Stollery had a special collection box made – an exact replica of the Clubhouse, the club colours being flown upside down to denote distress and the need for funds!

By 1931, Mr Stollery felt that the Nissen hut was becoming too small for meetings and that it was suggested that it was time to consider building

1932: The scene at the opening on Whit Monday. Mr Alfred William Stollery
Commodore introducing Mrs Waller or Mrs Wickman or both [371]

By 1933, the name was changed to Waldringfield Sailing Club (WSC) and subscriptions were raised to 5/-. A newspaper cutting also from 1933 described the week of regattas. Woodbridge started the regatta on Monday, Bawdsey followed on Wednesday and on Friday and Saturday, WSC held their 11th annual event which was spread over 2 days and had record entries and a record crowd. Friday was devoted to Club races and a few children's shore events, and Saturday the Open events and remaining shore events. It was noted that the younger yachtsmen tended to flock to the Waldringfield event and the other two were popular with 'men of more experience'. Throughout Saturday afternoon a humorous and interesting commentary was given by the Commodore through the medium of electrical amplifying apparatus. The novices held an impromptu race and Billy Garnham who came in first in *Rigaud* received a string of beads as there were no cups to spare from the prize table. An orange was the second prize and Mrs W Brett, who presented the awards, was so impressed with the performance of the scratch boats that she divided the third prize (an apple) into halves.

The Club came up with suggestions for rules and these were printed in the handbook in 1934:

'Thou shalt honour thy sClub and do thy share to make it prosperous.
Thou shalt not curse thy handicap, nor thy handicappers, for their's is a thankless task.
Thou shalt not worry the Club Officers immediately before any race is about to start'
There was also a scheme put forward for the provision of beacons at certain vital points of the sailing courses "which might stop the habit of some club members for finding the mud".'

In July 1933, Capt WE Pitt Miller of Kyson Point organised a 'Cork Cruise' where all Deben craft were asked to join the fleet as it moved down the river and sail out over the Deben bar. They proceeded around the Cork Lightship and back into the river. Forty boats took part that year with half going around the Cork.

The 1935 Regatta took place at the beginning of August and the shore events included 'Filling the pail' and 'Untie the String' event. Each competitor was given a mass of knots or a 'bunch of beggars' as rivermen might say and were charged with untying them. There was also a greasy pole competition off the Quay and a shovel race always with the proper malt shovels as used in the maltings at the time.

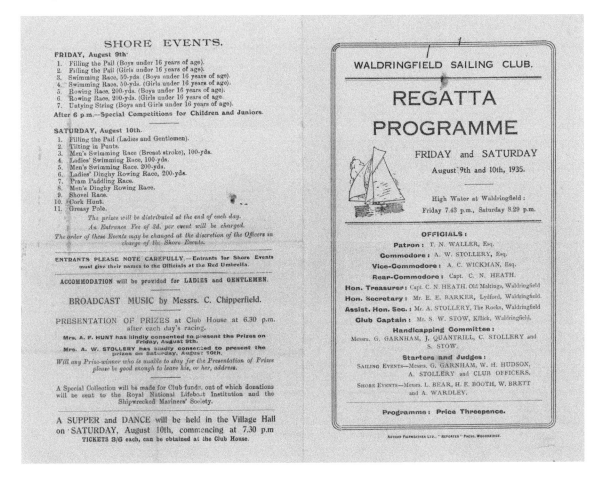

The Programme from the 1935 Regatta [372]

Membership in 1936. 2nd row: Cyril Stollery, George Garnham, Arthur Stollery, Ed Barker, Mr Booth, Stan Stow, Jim Turner, Jimmy Quantrill, Alfred Stollery, Jack Olson, Bill Garnham, Roy Mace, John Venmore-Rowland, Frank Mace, Lucy Stollery, Ken Palmer, Jack Fisk. Front row (sitting): Ioan Venmore-Rowland (a.k.a. Joe Rowland), Andrew Haig, Peter Olson, George Turner, Hamish Fraser [373]

In 1936 the subscriptions were again raised, this time to 10/-.

Among the members helping to take responsibility were Donald Spear, Alfred Curjel and Ernest Orvis.

1936 was the first year of the National 12 foot class and 4 of this new class are racing identified by N in front of or above the number. Scratched on the bottom of the photo are the names *Cain* R14, *Able* R15 and *Terror* N87. All 3 had ownership connections with Cyril Stollery and Ken Palmer. Here they were testing their new boats and looking forward to the first National 12 Championship at Poole later in the year.

A week before Poole they trialled these two designs on the river and chose to take the Uffa Fox-designed *Itch* N153 to the national championship, a decision which Cyril

Waldringfield Regatta in 1936, showing the very first racing of National 12's at Waldringfield (sails with an 'N'); along with the earlier International 12-foot dinghy class; the 14' Restricted Class (denoted by the 'R') and other non-class dinghy [374]

Picture of Ken Palmer and Cyril Stollery with the National 12 [375]

later regretted because *Terror* was a much better heavy weather boat and it blew hard! Cyril and Ken won the 1936 Burton Cup and the Championship week in *Itch* N153 beating the future 1952 Finn Olympic medalist, Charles Currey into 2nd place, demonstrating the high standard of sailing at Waldringfield Sailing Club.

By 1937, membership of the club stood at over 100. Mr Hunt presented the Cup for which the Ladies still compete.

The scrubbing posts were handed over to the Fairway Committee, and the Gear Shed, presented by the sons and daughters of Arthur Stollery, was erected. A one-day Regatta was suggested in 1939 because of the uncertain times, but nevertheless, plans were put in place for a two-day Regatta and a dance in the Village Hall on 12 August was to be arranged.

Then World War Two broke out and everything was on hold for what became six years.

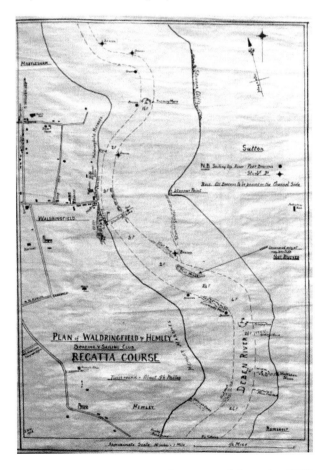

Courses used for racing [376]

189

Waldringfield's Contribution to the War Effort

[377]

Village Contribution to the Home Guard and Local Defence Activity

On 14 May 1940, as the Nazis invaded the countries closest to Britain, Secretary of State for War Anthony Eden made a broadcast calling for men between the ages of 17 and 65 to enrol in a new force, the Local Defence Volunteers (LDV). By July – with invasion expected imminently – nearly 1.5 million men had enrolled and the name of this people's army was changed to the more inspiring Home Guard.

Initially the Home Guard had make-do uniforms and weaponry. Yet it evolved into an army of 1.7 million men. Men of the Home Guard were not only ready to defend against invasion but also performed other roles including bomb disposal and manning anti-aircraft and coastal artillery.

Since those days the Home Guard has become TV's much loved 'Dad's Army'. In Waldringfield Captain Mainwaring's equivalent was Cyril Waller followed by Stan Stow; the local Sergeant Wilson was Roy Matheson.

The role of the Home Guard was to provide security for the village. This included manning various checkpoints – one beside a pillbox at the Chapel crossroads, one at the junction of Mill Road and Cliff Road, another close to the junction of Fishpond Road and Sandy Lane, and one on the river wall below Manor House. Initially their equipment was rudimentary and consisted mainly of shotguns and other agricultural implements. As time went on, uniforms, machine guns and a Bombard mortar became available, although the late Doug Canham used to claim that they never received the more modern Lee Enfield rifles. During the early months of spy and invasion scares there were incidents of folk being accidentally shot-at close to checkpoints.

The platoon had its share of First World War veterans. These included Walter Canham, Eddie Moules, Chinnie Gladwell, Sidney Aldis, Ellis Parken and Bill Thompson. The local company commander, responsible for their state of readiness and training, was Major Lampriere. Their HQ Hut was on the site of Micklegarth, on the sea wall just north of the Quay. The hut still stands, but is now to be found beside Martlesham Creek.

Other people with local responsibility included WW1 RNR veteran Donald Haig as senior ARP Warden and Ernie Nunn as Chairman of the Parish Council and senior Special Constable. He usually presided at meetings of the Invasion Committee which also included Dorothy Haig (who had served in the WRNS in WW1 and now took a leading role in the Women's Voluntary Service), Mrs Wishert (First Aid), Mr AC Bloomfield (Parish Food Organiser), Rev Canon Waller, Mr Wishert and PC Clarke. Minutes

Gwen Waller, member of the Invasion Committee and WI Rep [378]

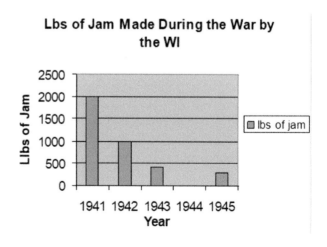

Jam Production by the Women's Institutes [379]

of their meetings reveal an impressive degree of attention to detail even when the subject matter was potentially chilling. On the 4th November 1941 for instance a minute reads:

'Mortuary: The military having taken over the Old Maltings, the garage there was no longer available as an emergency mortuary. An alternative was suggested in the garage at Rivers Hall if Mrs Glossop would consent.'

Although historians now know that the danger of invasion had almost entirely diminished after Hitler cancelled Operation Sealion in the autumn of 1940, it clearly didn't feel like that at the time. A Parish Meeting minute for 31st March 1942 records an alarming talk from Major Lampriere on food and the likelihood of invasion:

'Hitler hates us most and if he beats us will wreak his greatest cruelty. All must assist defence to the utmost. Bombing will be heavy, gas follows then paratroopers to get to the aerodrome. Scores of gliders each with 40-50 men. Dig slit trenches 2x2x7 long. Don't look out of doors or windows. Lie down in back room. Fill in holes (own shovel) when ordered.'

There were even annual reports concerning the quantity of jam produced. This communal activity was organised by the WI but open to anyone prepared to assist. In 1940 Gwen Waller reported that they used 9.5 cwt of sugar and ½ ton of local fruit.

Both evacuee children and military personnel were billeted in the village and the Village Hall (constructed from former WW1 huts) was in full use both as an overflow school area and also a canteen. Walter Aldis remembers that his parents had two RAF personnel, as well as a child evacuee, billeted with them:

There were also many evacuee children billeted in the village. The posh people tended to have the posher children and the poorer people had the rest. The evacuee children mostly came from Dagenham and West Ham, many of them the offspring of Ford workers at Dagenham. They came with their own teachers, both male and female, who must have

Monty Fellgett and friends [381]

also been billeted in the village. Kesgrave School was closed to villagers, so all the children remained at Waldringfield School until they were eligible to leave. The school had to overflow into the Village Hall. He said the children arrived by bus and later swarmed down to the river and thought they were in seventh heaven. They gradually adapted to country life and loved the freedom. Many of them after the War did not want to go home.'

Many service personnel were billeted in the village, never more so than during Operation Quicksilver. This increased the military traffic in the village resulting, tragically, in the death of Mr and Mrs Bertie Bell's only son outside their Cement Cottage on Cliff Road, renamed Bell Cottage in his memory.

Village Contribution to the Army

Many sons and daughters of the village signed up to serve in the Forces, mostly in the Navy or Air Force, but some joined the Army. They included the Fellgett brothers from Waldringfield Heath, two of whom, Monty and Stanley, died on the Burma-Thailand railway

Stanley Fellgett's gravestone in Kanchanaburi War Cemetery, Thailand [380]

in 1943 and the other, John, who was badly injured during one of the final pushes into Germany early in 1945.

Cyril Waller was called up early on in the War, causing him to relinquish his role in the Home Guard. Ernie Plummer fought in Burma and Felix Moules served first in the Royal Artillery then, later, in the Royal Army Service Corps. William Barker was a private in the Royal Engineers, Ivan Brook in the Royal Artillery. Later village residents who distinguished themselves in the Army included Bob Garnham and Tony Pyatt who stormed ashore on D-Day with 1st Suffolks and 48th Royal Tank Regiment respectively. John Savage won a DSO in Germany commanding one of the armoured assault engineer regiments which had trained in preparation for D-Day on the Orford Battle Training Area.

Joe Lubbock who, having helped RJ Mitchell and Barnes Wallis design the Spitfire and Wellington bomber before the War, was evacuated from Dunkirk, defused bombs, and helped build the railway from the Clyde to Faslane.

George Turner [383]

and the beach were out of bounds; the only civilians allowed access to the beach were Jimmy Quantrill, 'Shaver' Mills and Albert Hill. There were criss-cross pole obstacles on the beach as well as barbed wire and there were anti-tank ditches at various access points. There was a lookout post at the top of the cliff path. A small gun was emplaced at Gorse Cabin just beside the sailing Clubhouse, and there was even a small patrol craft, variously called *Gary Jane* or HMS *Sylph*, being operated off the Quay, initially by Jimmy Quantrill, Bob Button, Ernie and Harry Nunn, and young George Turner.

Presumably the craft didn't operate during the RN's disastrous attempt to mine the river in 1940. This resulted in many seamines detonating due to entanglements with weed and seabirds. Many dragged or were lost completely only to be found after the War by alarmed yachtsmen, one as late as the early 1970s. Ultimately, Albert Hill, the publican and a character of great ingenuity who also worked as a mechanic at the Motor Torpedo Boat base at Felixstowe, devised a framed explosive that could be used to detonate and so remove the worst of the menace.

As a riverine village, it seems entirely appropriate that many in the village served in, or supported the efforts of, the Royal Navy. That support started even before the outbreak of War when in July and August of 1939, both Donald Haig and George Jones embarked with friends on separate yacht-borne reconnaissance cruises of German naval activities and coastal installations in the Baltic. Andrew Haig recalls his father getting home on August 23rd 1939 and saying to his mother 'I am afraid War is inevitable'. Andrew Haig remembers some of the wilder stories going around the village – that his father was a German spy; that their house was a concealed gun emplacement and that, when Stan Fellgett's milk lorry stopped outside Shottisham, the cause might have been a death ray. 'Of course we knew something was going on at Bawdsey, but we hadn't a clue what.'

Many villagers trained in or served at local bases like HMS *Ganges* at Shotley, HMS *Badger* at Harwich, and HMS *Beehive* and the RNAS Seaplane base at

Joe and Ruth Lubbock on their wedding day [382]

Village Contribution to the Security of the River and the Royal Navy

Given the proximity of Waldringfield to the sea and the consequent threats of espionage, coastal raids and invasion, security in WW2 was of paramount importance. From an early stage both the village

Felixstowe. Others served on ships around the world. John Brown was severely wounded whilst serving in the battleship HMS *Warspite*. Philip Gladwell served on an MTB (Motor Torpedo Boat) out of Malta. Jim Turner survived the Battles of Spartivento and Crete in the Mediterranean on HMS *Kelvin*, then was posted to the heavy cruiser HMS *Cumberland* to support the Burma campaign.

Harry Whyard did escort duty all over the Far East and Australasia. Slightly closer to home, Leonard Reeves and his son-in-law Christopher Ellerby were involved in minesweeping in the North Sea, and George Turner served on an LCT supporting D-Day and later coastal operations in Belgium. Tragedy struck in 1941 when Eric Read of Hemley was lost in HMS *Barham* off the coast of Libya, and again in 1945 when Fred Rix was lost to a mine in the North Sea.

Some postwar residents of the village also served with distinction in the Navy. They included Edward Stanley who won both a DSO and a DSC commanding a succession of submarines, particularly as part of the 'Fighting 10th' Flotilla in the Mediterranean. Arthur Gilbey commanded a landing craft at Anzio and was Mentioned in Despatches. He was also torpedoed in the Thames Estuary. Buck Taylor was torpedoed and sunk three times – apparently without getting his feet wet! Jack Jones commanded Motor Launches at both Dieppe and D-Day. George Jones served on support ships in Scotland, Canada and Sierra Leone and was finally posted to nearby HMS *Badger*. Tom Lillingstone, Anne Hebblethwaite, and Jane Haig were all involved in naval intelligence and, more particularly for the latter two, in the code-breaking activities of Bletchley Park.

Jim Turner as a Chief Petty Officer in the 50s [384]

Lieutenant Commander Edward Talbot Stanley DSO and DSC [385]

George Jones in Sierra Leone [386]

Nearby Airbases and the Village Contribution to the Royal Air Force

It is almost impossible to imagine the degree of aerial activity going on above this part of East Anglia during WW2. Ever since the Battle of Britain in the summer of 1940 there would have been an almost constant buzz of aircraft. Martlesham was one of the busiest military aerodromes in the UK and there were frequent incursions of German bombers focused primarily on the docks and factories of Ipswich. Increasingly, these were replaced by armadas of allied bombers returning the favour over German-occupied Europe.

A number of villagers worked at Martlesham and other nearby bases; these included Nelson Sharpe and Ted Green at Martlesham Heath, Ted Edgar at Ipswich Airport, and Pam Harris-Last (later Turner) at the important CGI (Ground Control Interception) station at Trimley Heath. This was a method of using very short wavelength arrays rotating to beam their transmissions. These

Pam Harris-Last. She married George Turner in 1953 [387]

RAF Martlesham Heath Control Tower (later the USAF 356th Fighter Group base) during winter 1944 [388]

were translated into bright blips on Plan Position Indicators. Operators then radioed this information to guide night fighters to their targets.

A number of airmen were billeted in the village and an all-black American airfield construction company was based at the Old Rotary Club ground between Walk Farm Wood and what is now the Moon & Sixpence caravan site. The construction company, still subject to the ethnic segregation rules of the US military at that time, was tasked with tarmacking many of the growing number of airfields in the vicinity, including the upgrading of existing runways such as Martlesham. Vast amounts of shingle were brought

from the coast to act as a base layer for the tarmacking process.

There was a mobile radar site near the Chapel crossroads and barrage balloons would have been visible over Harwich Haven and Ipswich. At night a decoy light illuminated the sky over Shottisham Creek in an attempt to encourage the German bombers to drop their bombs there rather than on Ipswich. This did not prevent stray bombs landing on the village, however. Inevitably there were also aircraft which crashed nearby, most notably a Heinkel 111 near Early Creek, a JU-188 near Church Farm at Hemley and a B17 Flying Fortress in the river at Ramsholt.

Tad Kaznica from Poland, had been released from captivity in Russia in 1941 and came to England to

Martlesham Heath Rotary Club Ground [389]

Tad Kaznica in the cockpit of a Mustang. He worked as a mechanic on these US-built fighters [390]

serve in one of the RAF's Polish squadrons. He married Barbara Turner, and stayed in the village for the rest of his life, acting as the sailing club's bosun for 40 years.

Leslie Bear (later editor of *Hansard*), Robert Bloomfield (of Oak Garage) and Roy Wardley all served in the RAF. Another resident serving in the RAF, Edward Stevens, became the first village fatality of the War when he was lost in a Whitley bomber over Duisberg in November 1940. His widow, Dorothy Stevens, went on to turn their poultry operation at Oak Tree Farm into a major concern. She sold plots of land for the development of Sullivan Close and Sunnyhill, and gave the playground opposite the school to the village.

Some postwar village residents also served with distinction in the RAF. These included Joe Gissing, Arthur Hebblethwaite (awarded the DFC), and Paddy King who served respectively in Halifax, Lancaster and Stirling bombers. Joe and Arthur were shot down over Holland and Germany, after which Joe was involved in the infamous 'Long March' of POWs westward from Poland in front of

John Foster [392]

Harold Walmsley DFC & Bar [393]

the advancing Red Army. John Foster flew Typhoons followed by Tempests whilst Harold Walmsley (DFC & Bar) flew the later versions of the Spitfire. John Foster and Harold Walmsley were sent respectively to Canada and Rhodesia for flying training, before being based in Kent and, later Belgium, where Harold was shot down by US 'flak' over the Ardennes.

Many others from the village served either in uniform or as a civilian but all were involved in supporting this total War effort in some capacity or other. It was a time of national emergency which required levels of commitment and stress that few of us can imagine now as we enjoy the freedoms and peace they fought so hard to uphold and preserve. They all unquestionably deserve our admiration and gratitude, and we should never forget their sacrifices on our behalf.

RAF Martlesham Heath [391]

Wartime Locations of Interest
around the Village, 1939-45

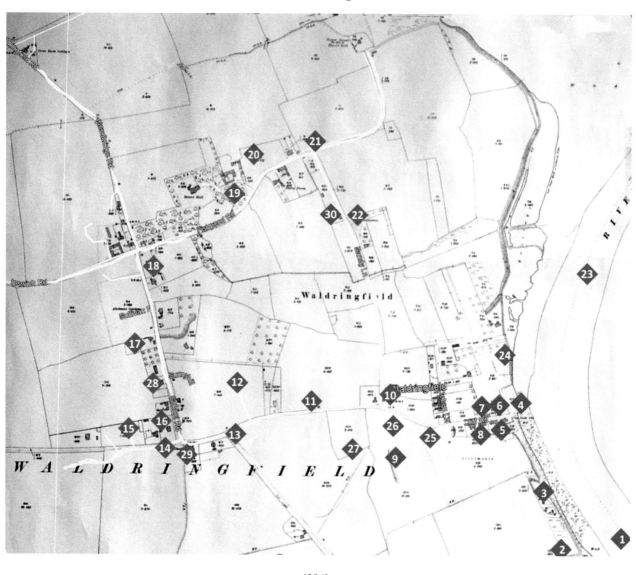

[394]

1. 66 fake tank landing craft constructed and moored in pairs between Ramsholt Quay and Waldringfield by the end of June until September 1944

2. Once Sedge Close and now the dinghy park. Four 'Bigbob' fake landing craft were assembled here every night for three weeks in May and June 1944

3. A gun emplacement was put in Gorse Cabin, itself originally a WW1 hut; ammo markings and the soldiers' Morrison air raid shelter still exist

4. The Quay was used as a Navy Patrol base and the Army also had a hut on the site

5. The Maybush had extra beer rations when the Bigbob training was underway. Albert Hill, the publican, was a civilian mechanic working at Felixstowe MTB base

6. The Old Maltings was used as HQ for Home Guard and then latterly as the HQ for those training the 700 men in building fake landing craft

7. Now Greenaway used by Ransome's for manufacture outsourced from its Ipswich works

8. Bell Cottage was the home of Maurice Bell who was run over and killed by an army lorry while playing snowballs

9. Bomb dropped

10. Frost's shop

11. Killick was bombed on 9 Feb 1941 and was home to Sgt later Capt Stan Stow of the Home Guard. Mrs Stow was badly injured and taken to hospital

12. A Bomb fell around here. Several chickens were killed but there were no houses here until the 1950s

13. A checkpoint manned by the Home Guard and at sometimes Red Caps (Military Police)

14. Village Hall. The old one replaced in 2000 was made from Army WW1 huts. Some Annual Parish Meetings held there and also used as a school and/or canteen for the school

15. Quietways – RAF billeted here and breached blackout regulations!

16. Broomfield – First Aid Station in the coach house

17. A bomb landed at the back of the garage – got stuck in a tree?

18. The Lilacs – Soldiers billeted here.

19. Rivers Hall, Coach House designated as Mortuary (not used)

20. Turner's Yard – soldiers camped here.

21. Home Guard Checkpoint sealing off the river

22. Novocastria, HQ of the Invasion Committee. Field Kitchen in the grounds under tree cover. Some Parish Council meetings were also held here

23. Mines were put in the river early in the War but kept going off. We are not sure of actual locations

24. The Home Guard had their HQ hut on the site of Micklegarth. The hut still exists near Martlesham Creek

25. Deben House used as a Billet

26. Homewaters used as a Billet

27. Broomstubbs used for some Invasion Committee meetings and Warden Post, also as a Billet

28. Cartref used as a Billet

29. School

30. The Orchard was the home in WW1 of Captain Hammond who was a pioneer of aerial photography

Operation Quicksilver and the Story of the 'Bigbobs'

Dummy 'Bigbob' landing craft moored downriver [395]

There can be few more extraordinary events in the history of Waldringfield than the construction and positioning of fake landing craft in the river during the summer of 1944. This was part of the deception plan, Operation Fortitude, designed to persuade Hitler and his generals that the main allied landings would take place in the Pas-de-Calais area. Quicksilver III was the section of the operation that called for large quantities of fake landing craft, 'Bigbobs', to be constructed and positioned in various harbours and rivers from Folkestone to Great Yarmouth, thus simulating the means by which the fictitious First United States Army Group would be transported across to France.

In January 1944 two battalions from 61st Infantry Division, the 4th Northamptonshire and the 10th Worcestershire, were assigned the task of constructing and launching these craft at night. Their training in Waldringfield started on February 2nd 1944. Some service personnel were billeted around the village, but most were in tented accommodation in the field behind the sailing club and huts. The site for construction and launching was in the vicinity of what is now the Sailing Club's dinghy park.

There were two types of 'Bigbob' dummy landing craft, although most were designed to simulate the new Mark 4 Landing Craft Tank (LCT). Both came in kit form and consisted of lightweight tubular steel piping mounted on oil drums for flotation. They were covered with painted canvas to replicate what such a craft would look like from both the air and ground. The larger LCT replicas were about 160 feet long by about 30 feet wide, whilst the smaller ones were shorter and wider. It took a trained team of 30 about six to seven hours to complete one 'Bigbob' in the dark. Once completed the fake vessels were launched down a slipway into the river on a wheeled undercarriage. Royal Navy personnel then took them off to be moored in pairs down river between Waldringfield and Bawdsey, where the deception was maintained and enhanced by skeleton crews; white ensigns were raised and oil burners were lit to simulate smoke from false funnels. Sixty-six of these 'Bigbobs' had been completed and deployed on the Deben by mid-June, with a similar number launched from Woolverstone on the Orwell; the deception was complemented by a mix of real and fake camps.

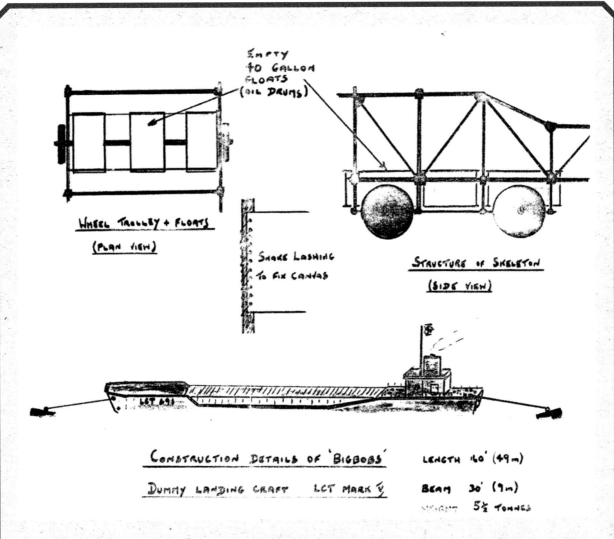

EMPTY 40 GALLON FLOATS (OIL DRUMS)

WHEEL TROLLEY + FLOATS
(PLAN VIEW)

SNARE LASHING TO FIX CANVAS

STRUCTURE OF SKELETON
(SIDE VIEW)

LCT 691

CONSTRUCTION DETAILS OF 'BIGBOBS'   LENGTH 160' (49m)

DUMMY LANDING CRAFT   LCT MARK V   BEAM 30' (9m)

WEIGHT 5½ TONNES

Plans for the 'Bigbobs' [396]

A slight irony is that, because of the Allied domination of the skies by this stage of the War, any German aerial reconnaissance is likely to have had extreme difficulty in getting through to detect and photograph what was moored in the Deben. The success of the deception is generally now attributed, in the main, to the activities of our double agents and the German intercept of the false allied wireless traffic. Nevertheless Waldringfield's 'Bigbobs' can still claim to have played their part in reinforcing this false picture. Certainly, never again are we likely to see the river filled with such unlikely looking craft.

Construction and accommodation site for the 'Bigbobs' [397]

199

A Walk along the River in June 1944

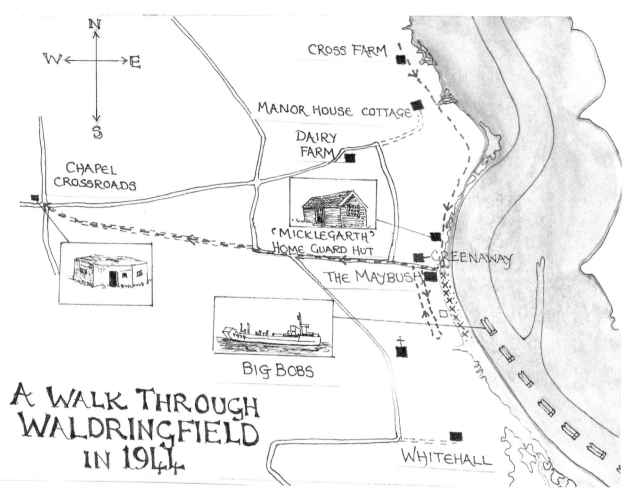

The route of the 1944 walk, painted by Jackie Brinsley [398]

To some it may seem odd to find a walk based purely on one particular month and year. But June 1944 was, of course, no typical month or year. It was the month of D Day and the invasion of Europe by Allied forces towards the end of the Second World War. The country had been at War with Germany for five years and Japan for three. It would be another year before either conflict came to an end. Britain and, for its part, Waldringfield and this corner of Suffolk were in the grip of an all-consuming 'total War' which affected the lives of everyone in one way or another – and for most in a very significant way indeed. As we take this wartime walk through Waldringfield, we shall try to relive this extraordinary period and highlight some of the unusual activities taking place in and around the village at the time.

Before doing so, just a few words to set the scene. Firstly, the village had been largely closed off to all bar its permanent residents since 1940, when the East Coast was seen as part of England's front line against invasion. Now, in 1944, access for civilians has once again been tightened for the whole East Coast from Margate to the Wash and ten miles inland. But this is for a different reason – and all letters from servicemen in the area are being censored so the secrets do not slip out.

The Home Guard (previously known as the Local Defence Volunteers), the Army and the Navy control access into and within the village, so just taking a walk isn't at all easy. There are also numerous wire entanglements, anti-tank ditches, beach obstacles, checkpoints and even mines to impede or limit your progress in many areas.

Waldringfield's Home Guard platoon.
Back Row: George Everard, Jim Scales, Walter Canham,
Todd Singleton, Eddie Moules, Harry Nunn,
Chinnie Gladwell, Mr Jennings, Bill Mather.
Third Row: Sidney Aldis, Jim Codling, Bill Keeble,
Wilf Spall, Charles Dickerson, Bertie Bell,
Hugh Leech, Doug Canham.
Second Row: Cpl Norman Greenfield, Sgt Maj Roy
Matheson, Capt Stan Stow, Maj Lampriere, Officer
visiting from HQ, Sgt Eddie Barker, Cpl Bill Brett.
Front Row: Bob Saunders, Ellis Parken,
LCpl Frank Brooks, LCpl Bill Thompson [399]

Whilst the initial threat of invasion has long
receded, there was still an aerial threat from planes,
both hostile German ones and damaged Allied ones,
stray bullets, spent casings and bombs. Hitler has
threatened 'vengeance weapons' to be fired from sites
just across the water in Holland and northern France
– but no-one's quite sure what these will be. What's
more obvious is the unusual wartime road traffic,
often being driven by inexperienced, tired, often
frightened, young men (and women). There's a wide
diversity of folk in this small village, ranging from
busy and preoccupied servicemen, to locals trying to
carry on as usual whilst remaining alert to strangers,
and of course ever-inquisitive children excited by the
activity and occasional detritus of War they find all
around them.

With these thoughts, let us start our walk in the
same place as the others – in the vicinity of the Parish
boundary with Martlesham to the north of the village
– and proceed in a roughly southerly direction beside
the river and through the village towards Hemley to
the south. Early in the morning of one of those days
in June 1944, the first thing you are aware of is the
sight and noise of aircraft overhead, as well as others
landing and taking off nearby. You might well see a
damaged RAF Lancaster or Halifax bomber limping
back from an overnight raid over Germany and trying
to line up for a safe landing at the nearby emergency

'Lancaster Legend' by artist Philip E West [400]

runway on Sutton Heath just over the other side of
the river. The Sutton Hoo dig – which was exciting
news in August 1939 – has been securely covered over
and many trees cleared to make the space accessible
to heavy duty aircraft. This has been open for a year
now and has been a godsend to tired and sometimes
wounded crews who had no chance of reaching
their bases further north in Lincolnshire and the like,
although sadly many crews crashed trying to land.
June Scott, who will come to the village soon after the
War, has heard her eldest brother saying that it was his
proudest moment as a navigator, when he guided his
Lancaster to land at RAF Sutton Heath with their fuel
tank empty.

US B17 Flying Fortress bomber formation contrails [401]

Even if you didn't witness one of these, you couldn't
fail to miss the sight high overhead of the contrails of
the 8th USA Air Force B17 Flying Fortresses forming
up from their many bases in East Anglia before flying
their daylight bombing missions over Europe. You
are equally aware of the sound of other planes taking
off from nearby Martlesham Heath. These were the
P47 Thunderbolts and P51 Mustangs of the US 356th
Fighter Group, whose primary task is to provide long-
range fighter escort for these bomber formations and
help protect them from attack by German fighters.
Later in the day you might witness their return, with

Suffolk Punch ploughing [402]

A mine come adrift amongst the boats
laid up in the mud berths [404]

one or two smoking casualties struggling to make it back to their bases. All of these sights are replaced on June 6th – D Day – by a vast armada of transport planes and bombers towing gliders full of troops heading over to Normandy to drop paratroops ahead of the two flank beach landings codenamed Sword and Utah.

But now peel your eyes away from the activity overhead and witness the more gentle life going on largely unchanged below on the land around Cross Farm and the Dairy Farm. At this time of year, you might well see the likes of Doug Canham and old Nipper Gray haymaking with the help of their sturdy Suffolk Punches and Clydesdale horses. Also helping out, not so unusually at this stage of the War, might be a group of German or Italian prisoners of War, let out for the day under armed guard to help with the harvest and other agricultural work. Meanwhile, the dairy cows will be heading back out to pasture, having been milked at David Parken's farm with the help of one or two Land Girls from the Women's Land Army, set up in July 1939 to provide much-needed support to Britain's depleted agricultural workforce.

Land Army girls harvesting near Dairy Farm [403]

Having witnessed all this early morning activity, you now set your sights on the path along the river wall, which will take you past the gap left by a discarded German bomb earlier in the War as well as Manor House Cottage, before leading you into the village itself. The wire obstruction put across the lane to Manor House Cottage early on in the War has been removed but you can still see some rather unusual sights out on the saltmarsh to your left and even in the distance down the river ahead of you. The one or two silver stream-lined objects you can see lying in the saltmarsh are fuel drop tanks carried by the US fighter escorts from Martlesham Heath, who often discarded them in the river before landing for safety reasons. They were usually recovered, but some were brought up by the tide into the creeks and others were claimed, along with any other souvenirs they could lay their hands on, by local children like Roger Price and Noel Edgar.

More ominously though, there is also lying out there on the mudflats exposed by the tide, a much larger black spherical object. This is one of the last of many sea mines laid in the river early in the War, most of which exploded when they came into contact with drifting weed rather than the German invasion barges and E boats they were intended for.

You might also notice a number of yachts, many of them well battened-down and secured in mud-berths, all along the riverside saltings. These are pleasure craft that have been laid up by their owners for the duration of the War, and Jimmy Quantrill and 'Shaver' Mills, who are the only locals allowed access to the beach, keep an eye on them.

As the splendid vista of the river starts to open up, you catch a glimpse of some larger objects much further downstream, but at this range it is difficult to make them out. However, you are quickly distracted by the sight of a uniformed sentry on the river wall, who asks you what your business is and checks your

Bomb damage to the Stow's house 'Killick' [405]

papers. This is probably Bill Mather, Bertie Bell or one of the other members of the local Home Guard, who are commanded by Captain Stan Stow. Their hut is at Micklegarth, just beyond Swans Nest, the old Cement Works manager's house, which is the first house you come to on the river wall. Fortunately, you are allowed to proceed, but not without overhearing the troubles of one of their platoon commander, whose wife is still struggling to recover from her serious injuries incurred when their house Killick was hit by one of a stick of five German bombs in 1942.

Rather shaken by this story of near-death, you now venture further into the village, first coming off the river wall just before the Quay and then passing several interesting sights when you get onto the adjacent Quay Lane and then the bottom of Cliff Road. You notice a particularly well-developed allotment and a rather strange-shaped shed, both adjacent to a pink-coloured red-tiled cottage called Windward. These two features are typical of most houses in the village at this time and can be explained by the government's encouragement of people to grow more of their own food, and to build something

Windward's Stanton air raid shelter [406]

The Army and Navy HQ at the Old Maltings [407]

like a Morrison, Anderson (or in this case Stanton) shelter to protect them from air raids. The latter are fairly rudimentary corrugated iron or concrete affairs in which families have spent many nights sheltering from stray German bombs, more likely intended for local military and industrial sites. It may have been their shelter that saved the Stow children.

Next to this pink cottage, you see a rather impressive three-storey red brick house called the Old Maltings which is currently in use as a billet for Army and Navy personnel. It's not looking quite as smart as it has done in the past. The Navy have been here since the early days of the War and, after the early debacle with the mines, have helped secure the river through regular patrolling in a grey-painted motor launch called HMS *Sylph*, which you can see tied up alongside the adjacent Quay. More recently though they – together with contingents from the 4th Northamptonshires and 10th Worcestershires – have become responsible for a rather more exciting and unusual arrival on the river, about which they are remarkably cagey.

You are not detained but, because of the barrier to the slipway and beach, which is still strewn with anti-invasion obstacles made from steel poles, angle-irons and the like, you decide to turn up Cliff Road beside the Maybush Inn which, at this time of day, is firmly closed. Beer is one of the commodities which has not been rationed (even women are encouraged to drink it, which shocks some people) but regulars grumble about the quality and wonder exactly how it is brewed these days. The publican, Albert Hill, is nowhere to be seen, probably because he also doubles up as a mechanic for the Motor Torpedo Boats based at Felixstowe. His wife, Grace, is a capable manager however – like many of the women who actively took over the running of pubs during WW2. For

The Maybush Inn [408]

many people, the Maybush is the social heart of the village and is not surprisingly the favourite haunt in the evenings of the Home Guard and the various servicemen around. This diversion from the beach prevents you from seeing the Lookout at the top of the Cliff and the small gun emplacement at Gorse Cabin just beyond the Sailing Club's closed Clubhouse.

Just up from the pub on Cliff Road, and opposite the distinctive Cement Cottages on the left, is the coach house of the Old Maltings (later called Greenaway), which is being used by Ransomes of Ipswich as an outlying workshop for its huge factory in Ipswich.

Many women of the village are employed here although, given the understandable tight-lipped secrecy engendered by the War, it is unclear whether they are engaged in War Work (munitions, aircraft parts and the like) or whether they are picking up some of the manufacturing of agricultural equipment from a business mainly focused for the time being on War work. You decide not to ask one of the ladies,

who include Bessie Spall and Grace Turner, as they are just arriving for work. Instead you turn up the drive behind the pub that leads up to the field, now a car park, on top of the cliff.

As you broach the top of the rise your eye is drawn to an old derelict bull-nose Morris car, which seems to contain several wide-eyed and curious boys who appear to be bunking off school. As you approach, the noise level increases and it soon becomes clear that they are shooting at you from what they are pretending is a tank. Having sensibly decided to put your hands up and proffer your surrender, you engage them in conversation and learn that there is yet more to see before you complete your walk. Apparently the car park, and the field beyond it, leading down to the river, has been a hive of secretive Army and Navy activity every night for the last few weeks and the boys, despite their parents' reminders that 'loose lips sink ships', can barely contain their excitement. Even though this part of the beach and riverfront is out of bounds and closely guarded, the boys promise to show you a way around, as well as a peek at what all the excitement is about.

The boys lead you, through a slightly circuitous route, down to the far end of the cliff path, where the ground flattens out and there are several wooden beach huts. What greets your eyes both in the field behind the huts and beyond where the ground almost seamlessly transcends into a riverside beach, almost defies belief. Having circumvented a few desultory strands of barbed wire, you have come across something between a builder's yard and an aquatic launch-pad. The boys explain that this has only been here for about month or so, and the area has been a hive of activity ever since – but only during the night. Everything stops during daylight because the soldiers and sailors doing the work clearly don't want any stray German aircraft to see what they are up to.

Every night they have been constructing and launching fake full-size landing craft to be moored further downstream to resemble a potential invasion fleet for D Day. You discover later that they are building no less than 66 of these canvas and scaffolding-pole 'Bigbobs' which, together with similar 'fleets' on the Orwell and at Lowestoft and Great

Instigators in the setting up of the factory started by Waldringfield & Hemley Women's Institute (now Greenaway). L to R: Miss Saunders, Mrs Lily Button, Mrs Roy Matheson, Nurse Cook, Mrs Phyllis Brett, Mrs Stow, Mrs Turner and a lorry driver from Ipswich, Steps: ?, Mrs A Ward [409]

Yarmouth, are part of Operation Fortitude. This is just part of the extensive D Day deception plan designed to persuade Hitler (successfully as it turned out) that the Pas-de-Calais, not Normandy, was the Allies main invasion destination.

As you look beyond the newly built ramps, slipways and winding gear to the river, you realise that these were the larger objects you saw in the distance earlier on your walk. Looking downriver towards the Rocks, you can now clearly make out the outline of a very large number of realistic-looking landing craft sitting at anchor and even showing, with the help of an attendant naval party, steam coming from their funnels and other indications of readiness for action. These are designed to attract the attention of German reconnaissance aircraft and, thinking about it, you guess that any aircraft who do make it this far won't be shot at too accurately by anti-aircraft guns. Everyone wants to ensure that Hitler and his generals are fully taken in.

Having discovered a major secret of the D Day operation, you decide that discretion is the better part of valour and, rather than battling on towards Hemley in the hope of seeing the wrecks of the Heinkel 111 near Early Creek or the advanced variant JU-188 downed near Church Farm by an RAF Mosquito in October 1943, you beat a hasty retreat to the car park and thereafter to Cliff Road. From here, you ascend Cliff Road, past Mrs Turner's guest house, now Deben House, where some of the officers responsible for building the 'Bigbobs' are billeted, up past the checkpoint at the top of Mill Road and eventually back out of the village to the Chapel crossroads on Waldringfield Heath.

There, just beside their concrete pillbox, now long gone, you are stopped again by the Home Guard, who are very interested to know what you have been up to inside the village perimeter. This unauthorised activity is going to have to be referred to their platoon commander and on up the chain of command. You sense you are in trouble.

Before matters can be taken any further, however, everyone's attention is completely taken by the noisy approach overhead of two things – first, a cross-shaped flying object making a throbbing noise and pulsing a flame out behind it, then an excitingly new RAF Tempest fighter plane. Rather than firing at this flying object, it soon becomes clear that the Tempest pilot is trying to fly wing-tip to wing-tip alongside it. No sooner does he achieve this, than he flips his nearest wing up and this object, which you now know

Ladies of the village doing War Work for Ransomes at Greenaway [410]

to be a V1 Flying Bomb, comes crashing down to earth just short of the Martlesham runway. You are all agog to see whether the Tempest sports the distinctive RB call sign of the famous test pilot Wing Commander Roland Beamont but it's already too far away.

As the Home Guard boys cheer, you realise that this minor miracle gives you your chance to slink away in the confusion and euphoria. You hope it's a sign that not only have you got away with your little adventure but that all is going to be well with the ongoing invasion operation. You live to walk another day and promise yourself that you will return to see what becomes of Waldringfield and its river when the dangers of War are over and the safer certainties of peace are established once again.

Tadeuz Szimanski, Spitfire pilot showing June Scott his dented wing after flipping a V1 rocket [411]

Post-WW2 Yachting, Waldringfield's Golden Age?

'May the good winds bring comfort and the tides prove allies'
Maurice Griffiths, 1946

[412]

German E-Boat S 204 surrenders at Felixstowe on 13 May 1945 [413]

In practical terms there was a great deal to do before sailing for pleasure could resume in 1945. Beaches had to be re-opened, coastal defences dismantled and the massive work of mine clearance begun. When the German E-boat fleet surrendered in Felixstowe on May 13th 1945 they handed over their charts of their North Sea minefields. George Jones was among those who would spend another year in uniform. He was working at HMS *Badger*, Harwich, for Captain Marsh who was responsible for this major clearance operation.

The Home Guard had been stood down in December 1944 when the invasion threat was finally over. Beach and river defences were dismantled as soon as practicable. Dinghy racers and river sailors were quick to get back onto the water but cruising yachtsmen were not too far behind.

Nunn Brothers Boatyard was among many businesses making a welcome switch back from wartime production to assisting yacht owners to

recover the boats that had been laid up for the duration. They had to assess their condition and either fit them out for the chance of some late summer sailing or regretfully decide that the deterioration had been too great.

Some owners, like Humphrey Mason (son of former Cement Works proprietor Frank Mason) whose handsome motor yacht *Deben Rover* had been requisitioned by the Navy in 1939, declined to have her returned to him and Douglas Kennedy's *Chequers* was left 'to a slow death on the mud'. Among the disappointed owners was Arthur Ransome whose *Selina King* had been laid up in Oulton Broad. She had deteriorated and – over six years – so had he. His was one of the first new-build orders to be recorded on the East Coast in 1945 when he commissioned Jack Laurent Giles to design *Peter Duck* – a yacht, built at Pin Mill but which would later make Waldringfield her home.

The Palmer family on *Cormorant* [414]

Cormorant was one of Waldringfield's survivors. Before the War she had been owned by Sir Arthur Ernest Eborall. Katherine Eborall had married Rev Arthur Henry Naunton Waller in 1938.

In 1946 Kenneth Nicholls Palmer, a leading member of the WSC bought *Cormorant* for his family and kept her until 1954 when he commissioned a new yacht *Sea Rhapsody*. *Cormorant* later fell on hard times and was blown onto the saltings in a storm.

She was pulled off by the captain of a Thames barge and has since been beautifully restored.

Immediately after the end of the War money and materials were in short supply. Jack Jones's first successful postwar design commission was for a 16' 'sharpie' day boat which *Yachting Monthly* readers with even moderate carpentry skills could build for themselves. Kit boats were very much the flavour of the later 1940s and 50s – eg in the Cadet and Enterprise dinghies.

Conversions were also popular. Stan Stow, a teacher whose wife Vera had been injured by a wartime bomb, spent years working on his conversion but achieved a handsome ketch.

The Rowe's and the Stow's go for a sail in the 1930s. Vera Stow on the right [415]

Left to right: Stan Stow, Norman Greenfield, Bob Starling, by the Dinghy Park [416]

Stan Stow's boat finished some years later [417]

Cormorant on the saltings [418]

Cormorant after restoration [419]

June Jones on *Barnacle Goose* off Dunkirk [420]

Green Dragon, built 1951 for Mr Thomson
and Dr Roy Webb by Ernie Nunn [421]

Green Dragon [422]

Nevertheless as prosperity returned the 1950s and 1960s would be a golden age in the designing and building of wooden yachts, for Waldringfield and other Deben yards. Yachts designed for family cruising became increasingly popular as many people who had been parted for the duration of hostilities decided against the former 'Corinthian' ideal of the lone male adventurer and built their holidays around family life, whether enjoying the simple pleasures of the river or venturing further.

In June 1949 young business man Mike Spear sailed from Waldringfield in his father's yacht *Privateer* for a three week cruise with friends. Visiting Willemstad in Holland they noticed the effects of the heavy Allied shelling on the town and also the comparative absence of younger middle-aged men. Sailing on down the coast of Belgium to Nieuwport they were shocked by the visible reminders of War. George Jones noted:

> *'Great hotels which look undamaged from the sea were found to be empty shells, burned out and with small arms and artillery pockmarks.'*

The Low Countries soon regained their pre-war status as favourite cruising grounds for Suffolk sailors. The next time George was at Dunkirk it was with his wife June in their own small cruising yacht.

Waldringfield Boatyard

As people sailed with their families and without paid 'hands' they wanted yachts that were easy to handle and this often meant Bermudan rather than gaff rig and engines installed as standard. As well as the Dragon class, the Bombay Tomtits and a number of fast racing dinghies, Nunn Brothers built some particularly attractive cruising yachts through the 1950s and 1960s. Their reputation was high.

One of the first was the 7-ton auxiliary sloop *Green Dragon* designed by JD Calder and built for Mr Thomson and Dr Roy Webb in 1951. She had a Stuart Turner engine (many yachtsmen of that era have tales to tell about their Stuart Turners...). Sourcing good quality wood was not easy in the immediate postwar years but *Green Dragon* was built from timber stored during the War, larch on oak with both sawn and steamed frames. A subsequent owner described her as kindly and flexible and she has also proved durable. *Green Dragon* was most recently heard of sailing on Loch Fyne in Scotland.

Green Dragon's sister ship *Sea Rhapsody* was built for Dr Nicholls Palmer and family in 1955, displacing the pre-war *Cormorant*.

Sea Rhapsody built for the Palmer family [423]

Barleycorn, a 12-ton auxiliary sloop, was designed by Fredrick Parker and built for Colonel Richard Hubert Courage in 1957. The commission was an important one for the Yard. Not only was Colonel Courage instrumental in expanding Courage's in the 1950s and 60s into one of the largest beer groups in Britain, he was a keen sailor and kept *Barleycorn* at Waldringfield. He also wanted her built to the highest standard 100A1 at Lloyds. It nearly went wrong at the last possible moment. Mike Nunn relates:

> *'They had a large launching party at the Maybush but she didn't get launched all the way as she got stuck halfway down the slipway. The apprentice boy had failed to check that the wood guides were parallel and the cradle jammed. Next morning before Ernie arrived, one of the boat builders climbed down the launching slip and crowbarred the middle of the guides up and* Barleycorn *slid down on her own. When Ernie arrived, he said "Well, I'll be blowed, she has launched herself." The boy's job was safe. Ernie was never told.'*

The Fraser family were among those who had learned to love Waldringfield holidays before the War and were soon visiting regularly again. In 1965 Ernie Nunn built the Yard's second Kestrel *Sally Brown* for the Fraser family. Unlike *Flare* (built ten years earlier) *Sally Brown* was Bermudan-rigged. She proved versatile for both pleasure sailing and club racing and became a much-loved family member for four generations.

Launch of *Barleycorn* for Col Courage from the shed. The boat is stuck on the ramp! [424]

Barleycorn on the river [425]

Sally Brown [426]

Brambling [427]

Kim Holman, Mike Spear and Offshore Racing

Much of the creative and entrepreneurial influence exercised by Waldringfield through this period stemmed from the relationships that were developed. Kim Holman from Cornwall had done his wartime training at HMS *Ganges* and studied naval architecture at Bristol University. When the time came for him to find a placement in a design office, he chose to return to the East Coast and joined Jack Jones at the Old Maltings. While the practical skills and experience passed on by Jack were important, Holman's creativity seems to have been more effectively shaped by his friendship with Mike Spear and his introduction to offshore racing.

Mike's first taste of the water was as a boy sailing dinghies at WSC. Following this, he raced with his father for many years on the family yacht *Brambling*. In 1959, aged 22, Mike attended the inaugural meeting of the East Anglian Offshore Racing Association (EAORA).

Holman enjoyed racing but had not intended to make a career as a yacht designer. When he finished at the Old Maltings he moved to West Mersea where he bought a share in a sail-making firm. In 1956 however he designed the yacht *Phialle*, which was built by Whisstock's of Woodbridge. She won the Waldringfield Cork Plate in a near gale of wind because no other Dragons or yachts dared to venture out. Her

Vashti [429]

reputation led to further commissions. *Phialle* was designed in a rush to win the Pattinson Cup at the 1956 Burnham Week Regatta, which she did by a large margin. She went on to win the Harwich to Ostend race, later that season.

In 1958 Holman designed the 38' *Rummer* for his own use. She too was built at Whisstocks and although he said he had intended her for cruising, she too won many offshore races. The beautiful *Vashti*, *Rummer*'s great competitor, designed by Alan Buchanan also in 1958, can still be seen in Waldringfield.

Among subsequent commissions for racing yachts was one from Mike Spear. This was *Maleni* (1962) built by Everson's in Woodbridge. As well as racing

WSC member David Copp sailing his Stella *Shaula* [428]

successfully she proved a good family cruising yacht. In 1985 the Garnham family transported *Maleni* overland to Venice where she was launched and cruised down the Yugoslavian coast for 7 months. They then overlanded her back to Waldringfield for the winter.

The design for which most people remember Holman is the Stella. *La Vie en Rose*, the first built, won her first seven races in Burnham week so convincingly that competitors assumed the racing office had made a mistake.

Hoodwink at the Yachtman's Service [430]

For many years one of the loveliest yachts in the Waldringfield anchorage was *Hoodwink*, also designed by Kim Holman, built at Everson's in 1968, and owned by John and Penny Palmer for almost 40 years. *Hoodwink* is a Twister.

The story goes that at the beginning of the 1963 season, Kim, having sold his Holman 26, wanted a boat of his own at short notice. He phoned his brother Jack at Brixham in Devon, who promised one for the middle of the season if Kim hurried. In a few hours, he sketched out a 27ft 8in (8.4m) 'knockabout cruising boat for the summer with some racing for

fun'. The class was officially called the Holman 27 but became more popularly known after the name of that first boat: *Twister of Mersea*. Twisters dominated the East Anglian circuit throughout much of the 1960s.

Hoodwink is a little different from many of the Twisters and also no longer lives at Waldringfield. She lives in the Suffolk Yacht Harbour at Levington. This was established by Mike Spear, Charles Stennett (a landowner) and Eric Wright (a boat builder). Early in the 1960s Spear had a vision of transforming flooded farmland adjacent to the River Orwell into a marina, so yachtsmen could walk dry-footed to their boats instead of getting in a dinghy. The yacht harbour would also offer more immediate access to the North Sea at all states of the tide – no more need to calculate the depth of water over the Deben Bar when hurrying to get to the start of a race.

The trio of entrepreneurs was soon joined by Christopher Carter Jonas (a chartered surveyor and WSC member), John Adams (an architect), Geoff Hubbard (a refrigeration engineer) – and Kim Holman. Suffolk Yacht Harbour was one of the first of the marinas which have transformed the experience of sailing for many people. It was Spear who had identified the site where a freak tide had breached the river wall in 1942 rendering the land useless for agriculture. Planning permission was granted in 1967. The initial challenge involved moving half a million tons of mud. Phase One, offering space for 40 berths, opened in 1970. Among the first yachts to enter were Mike Spear's *Maleni* and Christopher Carter Jonas's *Zeelust*, both from Waldringfield. The yacht harbour and its associated facilities continued to grow until today it offers space for 550 boats of all sizes. Projects such as this have had a long term impact on neighbouring rivers, such as the Deben, enabling leisure sailing to continue to expand without rivers becoming completely clogged by moorings. In more recent years an East Coast Classic regatta has been established bringing wooden boats from 1920-1970 into contention – with a particularly strong and successful class of Stellas.

Mike Spear, WSC Commodore 1963-65 [431]

Woodbridge and Waldringfield

The interchange between boatyards and people in Woodbridge and Waldringfield remained strong.

Item Smut is a Deben 4-Tonner built by Whisstock's. Dick Larkman was apprenticed at Whisstocks Boatyard and in 1952 trade was a little slow, so he was able to use one of their sheds to build the hull and he then moved her outside under a tarpaulin to complete her to a basic standard. She had no engine and a fairly bare interior, with just a primer coat of grey paint when she was launched in 1954. She got her name because she was entered for a race at Waldringfield and the entry list said '?Item', so being somewhat drab and grey the answer was 'Smut'. This resulted in her being called *Item Smut* from then on. She had a very enjoyable and successful time in the Yacht class at Waldringfield and on the Alde and Ore.

The Larkmans spent the first night of their honeymoon on board *Item Smut* and woke in the morning to see some wellwishers waving to them from the shore unaware that Leigh Belcham and Dennis Mossman had rowed out overnight and written 'Just Married' along the hull in lipstick. But they can't remember whose lipstick they had used. She became the Larkmans' first home for 3 months until a house became available. She was later owned by Harold Keeble and Harold Walmesley, and had lots of trips around the English coast and Dutch Waterways. They eventually bought her back from Alan Matheson and she is now retired ashore.

Nigel Pusey, a former member and Commodore of WSC, relates that his first encounter with *Item Smut*, was a crossing of masts off Kyson Point during Deben Week one year. Dick held his course on the premise that 'bigger' had right of way and Nigel's

Item Smut, a 4-Tonner owned by Dick Larkman [433]

boat, an Enterprise dinghy, subsequently spun like a top and sank. Youthful profanities were met with a shrug of the shoulders from the disappearing yacht.

Woodbridge had more capacity for winter storage than Waldringfield. *Peter Duck*, who was moored in the anchorage every summer from 1957, was one of many yachts who retreated upriver when winter came.

Arthur Ransome, who had commissioned *Peter Duck* in 1945, had only a season's cruising in her before he returned yet again to the Lake District. She lived on the South Coast before George Jones, who, as a yacht agent, had been deputed to sell her, bought her instead. She was based in Waldringfield until after George's death in 1983.

In 1987 *Peter Duck* was brought by Greg and Anne Palmer from New Zealand and entered a new, adventurous period. Greg Palmer first took her on a British Isles circumnavigation, then sailed twice to Russia. On the first attempt she was turned back by a gun boat but reached St Petersburg successfully on the second voyage. There she settled until Greg's premature death in 1997 forced a return to England where she was bought by Julia Jones and Francis Wheen.

Peter Duck by the Rocks [432]

Arthur Ransome on *Peter Duck* [434]

William Maxwell Blake was a Woodbridge-based designer who died in 1939. Some of his portfolio was inherited by Jack Jones and in the years after the War two of his yachts, *Mirelle* and *Florence Edith*, were moored in the Waldringfield anchorage. *Mirelle* was owned by Philip Allen who wrote the first Atlantic Crossing Guide and *Florence Edith* by Francis Chichester (though in his ownership she was moored at Pin Mill). He had her substantially rebuilt by Whisstock's and renamed her *Gypsy Moth II*. He enjoyed the East Anglian offshore races as well as adventurous cruising. Francis and Sheila Chichester became friends with Ralph and Dorothy Hammond Innes who came to live in Suffolk after the War and brought their first small boat at a Woodbridge auction.

For Hammond Innes, Waldringfield and the Maybush were special places:

> '*Drinking beer on the Maybush lawn, face burning after a day in the wind and sun, relaxed at the end of a good sail – an hour to savour, it is so quiet, so beautiful. That on-shore south-easterly breeze which often blows as hard as a force 5 on the quietest of North Sea days as the land sucks cold air in from seaward, is dying to a zephyr now. There is not a ripple on the water and everything is very bright and still in the evening light, the moored yachts tide-rode to their reflections.*'

Their first yacht *Sonia* was not sufficiently sea-worthy to go out of the river but with their second, the Laurent Giles-designed *Triune of Troy*, which

Mary Deare in Norway, 1961 [436]

they moored at Waldringfield, they were able to join the off-shore racing set and also to cruise more extensively. Their third yacht, *Mary Deare* (bought with the proceeds of success rather as *Nancy Blackett* had been 20 years earlier) was purchased as a steel hull in Holland and fitted out at Whisstock's. They explored Brittany and Scandinavia then set out for a new base in Malta. As they left the Deben for the last time in 1962, 'it was with a catch in our throats that Dorothy and I saw the landlord of the Maybush raise a loaded tray of drinks high above his head in farewell.'

Florence Edith and others off the Maybush [435]

Influences from Abroad

Hammond Innes described the Deben as 'a sort of "yellow-brick road" leading to the enchantment of foreign lands.' He also loved returning to the river, describing 'the sudden embrace as we cross the bar, of quiet waters, and a land as beautiful as any we have ventured into.'

Some of the yachts that came up this watery yellow brick road brought elegant foreign designs to Waldringfield.

Godiva of Deben was the first of the GRP boats designed by Dutchman EG van der Stadt with the design name of *Pioneer* in 1958. This 9-metre-long sailboat design matched the name because there were some beautiful details included. Van der Stadt recognised the potential of glass fibre with smooth clean lines, particularly the companionway which didn't have an awkward looking hatch but a raised up section with lines flowing into the cabin at the top. This light design won many international classes and was a great success. She was sailed for a cruise by the Coventry family to Denmark in 1971.

Ondine has become one of Waldringfield anchorage's best loved residents. She was built in Sweden at the Halberg Yard. Joe Lubbock bought her from the 1956 boat show. *Ondine* is a King's Cruiser 28, an 8.5m sailboat and was designed by the legendary designer Tord Sundén.

Joe Lubbock graduated from Cambridge University with an Engineering Degree and was involved in developing the Spitfire fighter plane and the Wellington Bomber. During the War, he specialised in defusing bombs with a time delay on them. He moved to Suffolk in 1963 and took up sailing Flying Fifteens often racing on the South Coast. He also enjoyed ocean racing with Uffa Fox and once beat the Duke

Joe Lubbock and his neighbour Neil Winship, sailing *Ondine* in 2010 when Joe was in his mid-nineties [438]

of Edinburgh's yacht to first place in a race during Cowes Week.

He lived in Waldringfield but travelled to uncommon destinations such as the Antarctic and the Galapagos Islands. Joe published fifteen books featuring original prints of the natural world, etched onto copper plates and printed onto handmade paper made with equipment he designed.

Joe was still sailing into his 90s and when his wife Ruth died in 2017 at 100 years old, they had been happily married for seventy-six years.

Joe Lubbock's boat was launched and 'dressed overall' by Mark Barton of the Boatyard on the day of Joe's funeral in 2019. He died at the grand old age of 103 and remained very active well into his 90s despite once being declared unfit for active service.

Godiva of Deben [437]

Ondine, Joe Lubbock's boat in 2019 [439]

[440]

Intrepid Exploits

In the early postwar years many WSC members ranged more widely as they achieved racing success in their yachts: *Brambling* won the Dover-Marstraand, Sweden, RORC race (crew Mr AD Spear, Mr CH Thomas, Mr D Lewis, Mr RJ Garnham and Mr B Marriott). In the Fastnet race of 1954 Mr CR Holman, Mr RJ Garnham, Mr D Lewis, Mr B Marriott and Mr F Pearce crewed in *Jocasta*. In the 1969 Fastnet Race, Dennis Mossman crewed in Mr Harry Jonas's yacht *Andorran* and Mr RJ Garnham also crewed with Geoff Pattinson in the Sydney-Hobart race (they came 2nd overall). Mike Spear raced the Brent Walker Cup from Brighton to Cadiz. Nigel Pusey sailed with Mike Richardson (OK National Champion) at a Quarter Tonner World Championships in France.

In the 1960s many sailors were inspired by the singlehanded exploits of men like Francis Chichester. It wasn't always about speed. The Deben had its own round-the-world yachtsman in Sir Percy Wyn-Harris who took several years, sailing his Dutch-designed yacht *Spurwing*. Young people from Waldringfield and Woodbridge found work delivering yachts and other small vessels all over the world with the Woodbridge Company Small Craft Deliveries. Advances in electronic navigation made a huge difference to people's confidence and, from the mid-1980s concepts like the Atlantic Rally for Cruisers (ARC) encouraged people to sail long distances in company.

Maid of Wyvern, was built for Lewis Worsp of Wivenhoe, who owned the North Sea Canning Company on the Quay. Margaret Lamb, family and friends joined in one of the ARC Rallies to the West Indies and back in *Maid of Wyvern*.

Kim Mayhew (née Lamb) tells the story:

'I was on board so know the trip well ... we left Shotley Marina on the 6th September 1991 ... I had just turned 21, my brother Charles (also a

cadet sailor) was 23 and Mum ... we got caught in the massive storms of southern England and limped into Poole with the help of the RNLI ... that storm unbeknown to us put salt water into the engine which caused us greater problems later ... we eventually made it to Madeira where we bumped into the Aubers who were climbing the same hill ... onwards to Las Palmas for the ARC 1991 – we won the spirit of the ARC award and Charles was youngest skipper ... a fairly uneventful crossing apart from the engine failing due to the water earlier on and Mum cracking her ribs while trying to Swim mid Atlantic! So we were towed into Rodney Bay some 29 days after leaving ... just in time to buy a turkey to cook for Xmas day...

Many adventures were had from Trinidad to Bermuda – top tip – don't try and dry your washing at The Royal Bermuda's Yacht Club on your rails – they don't like it!! A very windy crossing home with gusts at over 80 knots ... we steered the last 1000 miles on 2 blocks and tackles into the rudder stock as the hydraulic steering broke!! We arrived back to Brest to the Classic Boat Festival in 1992 having had a trip of a lifetime...

One of the unknown stories was that Dad had helped build her when he was an Apprentice at the Boatyard in Rowhedge ... she was an amazing boat who looked after us every step of the way...'

Maid of Wyvern [441]

215

Juliet, Charlie, Alice and Pippa Dearlove on *Keoma* [442]

Blue Water Cruising & Other Challenges

Sailing from Waldringfield has inspired people to seek some exotic destinations and unusual routes. These are just a sample – one per decade after *Mary Deare* left for three years in the Aegean in the early 1960s.

In 1977 Mike Richardson cruised the West Indies after competing in the ¼ ton world series in the Gulf of Mexico. In 1983 Peter and Mary Fraser took Reflections down to the Mediterranean though Paris and the Canal du Midi, crossing a three lane motorway on a viaduct. In 1997 Mike and Rosemary Nunn canoed the Zambezi.

In the 21st century some young families have taken time out to explore the world whilst older couples have also appreciated the greater space, comfort and easy handling of modern yachts to travel in their retirement.

Charlie and Juliet Dearlove completed the 2005 ARC. They, together with their two daughters Pippa (then 6 years old) and Alice (then 8 years old), sold their house

and sailed/raced from the Canaries, together with occasional extra crew, to the Caribbean in their yacht *Keoma* – finishing in St Lucia a very notable 9th overall and first family boat. Juliet wrote about their experiences in *Atlantic Children*. Today both Alice and Pippa continue to seek adventure.

In 2008 Anthony and Celia Mason went transatlantic in their yacht *Tomia*, They set off from England and spent the next 3 or more years sailing around the Caribbean and up the east coast of America before returning to the Deben.

Some Waldringfield sailors are content with the ever-changing beauty of the Deben: others like to set themselves challenges.

In 2010 Fran Gifford sailed around the UK in her Wayfarer *Viper* in 72 days, starting and finishing at WSC. Twenty-two Club members joined for various different legs. Starting from Waldringfield, Suffolk, and sailing between 25 and 30 miles a day, they reached Penzance by 25 May, rounded Land's End, called at Lundy Island, Wales, the Isle of Man, went through the Crinan and Caledonian Canals, along the east coast of Scotland and did not reach England again until arriving at Newcastle. Some days they were on the water for up to 12 hours and covered nearly 50 miles.

In 2012 Geoff Sinton's yacht *Quickstep* took part in the Three Peaks Race which involved a start at Barmouth (for Snowdon), then Whitehaven (for Scafell Pike) and Fort William (for Ben Nevis). Team *Quickstep* came second out of 12 although Geoff, after doing all the planning, was unable at the last moment to skipper the boat himself.

Tomia off Guadeloupe [443]

Quickstep, a Contessa 33 designed by Rob Humphreys and built in Lymington by Jeremy Rogers. She was the race training boat for East Anglian Sea School at Levington and has competed in many regattas including the Fastnet. In Geoff Sintons ownership she has competed with success (with WSC crews) and cruised extensively [444]

The final finisher of the 2013 Fastnet Race was *Duet*, who crossed the line and arrived in Plymouth, in 6 hours, 31 minutes & 27 seconds. Christopher Courtauld's 101-year gaff yawl was skippered by WSC member & Squib Helm David Cannell as she tackled the 608 nm course and raised more than £20,000 for the Cirdan Sailing Trust. This Charity provides opportunities for disadvantaged young people to experience the challenge and adventure of life at sea on large sailing vessels.

Jesus, however, remains on the Deben. This distinctive small motor boat was owned by the late John Waller, Rector of Waldringfield and has been moored in the Waldringfield Fairway for many years – often with a crate of beer cooling over the stern. She is believed to have been built at Fox's of Ipswich and was originally called *Sea Stream*. There was a tender named *Baby Jesus* and John Waller also owned an open fishing boat called *Joshua* and another larger motorboat called *Compass Rose*. They were moored off the beach between the Maybush and WSC.

Jesus was sometimes used to take the ashes of parishioners down river if they had asked for them to be scattered at sea.

The motor boat was also used as transport down to Felixstowe Ferry for the Master Mariner's Lunch. On one occasion, around the beginning of December, fog set in as they were leaving the Ferry on the return journey and *Jesus* ran aground on the Horse Sand. It was a falling tide so Rev Waller and his companions dropped anchor, disembarked into *Baby Jesus* and attempted to navigate back up the Deben almost completely blind. Despite knowing the river very well, it took several hours to get back by looking at mooring buoys and deciding which way the tide was running. There was much weaving about from one bank to the other.

When they eventually arrived back at Waldringfield, all very cold and damp, one of the crew was heard to say that they had just found a compass in their pocket! At 0200 after the tide had changed and the fog had lifted, John returned to Felixstowe to rescue *Jesus*. He arrived back home, safe and sound, at about 0430. The next day he declared 'There's not many who can say that they have lost and found *Jesus* in 24 hours!'

Jesus, owned by Rev John Waller and used for the Yachtsman's Service [445]

The Waldringfield Fairway

The beach chains have proved a valuable form of dinghy mooring [446]

As the use of the River Deben by leisure craft increased during the 20th century, so did the need for control and regulation. To this end, a Fairway Committee was formed in Waldringfield in 1938. Before then, the channel was in a 'chaotic state' (extract from minutes of the Waldringfield Fairway Committee Public Meeting held on April 20th 1946). A 'fairway' is a navigational 'main road' which must be kept clear for vessels to pass through safely. It follows the deepest water and often includes buoys or other markers to indicate its course. Moorings must not be laid in a fairway and vessels may not anchor there. Swimmers and small rowing boats are wisest to keep out of the Fairway and, if they have to cross, they should cross quickly. Larger boats moving through the anchorage should each keep to the starboard (right hand side) and pass 'port to port' (left side to left side). Just how difficult this is can frequently be seen on Waldringfield race days when the dinghies are jilling about waiting for the start and yachts or motor boats are passing through. Race officers do their best but shouts are often heard and collisions narrowly avoided.

The Waldringfield Fairway Committee is a voluntary body which, from its outset, tried to ensure that it represented a balance of local interests. William Bateman and Ernie Nunn represented the Parish Council. George Turner and Harry Nunn represented the commercial interests and Donald Haig (the first chairman) and Jimmy Quantrill represented Waldringfield Sailing Club. At its first meeting held on 19th March 1938 at Broomstubbs, Ernie Nunn produced a rough chart of the moorings which showed there were already 63 in total at Waldringfield. Twenty of these were commercially owned, 41 privately owned and two were moorings for privately owned houseboats. The Committee agreed to charge commercially and privately owned moorings 2s 6d a year, and houseboats 10s 0d per year.

A glance through the minutes of those early meetings however, shows that the law governing the use of the river – and therefore control over it – was not at all straightforward. This was demonstrated by a letter to the committee by its lawyers.

> *'I am afraid, however, that the Fairway Committee will certainly not be able to carry out their suggestions.*
> *The ordinary public have very strong rights in a navigable tidal river, and these rights include anchoring, and mooring, without any liability to payment or tolls, or other acknowledgement to the owners of the river bed, unless such owners can show that some benefit is provided, in exchange for any fees charged.'*
> (Extract of letter dated 26th February 1945 from the committee's lawyers to its chairman)

The committee's aims are to keep the Fairway clear, to maintain navigational marks and to regulate moorings on a stretch of the river from Methersgate Quay in the north to Early Creek in the south. To

The Harbourmaster's Shed [447]

enable it to execute its aims, the Fairway Committee, through Trustees, leases this stretch of river from the Crown Estate, which in turn owns the foreshore of the Deben (the difference between the high and low water marks), and all of the river bed beneath low water.

Since the committee's formation in 1938, navigational aids, or beacons as they were called, have gradually changed and improved. The beacons were originally withies, long willow poles, planted in the mud. These were eventually replaced by buoys. In 1938, pilots were responsible for placing the beacons and at its first meeting the committee proposed that they take over responsibility from Waldringfield Sailing Club to pay the pilots one guinea per annum. After the war, when the river re-opened in 1945, this responsibility was taken over by the committee itself.

The 1945 Fairway Committee sketch of the moorings shows a small island to its southern edge called the 'Horse'. It has since disappeared but at the time it was a hazard to navigation. In 1946 the committee resolved to 'have channel beacons placed in position immediately. EA Nunn to provide the materials for same' (extract from the minutes of Waldringfield Fairway Committee March 23rd 1946). Unfortunately ice in the river during the severe winter of 1946-7 carried all the beacons away and they had to be replaced the following season when it was reported that 'the Horse Buoys were in position with suitable top marks, and all Channel Beacons in good order' (extract from the minutes of WFC held on July 18th 1947).

Over the years, the numbers of moorings and dinghies on the beach have sometimes caused friction, as has the procedure for allocating moorings. Furthermore, proposals for 'improvements' have not always been well received. In 1975 George Jones wrote to the committee secretary to thank them for:

'their public-spirited work towards the well-being of Waldringfield. I have sailed at Waldringfield for 47 years and have had a mooring there for 29 years. In a world of great change during that time, Waldringfield has altered relatively little – it still provides inexpensive sailing for good numbers of people yet still manages to remain unspoiled. This is in some measure due to the work of your committee which attends to navigation, moorings and beach chains in a quiet and efficient way and I feel the least I can do is record my appreciation.'

The secretary BG Illingworth replied:

'The committee wish me to thank you for the kind remarks in your letter. It is not often that anybody expresses appreciation – usually the reverse!'

Harbourmaster Tony Lyon in 2020 [448]

Costs had remained low: in 1975 a yacht mooring site cost £3.50 per year, a sailing dinghy £1.50 and a dinghy on the beach £0.50. Pressure was clearly mounting, however, as more people discovered the joys of the river. The Fairway Committee's decision to appoint a Harbourmaster, which took effect in 1976, must have lifted a burden from these volunteer members, as day to day issues could be dealt with as they arose and safety on the river improved. Costs rose sharply, particularly when the lease from the Crown Estate came up for renewal in a period of inflation. By 1982, the yacht mooring was £28, the sailing dinghy £14 and the dinghy ashore £3. Use of the scrubbing posts had risen from 25p to £2 per tide.

The present Harbourmaster Tony Lyon was appointed by the Fairway Committee in 2014. Here he summarises his duties:

> 'I cover the area downriver from Methersgate to Early Creek.
> The main duties are – maintenance of the navigation aids.
> To manage the dinghies on the beach – i.e. make sure they have the correct licenses, are fendered etc.
> To work with mooring contractors, as appropriate.
> To have close contact with mooring holders, and to help with any queries/questions.
> To help/direct visiting boat owners and members of the public as appropriate.
> To report anything untoward – this includes liaising with other agencies such as the Police, Coastguard, and Border Force etc.
> Other – general duties as required.
> I am also an Assistant Flood Warden.'

In his lively painting of a regatta in 1960s, the Waldringfield artist Arthur Henry Naunton Waller seems to have made the Fairway Committee's wildest dreams come true as he seems to have swept almost all the moorings from the anchorage to make way for the racers:

Waldringfield Regatta by Arthur Henry Naunton Waller [449]

Tony Lyon explains:

'We do a mooring count each year. Last year there were 211 moorings, and they are allotted within a specific area. There are no plans to increase the number of moorings, or move moorings from the specified area.'

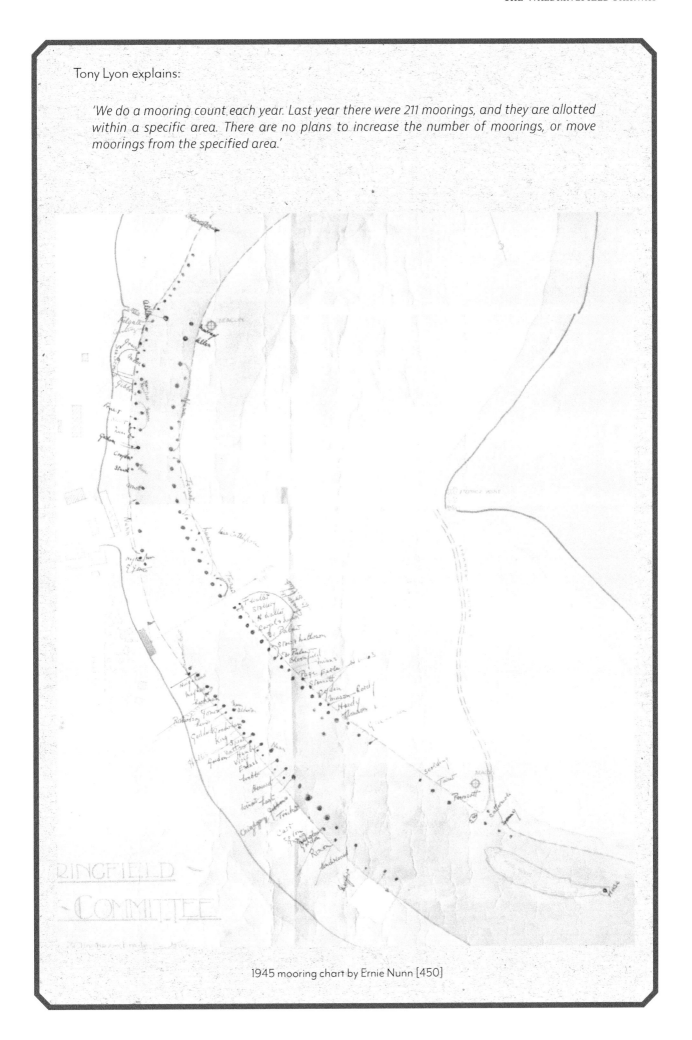

1945 mooring chart by Ernie Nunn [450]

The Caravan Site

Aerial view of the 'caravan park' on the car park. Also shows the allotments behind [451]

During the 1950s and 1960s, the pub and sailing club car parks were used as a caravan park with about 25 pitches. There was a building close to the pub which was the sanitation block.

Giles the cartoonist also used to caravan here. He also had the mooring closest to the Maybush.

Ted and Biddy Sudell had a caravan here in the 1950s and Biddy said that there used to be barbed wire along the cliff edge to stop people falling over. Apparently a Doctor McEwen managed to drive his

Sudells caravanning about 1965 [452]

Dennis Moore (owner of Dragonfly no 1) with family and friends on the caravan car park [453]

Camping on the campsite [454]

Albert Hill with his duck gun [455]

car over the cliff when he confused the accelerator with the brake.

The site was run by the legendary Albert Hill of Maybush fame, and he ran it with a rod of iron. The children were always a bit scared of Albert and never found him to be the easiest. He used to have regular site inspections and would not allow washing to be hung out. Apparently Bertie Bell used to allow people to dry nappies on his washing line in one of the nearby Cement Cottages. Albert was also keen on checking the rubbish bin. It had to be the right sort of rubbish. Any rubbish found lying around was often pushed through the window of the offending caravan. Obviously, he was a recycling pioneer.

Linda Wild remembers that Albert used to chase the kids off and around the site, accompanied by his spaniel dog. He presumably took his dog with him when he went wildfowling in his punt. He wore a trilby and had a patch over his eye and the kids were terrified that he would hit them with his stick, especially if he caught them scrumping from the adjoining fields.

Linda's 'boyfriend' in the photo to the right is Robin Adams, who lived at the house next to the footpath across to the Church from Cliff Road. It had a thatched roof in those days.

Despite Albert Hill's fearsome reputation, the site was always full and the Maybush caravan site must have been the place to be seen. The strict discipline made for a well-kept orderly site. Many of the caravan owners subsequently bought houses in the village.

Linda Wild and 'boyfriend' on the steps of a gypsy caravan [456]

Deben Week

This annual early August regatta was run jointly by WSC, FFSC and DYC and started in 1946. It attracted hundreds of sailors each year, but sadly no longer happens.

Start of a Deben Week race (shows Dorothy Jones with hand on the back) [457]

Year after year the same families came to Deben Week. Everyone knew if they came to WSC during the Week, they would meet up with friends and it was the week when all the dads tried to take a holiday. The racing took place at the sailing clubs at Woodbridge, Waldringfield and Felixstowe Ferry with extra passage races to and from each venue. At DYC getting ashore with 80 plus dinghies on a windy day between races provided a lot of excitement or trepidation but was rewarded with a great lunch.

George Jones wrote an account of the 1958 Deben Week in *Yachting Monthly*, saying:

Ted, Biddy and William Sudell in their Dragon – Going over the Bar and getting stuck! [458]

'The entries during Deben Week were excellent – Woodbridge Regatta on Bank Holiday Monday was a record and at one time at about noon your correspondent counted about 160 craft under sail between Methersgate Quay and Everson's Quay, although some of these were visiting craft moving up river to watch the racing. Entries at Waldringfield and Felixstowe Ferry were even heavier with the larger craft competing. [...]
In all the six days racing attracted close on 1000 entries and a huge number of visitors many of whom appear so enchanted with the Deben that they spent most of their cruise here.'

Tug o' war, cheered on by Annie Turner [459]

Greasy pole competition – Caitlin Smail (L) [460]

Deben Week cork hunt. Cooney, Mason, Marriott and Fish families get involved [461]

Fireworks on Ernie Nunn's barge [464]

At FFSC the dinghies would sneak in near the shore to avoid the ebb tide and hope for the eddy to swish them into the Deben. Often back puffs from the other boats caused them to go aground and general chaos ensued. The greatest fear was 'Going out over the Bar' through the treacherous passage between shingle banks.

Shore Events were on the first Saturday of Deben Week. These included: Tug o' War, Greasy Pole, sandcastle and fancy dress competitions, and rowing and swimming races. Everyone hoped to win prize money to pay for at least one ice cream a day for the rest of the holiday. Sadly there is no greasy pole event any more – health & safety! The grand finale was the firework display let off from Ernie Nunn's barge on the marshes.

Although Deben Week is no more, the Shore Events still take place on the Saturday of Regatta weekend and most of the traditional events, including the cork hunt, still happen today.

Fancy Dress Competition Regatta 2011 [465]

Setting the corks for the cork race 2011 [462]

Cork hunt at the Regatta in 2011 [463]

The Yachtsman's Service

Dressed overall! [466]

A Yachtsman's Service was started by Canon Arthur Waller (possibly at the instigation of his great friend Alfred Stollery) around 1936 and was originally held in Waldringfield Church. It was followed by a soiree in the Clubhouse. In 1949 the Reverend Trevor Waller moved the service to outside the Clubhouse partly because he was an enthusiastic sailor and wanted an excuse to get to the river on a Sunday.

Since 1952 the preacher has been escorted on the river by a parade of yachts from Ramsholt.

In the fifties and sixties, the Cadet dinghies used to go and meet them. They sailed towards the procession and as it approached the Rocks, four Cadets sailed either side of the Bishop's yacht, dipping their burgees in salute. The yachts were all 'dressed overall' which made an impressive sight.

In his account of Deben Week 1958 for *Yachting Monthly*, George Jones described that year's Yachtsman's Service:

1951

Yachtsman's Service in 1951 [467]

Another Yachtsman's Service in 1963 – with the service now being run on a yacht [468]

'The week began as usual with the Yachtsman's Service, conducted by the Rector of Waldringfield and attended by the Bishop of St Edmundsbury & Ipswich, Dr AH Morris, who preached from Dr KWN Palmer's 7 ton Sea Rhapsody moored a few yards off the foreshore. The service was attended by a congregation of over a thousand and there were upwards of 80 yachts (over 2 1/2 tons) in the anchorage, a fine sight. Prior to the service Dr Morris embarked at Ramsholt Dock on Sir Raymond Quilter's Silver Darling, which wore an enormous St George's flag on her masthead and was escorted up the river on a fine evening by dozens of craft of all types. The station-keeping was not quite so good this year, however, as in previous years.'

Yachtman's Service and it looks like the choir went too [469]

In 1973 it was negotiated to take place on the Sunday of Deben Week to allow the sailing to also take place on that day.

After Deben Week ceased to be a week-long event the service was held either on the Sunday of Regatta weekend, or another Sunday during July or Early August and often the Reverend John Waller led the procession on his boat *Jesus*.

Alvister was a large Felixtowe Ferry Motor Cruiser owned by Wilfred Barnard which used to attend most Yachtsman's Services – often during the service, it would drag its anchor causing mayhem.

The Excelsior Band from Woodbridge continues to attend on the beach and play the music for the hymns; the sermon is still given from a moored yacht in front of the sailing club on the theme:

> *'Our Lord got into one of the boats which was Simon's and he asked him to put out a little way from the land. Jesus then sat down and taught the people from the boat.'*

Yachts dressed overall parading for the Yachtsman's Service [470]

The Service from the Hansford yacht *Misbehavin* with the Spear yacht anchored further behind [471]

A Walk along the River in 1971

'Down the years there were happenings, Ernie stepping back to admire his handiwork and plunging from the quayside into the mud 20ft below, an amphibious Tiger Moth outside the Clubhouse, some idiot walking across the frozen river to the island, George Turner coming second, the starting gun blowing the window out of the Crows Nest, the floods of 1953 and the storm of 1987, a somewhat blue yachtsman dangling from a yellow helicopter and more recently a jet propelled Mini using the Quay as a launch pad.'

John Adams, *River Deben Association Newsletter* – Autumn 1997

Yes, Ernie Nunn very rarely fell into the water or mud and George Turner very rarely came less than first in a sailing race. And, yes, there are witnesses living in the village who say that one winter's day in the early seventies a Tiger Moth did put down opposite the Sailing Club; it is said that the occupants nipped to the Maybush for a pint and then left. The weather events are well documented and, let's face it, helicopter rescues in Waldringfield are par for the course – 2020 included. As for the Mini – who would have believed it was possible?

We will take our basic walk in 1971. At least twenty-five years have passed since the end of the Second World War. The army has long since reopened the beach; we can walk almost the complete length of the Parish shoreline. It is limited at each end only by broken sea defences.

At the start of our walk, to the north of the village, close to the Parish boundary with Martlesham, it matters not which decade we choose for our postwar walk for nothing much changes in this peaceful place except those natural features which vary from moment to moment – the water, the clouds, the wind and the light.

The same observations apply at the southern extreme of the walk, below White Hall, where the wind whistles in the long grasses of the saltmarsh and the scents of the Estuary contrive to create an immediate and lasting sense of well-being. Closer to the centre of the village, however, each decade brings considerable change. The population, for instance, has nearly doubled since 1931. (205 in 1931, 403 in 1981, 464 in 2011 and predicted 458 in 2018.) It is probably better, then, to consider each definable section of the walk and to look at the changes which occurred in that section between 1945 and the time of our walk and, in some instances, changes which occurred in later decades.

We start again on the shore close to the Manor House Cottage where the stream from upland Waldringfield Heath continues its passage across the marshes and into the Deben. The fields of Cross Farm, situated on the other side of the stream, and behind hedges, show little physical change from 1881 but the farming is now almost entirely arable, and any unpleasant aromas are those associated with fertiliser rather than industry. Tractors may be seen hauling pipes for irrigation and occasionally a large flock of sheep will be brought in to clear the field of cauliflower stalks or similar. Since the 1960s there has been a wooden jetty here. One is advised not to venture upon it – it is private, it is rickety, and it is slippery.

Manor House jetty, 2018 [472]

DRIVER IN QUAY PLUNGE DRAMA

A MOTORIST was being treated in hospital last night after scrambling from his sinking car when it plunged into a river.

The driver managed to clamber out through a window of his Mini as it sank into the River Deben before settling on its roof on the muddy river bottom.

Moments before, eyewitnesses said they had seen the red Mini tearing through the village of Waldringfield, Suffolk, at high speed.

It then sped through a chandler's yard, hit the edge of a concrete quay and somersaulted into

by RICHARD CORNWELL

the river. Last night, the male driver was being treated at St Clement's Hospital, Ipswich. He has not been named but is known to be from Colchester.

An eyewitness said the man ran off after climbing out of the river and tried to break into three cars before being captured by police.

Bill Drake, who lives on the waterfront at Waldringfield, tried to help the man on to the shore. "He said, 'Don't touch me – I'm in big trouble' and then managed to clamber up on to the quay," said Mr Drake.

Mr Drake said the man was lucky to escape from the car, which sank quite quickly about 35ft from the quay.

Another resident, Keiron McKew, said: "The man appeared to have a knife and the police officers had to bandage his wrists before they could handcuff him."

Police officers sealed off the scene while investigations took place into the man's personal circumstances.

At about 4pm, as the tide turned, a crane on the quayside hauled the car out of the river and on to dry land.

PROBE: The search for the car gets under way

E.A.D.T.

9th October 1996

RECOVERED: The Mini is dragged from the river

Photographs: JAMIE NIBLOCK

A jet propelled Mini used the Quay as a launch pad [473]

Stopping for a moment we see close by, navigating gracefully through the rising waters of the saltmarsh a cob and a pen, followed at a short distance by their two cygnets, their plumage still browny-grey but their size now sufficient to give them that graceful curve of the neck and the unique majesty of their breed. Across the water a few fine wooden yachts and a work boat are moored near Methersgate Quay; then we take in the Tips, its solitary farmhouse newly whitewashed and reflecting the early evening sun. Those same rays pick out the channel marker buoys and cause them to glisten intermittently as they bob in the gentle waves of the rising tide. The autumn evening light intensifies and picks out the varietal greens of the shoreline woods to the south of the Tips. The call of a curlew completes the ambience. All seems at peace in the world.

Looking back along the western shore of the River Deben the scars of less peaceful times are apparent. The river wall is in chaos as a result of bombs being discarded there by German aircraft returning home after a raid on Ipswich docks or Martlesham aerodrome. Of course, once there is a breach in the river wall the damage just keeps worsening and low-lying farmland becomes marsh or saltings.

Manor House Cottage

The Manor House Cottage is a white single-storey home built on the site of Rivershall Manor. It is surrounded by a well-tended garden. It last changed ownership in 1968. Although a building is depicted on this site on the 1839 Tithe map, the title of the land appears not to have commenced until the Will of

Manor House Cottage from 1968 Auction Prospectus [474]

The sad end of a clinker-built vessel, 2018 [475]

George Tomline of Orwell Park, Nacton, a Will which was dated 13.05.1889. The current building is said to have been built by Arthur Tuckwell, probably in the early part of the 20th century, since when it is known to have been extended. A Conveyance of the property took place between George Ravenshear and Arthur Hallam Roberts in December 1949. A small barn or fisherman's loft in the grounds, built in the Victorian style, was either built or reconstructed in the early nineteen fifties; Ray Whyard recalls helping his father with the bricklaying when he was a young lad at that time.

There are no further buildings between Manor House Cottage and the corner of Fishpond Road and Sandy Lane. We can wander up the lane to take a look.

There is a darkened patch of earth near the bend in the lane; this is the last remaining evidence of the wheel-wright / blacksmith's shop that was there when we walked this way in 1881. The old cottages at Barrack Row were demolished in 1914 or thereabouts and replaced in 1939 by a bungalow with excellent views of the river. Built by Ernie Nunn for his own use, it was completed the very evening before the Second World War broke out. The demise of Barrack Row, and possibly other buildings in this part of the village was associated with the loss of several local trades. No longer will a census boast the presence of a cowper or a shoemaker.

But we must retrace our steps and get back to the river wall.

Mrs Gilbey at Cedar Bungalow receives a letter from the Postmistress, Gladys Lillingstone [476]

The River Wall

The course of the river wall from the shoreline near Manor House Cottage to Swan's Nest is little changed from 1881. The mud wall is topped by an equally muddy footpath and immediately behind the wall is a very slow-moving stream, full of weed and sometimes pungent, particularly on the coat of the occasional labrador or spaniel which might chose to swim in it. It is likely that sometime in the next fifty years this river wall will prove to be inadequate. Both weather and tides can be extreme, as we saw in 1953 when the river overflowed and in 1963 when it froze.

Crises and Events Affecting the River Wall

1946-7	Extreme cold		Temperatures down to minus 20 degrees
1953	Major floods	Extensive flooding	Beach huts float away
1963	Extreme cold	Saltmarsh turned to ice	
1987	Hurricane winds	Major loss of trees	
2013	North Sea surge	Extensive flooding	Fortunately no wind

The original Micklegarth chalet [477]

As our walk takes us nearer to the village the chatter of sea birds increases volubly; they are gathered in their hundreds on the island, awaiting dusk. The rusting bow of Ernie Nunn's steel work boat serves as a useful landing stage for several oystercatchers. The seven-metre hulk of a clinker-built vessel lies disintegrating in the mud, piece by piece but very slowly.

Down to our right, in a small field adjacent to Marsh Sluice, there is a wooden hut about the size of an average garage. It is a Scout Hut but it started life in WW2 as a hut for the Home Guard. Walter Aldis was a teenage messenger in the Home Guard – he remembers the hut well.

Swan's Nest

The Cement Works' manager's house comes into our sight as we pass beyond the gorse which lines the path to our right – the house is now called Swan's Nest but its pebble-dash walls remain as grey as ever, as if in memory of the Cement Works. It is now one dwelling – it is rumoured that one of the rooms was once finely panelled in oak, a legacy of its time in the ownership of Mr Leslie Alston, the Ipswich furniture manufacturer. Mr Alston lived here during the 1960s and was responsible for having the river wall raised to its proper height after years of neglect. The current location of the oak panelling is not known.

Beyond Swan's Nest, we can see the first of the houses built on the site of the old Cement Works – the houses on Quay Lane. The Works site was sold to Alfred Everson, boatbuilder, of Woodbridge, in 1921; he drew up a plan which divided the site into 16 plots, 7 on the eastern side of the lane with river frontage and 9 on the western side of the lane. However, the plan was never strictly adhered to; purchasers were able to buy multiple plots and part plots so that the distribution of properties became very much as it is today with only ten properties in that area of the village.

As we walk the river wall in 1971, just after Swan's Nest we can see, on our right, a gate and a narrow, private path leading through to the orchard at Heron's

Not quite the same at Martlesham Creek [478]

Kiln in Deben Lane. Immediately after, the first property visible from the river wall is Cedar Bungalow, a wood-lap single-storey dwelling belonging to Arthur Gilbey and his American-born wife, Fredericka. Mr Gilbey's father, Captain Vincent Gilbey was an Olympian lacrosse player. Fredericka Gilbey is a keen grower and propagator of pelargoniums; the variety called 'Fredericka Gilbey' has been propagated by her and named after her by the Pelargonium and Geranium Society.

The next plot, Micklegarth, was first purchased from Alfred Everson in November 1931 by Edward Stuart Russell, an eminent biologist who lived in Hertfordshire. He worked for the Ministry of Agriculture and Fisheries and for some time administered the Lowestoft Laboratory from his London office, visiting Lowestoft at regular intervals. From 1940 to 1942 he was President of the Linnean Society.

There is a wooden chalet on the site which, presumably, was built for Edward Russell. During World War II the site was taken over by the Home Guard and a Nissen hut was erected where there is now a shed. The plot, the chalet and the Nissen hut were sold to Cyril Hewitt in April 1946. Three years ago, in March 1968, he passed the property on to his son-in-law, Raymond Atkinson.

The chalet was dismantled in 1975 and taken on two small barges, tied side by side, up the river to a new site in the woods at Martlesham Creek where, in the first instance, it served as a Scout hut in the care of Roy Ingham.

The next property, immediately adjacent to the river wall, is a recently built three storey, brick house with panoramic windows and a balcony overlooking the river. It was built for Bob Garnham and his wife Ann; they have called it Debenair. The new house replaced a wooden chalet on stilts, known as the Shack, and built for Bob's father, George, an Ipswich solicitor.

Next door and adjacent to the path is Windy Bank. The plot was bought initially by George Garnham in 1933 but he opted for the bigger site next door and appears to have sold the plot back to Everson in the same year. A series of owners followed including Mini Blumfield of Forest Gate (1933 – 1934) and the locally renowned William George Arnott, auctioneer of Woodbridge, who sold it, still as a plot of land, in 1935, to Lieutenant Colonel (Rtd) Henry Coupland of Bramford. It is likely that the current chalet on this site was erected for the Coupland family. It was built

Kiln Cottage on Quay Lane [479]

on oak piles which are still there (even in 2020). It is rumoured that it was run as a tea-house during the late thirties.

In 1943 the plot and the chalet were sold by Charlotte Simpson Moor, a widow of Bramford, to Milton Barham, a Woodbridge solicitor, and his wife, Lily. In 1952 the property was bought at auction, in the Maybush, by John Croydon, the Ipswich jeweller and it has remained in the Croydon family. The property was seriously damaged by floods in 1953 following which considerable renovation was undertaken, once the water had been let out of the building by the drilling of holes in the floor.

At the time of our walk (1971) the plot between Windy Bank and the next house, Quayside, remains undeveloped. It is known as Tides Reach.

We will step backwards and forward from 1971 for a moment to recount a rather romantic story about Tides Reach which at the time of writing is a neat built-brick two storey chalet between Windy Bank and the last of the homes on that part of the river wall, Quayside. Tides Reach was built in 1979/1980 by the then owner of Quayside, Vera Stewart. Sadly widowed, she lived there until the late nineties when the house was sold to the current owners (2020) who have been married for more than sixty years. They remember cycling out from Ipswich on their first date aged, respectively, 14 and 12; they walked the river wall which now passes in front of their house.

Back to 1971 (and beyond to the time of writing), looking westward between the north wall of Tides Reach and the flag-pole of Windy Bank we get sight of Kiln Cottage, a chalet built against the base wall of a kiln on the other side of Quay Lane. Those kilns were only about one hundred yards from the river wall.

Rickety Nook [480]

Quayside

In August 1931 Mrs Madeline Reeves purchased from Alfred Everson the plot of land which is known collectively as Quayside and Tides Reach. The property was put up for sale in April 1957 following the death of her husband, Leonard, the previous year. It was withdrawn from auction and sold privately for £3,000 to John and Vera Stewart.

George Arnott was the estate agent responsible for the sale. In days past, between 1937 and 1968 he would moor *L'Atalanta*, then his boat, just off Quayside so he knew the property well. An 'Office Block' mentioned in the sales information was Leonard Reeves' darkroom and the 'Studio' was used by Madeline for painting. To this day there is, in the garage, a sturdy old workbench which shows signs of being used for the building of boats.

In 1980 Vera Stewart would move into the then new Tides Reach and Quayside would be sold five years later to William and Joyce Drake who extended it in 1994.

But we are walking in 1971. The Boatyard perimeter prevents us from further passage along the river wall beyond Quayside. As we turn inland along a narrow footpath we can see ahead, on the western (opposite) side of Quay Lane, a tall pine tree and, behind it, a chalet called Rickety Nook. Behind that, at a higher level and close to the bases of one set of kilns, there are three cabins, the Cabin (or the Rocks), the Fo'c'sle, and the Quarterdeck. These used to be let as accommodation, mainly for holidays but, later, they became storage sheds for boat gear. Alan Matheson recalls taking up residence in 'The Rocks' immediately after marrying his wife, Susan, in August 1959. He also recalls moving out fairly rapidly a few months later because of the nocturnal rodents. The whole site belongs to the Venmore-Rowland family with Elsie Gwendoline Venmore-Rowland, née Harrison, having bought the plot from Alfred Everson in the late 1920s. Several senior citizens of Waldringfield recall holidays at Rickety Nook and one, in particular, recalls being put in the bath there.

It appears that in the 1950s Rickety Nook was a cafe-cum-shop serving home-made cakes, items of patchwork and Fair Isle jumpers made by Mrs Venmore-Rowlands' daughter, Betti Carrick-Spreat. There was also a 'gypsy' caravan on the site which provided great fun for the younger generation, including Lucinda Morrison, Betti's daughter.

Turning right into Quay Lane and effectively doubling back on ourselves we can see, on our left, two sheds on an 80 ft x 40 ft plot of land which, in the 1950s, was owned by a family called Stevens. In the 1960s, ownership passed to the Hawkes family of Hawkes and Slacks manufacturing confectioners of Chelmsford. From 1960 to 1968, in one of these sheds, in an area only 27 ft x 17 ft, Dick Larkman built 4 Kestrels with an improved sheer (one each for Arthur Mason, John Power, Len Cordy and one for Ken Wincer and Mike Jarvis). Also in this shed, which he rented from Bob Hawkes (aka 'Pop'), Dick built numerous Cadets, 14-foot Internationals and boat-parts such as masts for Finns and OKs.

The other shed on this plot is owned by Brian Hawkes, Pop's son.

As we stop to chat, we are told about an amusing incident which happened here on Quay Lane. Evidently, a land drain got blocked and there was difficulty clearing it. Bob Hawkes kept inserting more and more rods to clear the blockage and could not understand why yet more rods were needed. He borrowed even more rods from others in the village, unaware that Mr Reeves at Quayside, across the lane, had his drain cover up and as fast as Bob was feeding in the rods at one end so they were coming out at the other, having been deflected from their proper route.

Within a year of our walk Jem Goddard had a house built on this site and called it Driftwood. It was designed in such a way that it would withstand a 1953-type flood if there was a reoccurrence. He took up residence in 1976.

Further along Quay Lane, beyond a track leading up into land owned by Mr Maurice Heffer and his Canadian-born wife, Joan, who live in Deben Lane, there is another 1930s holiday cabin – the afore-mentioned Kiln Cottage, probably the most original of the holiday cabins we have seen on our walk. It is believed that this plot was purchased by Maurice Heffer's mother, possibly in the 1930s and it was she who had the present structure built with its lean-to abutting the wall of an old cement kiln. Then, in 1953, she sold the plot to Rev James Fraser. He bought it, after the floods, as a sailing holiday cottage for his family and it remains with the family to the time of writing.

Having explored Quay Lane, we can turn around and make our way back to the shore. We have to pass the Boatyard, still run by Ernie Nunn and his foreman, Jim Wicks, on our left and Rickety Nook, Windward, the Coal Shed and the Old Maltings on our right.

The Maybush and the bottom of Cliff Road [482]

Windward was built in the 1930s; it is destined, within a decade, to become linked with the Brown family who will purchase the Boatyard business from Ernie and run it until 2011. As we walk we can see Reg's 42-foot Colt motor cruiser out on its mooring. Reg is clearly preparing to swap his motor racing thrills for power on the water.

Now we can stand at the top of the slipway and take in the glorious view of the island and the river beyond. The Old Maltings, the Boatyard, the Maybush and the Sailing Club all feature in their own chapters and so, too, do the Beach Huts which line the inshore side of the path above the beach.

Perhaps we will venture inland a few hundred yards up Cliff Road toward the Village stores and bakery on the corner of Deben Lane. We pass between the Maybush and the Old Maltings, past Cement Cottages on our left and Greenaway – the new name for the old stables, now converted into a house, on the right. Then we pass Tony Brown's Boatyard, mainly used for storage, again on the right and just before the village post office and shop now run by Mr Davey.

The shop in the seventies [481]

Mr Spurgeon's shop [483]

235

This shop, on the near corner of a bridleway called Deben Lane, was built about 1902, about the same time as the six Riverview Cottages along Deben Lane on the left. We stop for a while to talk to Ray Whyard, a young man in his early twenties; he and his sister were born and raised in one of the cottages. Ray plays cricket for the village and he is a keen footballer. He recalls that in the early fifties they could buy freshly baked bread at the bakery on the corner and, if they had their ration books, they could buy sweets. (Ration books were required for sweet foods until 1954.) There was still postwar austerity and there were still shortages despite the best part of a decade having passed since the end of WW2.

In the late forties, if we were walking here, we might have bumped into Mike Nunn or the two young grandsons of Mr Spurgeon, the shopkeeper. John and Derek would deliver bread for their grandfather.

The sixties would turn out to be much better for most but by then the shop would be in the hands of Mr Davey who took it over in 1958. The late Peter Kaznica would be out on his bike doing the paper round during Mr Davey's days.

The seventies are better still: with Walls' ice cream cones in our hands, we return to the beach. There, Liz Ogden is returning from a sail. In 1976, Liz will marry Douglas Kennedy, and she will be sailing his dinghy, *Check*. We are not to know that Liz and *Check* would still be sailing together in 2019 and that in that same year Mark Barton, the owner, with his wife, Emma, of the Waldringfield Boatyard business, would make a mould of the clinker-built *Check* with which to make a fibreglass version.

Bidding good-day to the ever-smiling Liz we walk along the shingle beach, stopping from time to time to pick up what look like sharks' teeth. Looking up we can just see the tops of some of the caravans which now frequent the field at the top of the cliff. The site is administered by Albert Hill of the Maybush.

Our walk takes us past the Waldringfield Sailing Club and on to the dinghy park situated between the beach huts and the river. Just under ten years ago a reservoir was constructed, inshore from the river wall and below Church Farm; it serves to irrigate the fields through the hot dry summers. If, instead of continuing beyond the dinghy park along the river wall, we turn to the right and proceed a little inland we will find, first, this reservoir and then, further inland still, a deep pool all included within what was once called the Hilton inlet. It is very likely that somewhere in the environs of this pool there was once a Saxon water mill. The track up to Church Farm cottage, once

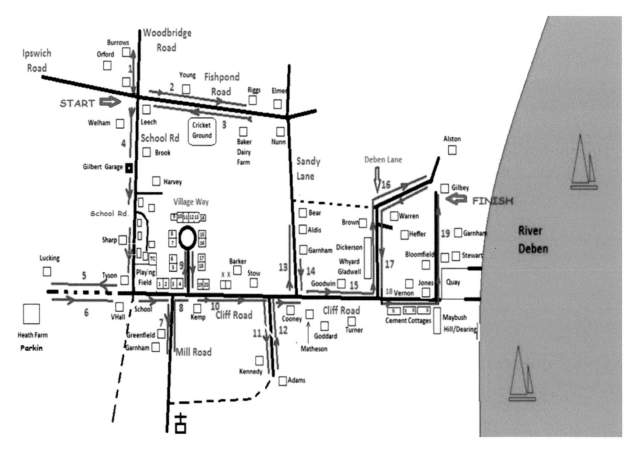

Evening Star Paper Round – 1962 to 1967 by Peter Kaznica [484]

known as Hilton Hall, is not open to the public but there is a footpath which passes between the reservoir and the pool and then on to the fields on the northern side of White Hall. But we will return to the shore for that is our remit. Here the river wall is less robust than the wall immediately to the north of the village but we can reach the fields on the other side of the inlet without difficulty.

As we walk along the edge of the field a glance to the left reveals nine parallel cuttings in the saltmarsh. Their purpose and their origin are uncertain. Looking beyond the cuttings there are moorings, the number increasing with each decade as 'messing about in boats' becomes more popular and more affordable.

We wander along the edge of two fields until we reach the small stream which marks the start of another section of the river wall. We have to take to the saltmarsh in order to access this southerly part of the defence but once we have done so we gain uninterrupted views to the south and to the south-east. With those views comes the fresh biting North Sea breeze. To our right, looking toward Hemley, there is a line of dead trees, marking the edge of the saltmarsh.

Across the Deben, to the south-east, off Shottisham Creek, a small fishing boat from Ipswich is trawling for mullet and, just south of Shottisham, along the shore, the Rocks awaits another day of visitors boating over from Waldringfield for picnics. Might that be *L'Atalanta* in the deep anchorage?

It is now getting late and time to return to the village. Were we to continue we would reach Early Creek which marks the southern boundary of the Parish and the end of the Waldringfield Fairway. However, our walk would be incomplete without looking inland toward White Hall, its barns now pulled down for the sake

On the river wall by the reservoir, 2019. Tidal waters lie to our left and the reservoir is to our right [485]

Two of the mysterious cuttings, seen through the trees, 2019 [486]

Away to the sea beyond Early Creek, 2019 [487]

White Hall [488]

of safety and the house and outbuildings now looking in need of a face-lift.

White Hall

According to the Deeds of White Hall, it was built in 1750 as a farmhouse. The land had passed into the ownership of the Wallers upon the marriage in 1639 of one Susan Goss, a landowner of Waldringfield, to Jeptha Waller of Woodbridge. The farm, being tenanted, is said to have fallen into a ruinous state. In 1830 it was rebuilt, very much as it is now because it was required for newly-weds, George and Anne Waller, who hailed from the other side of the river. Sadly, George died four years later. His young widow and their two children went back to Wood Hall in Sutton, and White Hall was tenanted through Trustees.

George Waller's grandson, John Henry Waller farmed both

White Hall and Church Farm from the 1870s until 1943 but otherwise, the property has been tenanted since 1834. Currently, it is a holiday let. It has enjoyed mains electricity for less than a decade and there is no mains drainage, but the view over Garden Field and the river is stunning; the sight of passing sails incites a desire to go down to the shore and take a closer look.

The barns at White Hall. These barns were in a poor state and, for the sake of safety, were pulled down not many years after our walk [489]

Peter Ducks, Pandoras, and Plastic

Looking out across the river in 1971 some of the boats appear to have cloned themselves. *Peter Duck*, who has been moored at Waldringfield since 1957, has spawned repro-duck-tions. These are the Peter Duck class developed from 1960, once George Jones realised what a seakindly yacht she was, and how well adapted for cruising (though not if you were in any great hurry). 38 Peter Duck class yachts were built through the 1960s and most have still survived, dispersed across the globe. Regulars moored at Waldringfield were *Scamp Duck*, *Goldeneye* and *Bar Goose*.

You can see other examples of wooden class boats in Waldringfield. There are the Kestrels of course and the Twister *Hoodwink*, designed by Kim Holman, and occasional Stellas. Nevertheless the writing is on the wall

Mallard, a Peter Duck, at St Malo [490]

for these wooden yachts – there are no more Peter Ducks being built in 1971 and the Stellas will cease production in 1972. Kim Holman himself has become depressed at the way yachts are developing. It's not just the new dominance of GRP (glass reinforced plastic) – he's usually been quite comfortable designing for that material – it's the loss of their aesthetic appeal (in his eyes) and the dominance of speed over comfort when at sea that troubles him. He spends much of his time out of England these days and is rumoured to have suffered a breakdown.

Some of the unique yachts, such as *Ondine*, are still there and there are new ones: Sir Harwood Harrison's *Amatory* is moored just ahead of *Peter Duck* opposite the Maybush and Carl Giles has a yacht there too. More controversially Giles also has a speed boat moored between *Peter Duck* and the shore. The anchorage has become much more crowded, and when there's a high wind or freak weather conditions the moorings drag, the boats get tangled and Ernie Nunn gets very angry. Then the owners have to talk among themselves hastily to see how best to calm him down and re-lay their moorings. Ernie doesn't like modern yachts and has begun to talk about retirement. Within a few years the business will be bought by Reg Brown, who is rumoured to prefer cars...

Ernie's nephew – Harry Nunn's son – Mike, has struck out on his own, founding Seamark Nunn, a company much more in tune with modern taste. Although he started building wooden RNSA boats, he's now become a dealer of pocket cruisers built by Rydgeway Marine. He sells 19ft Preludes and 22ft Pandoras such as *Blue Nunn*, followed by a Sadler 25 *Second to Nunn*. Gordon Harris of Rydgeway Marine responded with his own *Nunn Chaser*! A Pandora owned by WSC's Nigel Pusey called *Panic* is rated for IOR and completed some EAORA races winning the Lowestoft-Harwich race with a record elapsed time of 5 ½ hours.

Panic, Nigel Pusey's highly successful Pandora [491]

A Popcorn racing [492]

There's a lot of talk about the numbers of boats on the river and whether it is reaching saturation point – the Tide Mill Yacht Harbour is already established and there's talk of turning Martlesham Creek into an additional marina. The Tide Mill itself has been stripped to its skeleton ready for the smart new white clap board that's going to be completed in 1972. There are worries about how many more people will be attracted to the area. Waldringfield has become harder to sail through and there are tougher conditions made for the laying of new moorings. Many keen sailors are beginning to consider the new Suffolk Yacht Harbour at Levington.

Speedboats and the popular new sport of waterskiing infuriates many of the other river users because of the noise and the wash – they've not yet been confined to particular areas of the river and no speedlimits have been introduced. There are other unwanted noises too from the aircraft at the nearby

USAF bases as fighters scream suddenly overhead or heavy bombers drone round and round in circles getting their air time in, because this is the Cold War and the East of England is once again on the front line.

What's made the real difference to Waldringfield and other riverside villages over the years since the war is the advent of new ideas about boat design and new materials to build in. So many more people want to be on the water and bring their families with them, This has been the era of the boat built at home from a kit – not just the dinghies, like the Cadets, Mirrors and Enterprises, but larger yachts (though still small by 21st-century standards) – Silhouettes and Debutants, built first in cold moulded plywood (a postwar development) and then in the new wonder material GRP.

Maurice Griffiths, former editor of the *Yachting Monthly* developed some of these new designs – such as the Eventide and the Waterwitch – which could be self-built or mass produced. Griffiths and his yachts are often seen at Waldringfield. Even people like Jack Jones, who says he hates plastic, allows his Kestrels and other designs to be made in this material. Jack is about to retire from designing. His brother George gave up his yacht agency several years ago because he said there was no pleasure in selling mass-produced products. Today, if you look across the river to the Stonner shore or up to Methersgate or down to some quiet spot just above the Rocks, you might see George out in *Oystercatcher*, a little clinker built fishing boat designed by his brother Jack as the Jaunty class. He'll be trawling. Among his log entries for 1971 there are days when he catches 20 flounders, 10 plaice or sole. But even the Jaunty class included some models made of GRP. *Oystercatcher* still has a mooring at Waldringfield.

Nick and George Jones trawling on *Oystercatcher*, a Jaunty 19 [493]

Oil is still cheap in 1971 – and oil is a main component of GRP hulls – so the yachts of this era are built thick and strong and many will last well into the future. Every year at the Earls Court boat show more and more new models are unveiled: Westerlys, Contests, Mirages, Hurleys, Hunters, Contessas, Snapdragons, Fulmars. It's not only yachts that have gone into plastic – dinghes have as well. Classes like the Wayfarer, which has been popular since the mid 1950s, began being produced in GRP in the mid 60s. The first of the ultra fast Flying Fifteens, designed by Uffa Fox in 1947, was produced in GRP during the 1970s. The elegant Squib dayboats, which are popular at Waldringfield now, were first designed in 1967. A crash is coming but today, on our 1971 walk, we've no conception of it.

15th February 1971 was Decimal Day. It now costs 25p per tide to use the scrubbing posts instead of 5/-. In August this year the Prime Minister Edward Heath led the British team to victory in the Admiral's Cup, helming his yacht *Morning Cloud*. Any popularity will soon be lost in the grim winter ahead with strikes, record unemployment and the rising toll of death in the Northern Ireland troubles.

Working boats trading under sail are a thing of the past, but Frank and Christine Knights' smack *Yet* is a popular sight. When the Thames barge *Thalatta* comes up the river now, her cargo is likely to be children. She's a school ship and specialises in taking children out from East London and the former Docklands, giving them a taste of the coasting life. Hammond Innes has retired from his own adventures on *Mary Deare* but sails quite frequently with John Kemp and Jane Benham on *Thalatta* and is always ready to help George Jones with fundraising events. Years later he will leave all his money to the Sail Training Association to help future generations learn to love sailing.

Aquagem, a 1980s example of the very popular Westerly designs [496]

Geoff Sinton in his Flying Fifteen [497]

Thalatta in the 1970s [494]

Yet, Frank and Christine Knights' smack [495]

Waldringfield Sailing Club (WSC) Post-WW2

Waldringfield Sailing Club had always been a family club with all generations mixing in and helping each other and this culture intensified after the War. The club had originated from working boatmen like bargemen and fishermen keen to show off their sailing prowess in their leisure time in whatever boats they owned or had to hand. Then as the area became more attractive the more moneyed classes, some locals and some visitors (especially from London) became involved enjoying some cruising and competitive sailing in a lovely venue. Some stayed locally, others on their wooden yachts, many built by Suffolk boatyards and some employed the local professionals to helm their boats or teach them to sail. In the mid-1930s this started to develop into one design dinghy racing classes with the development of boats like the National 12 where the boats were all similar and the test was more down to level of ability. The fact that it was named a sailing club rather than a yacht club shows its unpretentious origins.

[498]

After the war, there was an increase in the number of these one-design smaller racing classes creating niches for different sized people and differing abilities. With the advent of the Cadet class, this meant the children could also be out on the water at the same time as the parents learning and doing their own thing. These boats, although wooden and many still locally built, were generally much cheaper to buy and maintain than the bigger yachts and this gradually caught on. The numbers of racing dinghies increased as the yacht racers declined. Yachts were now used more for offshore racing or family cruises to destinations further afield. As technology improved these destinations became even further afield.

Ashore

During the war years 1939-1945 the river and beach were put out of bounds and it was decided to

WSC around 1949 from postcard [499]

close the club. Things began to change in 1946 after demobilisation, and by April that year members were keen to get the Club back up and running again. The Clubhouse, which had been designed with a relatively small membership and left alone during the war, now needed a little bit of an uplift and an extension. So in 1948, an army hut was bought at a cost of £90 and club members joined together for many weeks digging foundations, moving earth, putting up electricity poles, digging a well, cesspit and a soakaway. Younger members of the club were lowered down on a bucket to do the digging of the soakaway. A deep well was excavated on the advice of Mr Bob Hill and drinking water was found.

Members were extremely generous with providing equipment and a full list of items donated, bought, and made, was kept. This allowed for the installation of Ladies and Gentlemen's toilets and a galley for serving teas and refreshments. The extension

Phyllis Brett(L) & Bessie Spall(R). Bessie and Phyllis also did the catering at the Village School at this time [500]

was opened in 1949 by Mrs Alice Stollery and a very successful 'Sherry Party and Dance' was held in celebration. Despite rationing, the Galley provided tea and sandwiches, although a record had to be kept of all food served to obtain the next month's ration of tea and fat. Phyllis Brett and Bessie Spall did the catering for the Club in those days.

In the 1940s a barrel of beer was arranged with Albert Hill of the Maybush and might include a supper of sausage and mash. Despite the increase in size in 1949 the Clubhouse still wasn't big enough to stage large events so Laying Up suppers were held in the Village Hall, with a cold meal supplied from Ipswich.

In the 1950s Mr T Oldham installed a loud hailer, microphone and record player for the cost of £86. During most summer evenings at the Club George Goddard played his Radiogram with speakers and the evenings livened up once the Pub closed for the evening.

Clubhouse addition of new Gear store around 1952 [501]

Laying Up Supper at Footman's Restaurant, in Ipswich.
This picture shows (left to right): Jill White, Ann Liddell, Mike Nunn, Richard Hopkins (sitting), David Porter, Jane Emus (later Hopkins), Ian Bye?, Dawn Edgar (Larkman), Chris Smith, Damien Reilly, Sally Goddard, Robin Spear, Mrs Vera Stewart, Mrs Emus, Peter Fraser peering over [502]

With membership numbers continuing to increase and more families becoming involved, the Laying Up supper now moved to Footman's Restaurant, Ipswich, having outgrown the Village Hall.

In 1955 it was also agreed to extend the Crow's Nest and partition off part of the entrance hall for a Secretary and Treasurer's office allowing for more storage space.

Also during the 1950s, it was felt that the land in front of the club was eroding fast and that steps should be taken to keep the water at bay. A wooden sea wall was therefore created in front of the club and huts. Being a club that has always worked on a voluntary basis where possible, all the work appears to have been done using volunteer labour and by hand. 1959 was a sad year as both Mr AW Stollery and Mr A Donald Spear died, but they had played a very important role in the birth and running of the club.

Two changing rooms were added to the Clubhouse in 1952 and the gear shed was moved. It was lifted bodily with the aid of boards screwed to the inside, by 20 members who walked it into its new position. `Canon Waller agreed to a dinghy park on its present site, although half the current size and very muddy. The club tie was designed. Following the immense amount of work done by the existing membership, it was felt that a new member joining fee should be introduced.

The membership now ran to 600 and there was a waiting list to join. Waldringfield Sailing Club was registered as Cadet Squadron 35 in the International Cadet Class and the children's section proved an attraction for many families.

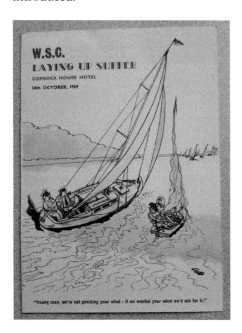

The Laying Up Supper Programme in 1969. Cartoon by Giles [503]

Building the new river wall outside the sailing club around 1957 (note the rudimentary steps behind) [504]

In 1963, with the increased membership numbers, discussions took place regarding rebuilding or adding to the Clubhouse. Mr CEB Thompson took charge of the fundraising scheme which involved interest-free loans. They raised £2,000 and Mr Adams drew up the plans. Mr Parker designed and constructed long seats with wood being given by Mr Arthur Mason. Mr G Goddard presented the blackboards on the south of the outer wall and the river was drawn on by Mr Alan Matheson, including the navigation and turning marks. These buildings were still wooden and based on old army huts like the pre-war buildings.

The Laying Up Supper continued to be a well-attended annual event with ever bigger venues to cope with the increasing membership. Giles was associated with the club for many years and presented several Cartoons to the club as prizes for their Annual Cartoon Trophy weekend, usually held after the summer holidays.

In 1966 it was agreed that the Club should again have a president and Mr Frank Mossman was elected. The idea of a Newsletter was also discussed and Mr Hyams agreed to produce and edit the booklet, and it proved very popular.

After winter gales the overhead electricity supply had become dangerous with wires dangling precariously between the trees on the cliff. The electricity board agreed to lay underground cables to the Clubhouse for £1,330 to the relief of the club. Up until then working in the galley had been hazardous, with lights flickering and power to the urns occasionally disappearing altogether.

In the mid-seventies, plans for a new brick-built Clubhouse were drawn up

A Cartoon Open Meeting prize showing the club cartoon presented by Giles [505]

and permission applied for but the club only had a three-year lease remaining. It was considered that this was not the time to spend thousands on replacing the old wooden buildings with brick ones unless a longer lease could be obtained. In 1979 plans were amended and revised several times before eventually being settled when the lease was extended to 31 years which also eventually included the car park. Gone would be the awning over the passage between the old office and the galley, where the salads were prepared during Deben Week. Previously this had provided little shelter especially when it rained. A massive fundraising drive ensued to raise enough for the building work and also a Car Park Committee to look into the possibility of buying the car park outright and guaranteeing access to the club. There were Discos, Auctions, 500 Club, raffles, gear sales, sailing courses and a 'Buy a Brick' campaign where people could sponsor a brick and have a plaque made with their name on it to be displayed behind the bar, for a fee. A sponsored sail was another fundraising activity. This was organised by Derek Bell Jones. Refreshments were passed to the sailors from a child's crabbing net held out from a stationary rescue boat and many doughnuts were lost overboard before the technique was finally perfected.

The Sailing Club as it was in 1979. Note the 'Old Lady' on the Gable End [506]

The grand reopening of the new Clubhouse in 1982 by Poppy Palmer (previous Poppy Orvis), with Rufus Plummer (Commodore), Anthony Mason (Vice Commodore) looking on and various other Flag Officers with their wives (note the old Crow's Nest has the loudspeaker and horn, later replaced) [507]

In the autumn of 1981, after sailing finished for the winter, the Clubhouse and gear shed were demolished and afterwards, everyone joined in to have massive bonfires on the beach. Any concrete or stone was barrowed along the beach for ballast to form the new dinghy park and any excess hard-core was used as infill between the two wooden slipways. Lorry loads of ballast were delivered to the dinghy park where Walter Cutting's Bobcat was used to spread and level it. Then a roller was used to flatten and compact it. Rogers Bros of Felixstowe was contracted to build the new Clubhouse and Dr Kenneth Nicholls Palmer refurbished the figurehead, the 'Old Lady', which had previously been placed on the gable end of the old extension.

Phase 2 of the Clubhouse build followed later and involved more fundraising. The old wooden, white-painted Crow's Nest which had stood for so many years was removed, complete with the hole in the floor! This hole had been accidentally made when the Officer of the Day (OOD) George Goddard had not managed to open the side window in time and had fired the gun into the wooden floor. The wadding from the cartridge plopped into a teacup of a lady member sitting below. On another occasion, Mr Steele fired the starting gun straight through the glass, thinking he had already opened the window.

With no Clubhouse available during the building work, a marquee was erected on the car park for the annual Easter Egg Open meeting. The changing facilities were a little draughty, but the event was a great success. The new Clubhouse was partially reopened on 23rd April 1982 with people mucking in to lay paving, tile changing rooms, fit out the galley and lots of other jobs. Roger Hansford was given a special mention as without his experience as a civil engineer it was felt the Clubhouse wouldn't have been rebuilt at all.

Poppy Palmer, the President's wife, officially opened the Clubhouse on 17th July 1982. John Waller held a short service on the terrace accompanied by Charlie Taylor on his accordion and there was a sail past of 80 yachts and dinghies.

Ted Kaznica led the procession followed by the police launch, The *Ian Jacob* and the 87 foot *Adelante of Heereven*, dressed overall. The Thames barge *Ena* also joined the celebrations. In the evening a five-course meal was enjoyed by all who could squeeze in.

Maisie Runnacles was the Secretary of the Sailing Club for 19 years, throughout the 1980s and was always on hand to help out. Her husband Bob was also involved, this time in the bar. He stood down in the late eighties and was thanked for his sterling bar work which had involved him serving beer and wine from the office through a small hatch, 18ins square, which was so low you had to bend down to see him.

In 1996 the club purchased its first computer and Graham Mills spent the winter uploading programs and data onto it. Ten years later broadband was connected and a webcam service provided.

Sail past of boats for the reopening [508]

Dr Kenneth Nicholls Palmer [509]

In December 1998 Dr Kenneth Nicholls Palmer died. He had been a member since the early days, Captain from 1945-1947, Commodore twice between 1949 and 1961 and President from 1976-1985. In 1982 he received an OBE. He had been a driving force behind the Dragonfly and Cadet classes. Not long afterwards another stalwart passed away; Charlie Taylor from Kirton was 75 years old and had been a Pilot of Sunderland Flying Boats at RAF Felixstowe. He had been involved in developing blind landings at RAF Martlesham Heath, worked on Atomic Weapons projects at Orford and finally at British Telecom (BT). In his spare time, he was a sailor of Dragonflies and Wayfarers and a musician and accordion player in the local band the 'Cornhuskers Barn Dance Band'. Charlie was very good friends with Father Sam Leader who reported that Charlie had gone out on the crest of a wave, as he was on holiday in Thailand and had been riding an elephant the day before he died.

2001/2002 saw the successful negotiations by Past President, Peter Fraser, of the purchase of the freehold of the Sailing Club from the Church for £27,000. The sites of the beach huts were sold to a new organisation, the 'Waldringfield Hut Owners Ltd' as one lot. This led to another round of fundraising but it meant long term security for the sailing club who now owned the freehold of the land from the slipway

The 24-hour race Jubilee mugs [510]

by the Maybush, to the dinghy park, including the Clubhouse site. About this time the club introduced the idea of a paid Galley Manager. Up until this time the Galley had been run purely by volunteers, but with increasing red tape and a very busy membership it was decided that now was the time to pay someone to take charge.

In June there was a second 24-hour Jubilee race, this time in celebration of 50 years of the Queen's rule. This fundraising event was successful in raising around £1,000 towards the target of £27,000 for the purchase of the Club's land.

Easter 2004 saw the installation of eco-friendly structures laid in between the launching areas. The eco-structure was laid in true WSC manner by volunteers who, because of the tides, started work very early in the morning, and some going on to work afterwards. Around this time a Weather Station, presented by the family of Ted Sudell in his memory, was installed on the Island. Ted started out as a Dragonfly sailor with numbers 34 and 43 then went on to sail Dragons, Squibs and yachts. He was also heavily involved in the Cadet class both locally and internationally over many years.

The Rev John Waller, the Honorary Club Chaplain, celebrated 150 years of Wallers at Waldringfield.

WSC Weathervane and clock made by members [511]

This photo was found amongst the belongings of Vivian Mason's late mother Dorothy Jones, who died in November 2008 at age 106. Vivian's father Bob Jones had made the weathervane and the clock was made by two other early members Ken Fish and

George Goddard. Both weathervane and clock are now well over 50 years old. Long term member Rosemary Schlee died on 17th April 2008 aged 80.

The long-standing issue of sand in the drains remained a constant battle and challenge to the Officers of the club. The Rear Commodore, House Committee and the volunteer BOBS (Band of Brothers and Sisters) Team has responsibility for the upkeep of the Clubhouse and other facilities and is often called out to investigate drain blockages.

The BOBS also meet regularly once a week to carry out other small improvements and maintenance tasks. Most are retired or semi-retired but happy to quietly carry out those unglamorous jobs that keep the club ticking over.

In the mid-noughties, the Galley was updated and the winter of 2011/2012 saw more building work at WSC. This time the changing rooms were extended. The Ladies Changing rooms had been very cramped for many years, probably harking back to the 1950s when sailing was much more a male concern. Many more young girls seem to be attracted to sailing these days.

The BOBS Team investigating a drain blockage, a not very pleasant way to spend an afternoon! [513]

Afloat

After the war, the sailing committee was formed under Dr Kenneth Nicholls Palmer. Interclub racing between Waldringfield Sailing Club (WSC), Felixstowe Ferry Sailing Club (FFSC), and Deben Yacht Club (DYC) took place and Mrs Nunn of the Ramsholt Arms prepared the tea at Ramsholt. Thus the first proper Deben Week was sailed. These weeks involved all classes of boat but gradually became more dinghy biased as more one-design racing became popular.

The advantage of one-design racing is that all boats should be the same so it is the skill of the competitor rather than the type of equipment that is being tested. This type of racing has been pursued at WSC since the war which may mean multiple starts but each race will be for the same class of boat. It is seen as a strength of WSC that this has carried on in the main to the present day. They are usually limited to around half a dozen types of class which have varied over the years as old classes die out and new ones come along.

The picture was taken by the *EADT* in 1950 and shows a Regatta start. Also written on the reverse: 'August 7th 1950 – Vivian Mason lying on the beach near the dinghy with two galley girls awaiting the time to make tea' This was later made into a postcard [512]

Some traditional Trophy races are still occasionally held for all comers but they only occur on certain days during the year and are limited. These races work by giving each type of boat a time handicap and they are either timed over the course and the results corrected afterwards or staggered timed starts to make the boats chase each other around the same course. Racing against people who are better than you and sharing useful tips creates a stronger fleet and everyone benefits.

In 1947 the Flag Officers commemorated the end of the war by presenting the Victory Plate Trophy which was contested for a race on the Whit Monday and this trophy is still awarded annually.

In 1949, the Cadet section was started and 2 Cadet Dinghies were presented to the Club for the use of the junior members. The launch of 16 Dragonflies was also a highlight of that year.

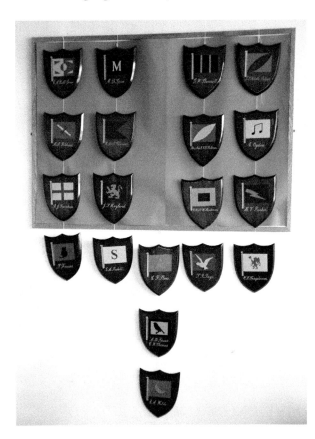

The Dragonfly shields [514]

These shields show the racing flags of the Dragonfly skippers. In earlier times the racing flag was very important. Between 1875 and 1982, the RYA had a rule that in order to be a legal entry for a race each boat needed to fly a rectangular racing flag. Failure to fly such a flag could lead to disqualification. This rule was removed when it became difficult to hoist such a racing flag on yachts with all the electronic gear at

Dragonflies racing in the 1950s [515]

the top of the mast. Of course, dinghies didn't really have the same issues but were then subject to the same rules. These plaques were never displayed on the boats but may have made identification from the shore easier. They stayed in the Clubhouse and were displayed around the clubroom but are now on the wall in the Mossman Room.

In 1954 the question of buying a Club rescue boat was raised. Until the birth of the Cadet class in 1950, rescue boats had not been dreamed of. If someone capsized another competitor went to their rescue – if you were lucky! In those early days, the Cadet fleet was followed by Felix White in his own boat *Beowulf*. In those days of cotton sails, no self-bailers and few buoyancy bags, one avoided capsizing like the plague. It was considered most unseamanlike to capsize or race in extreme conditions. Life jackets although more common were not considered mandatory and some sailors could not even swim so if they fell in they would have to hold onto to the boat and sort themselves out. Therefore in 1955, a second-hand boat was purchased and Ted Kaznica agreed to man it for rescue work during racing.

The beach before the river wall in the early 1950s (notice the old life jackets!) [516]

Squib Racing in the 1970s [517]

The Club Firefly was purchased in 1956 for £80. The first Cadet Week was planned and organised by Dr and Mrs Nicholls Palmer. This event has continued to the current day and Waldringfield has always had one of the largest Cadet fleets in the country.

The early 1950s saw the start of the National 12 and the Firefly fleets class racing at the club and The Easter Egg trophy for 12' Class boats was held on Easter Monday in 1952. Impromptu Wednesday evening racing commenced and serious points racing started in 1953. In 1967 the Cadet Squadron was asked to donate a cup to the International Cadet Week at Burnham-on-Crouch. WSC duly obliged.

Dinghy racing continued to become popular with more classes being involved and as a cheaper option to yacht racing and they gradually started to take over.

The Enterprise Class had been introduced in 1960 and in 1967 a record entry of 37 boats took part in the Easter Egg Open Meeting (prizes being Easter Eggs).

Some classes were singlehanded like the OK or the Laser, which also meant you didn't have to rely on a crew and the cost of all these boats was coming down. Deben Week in 1970 commenced at Woodbridge on Monday culminating in passage races to Waldringfield for the next two days racing there. There were 17 races each day and the total number of starters at Waldringfield totalled 869.

Shore events would remain at Waldringfield on the first Saturday followed by the Yachtsman's Service after racing at Waldringfield on the Sunday. This continued until the 2000s. Although the modern trend has seen a move away from week-long local sailing events (apart from some Nationals events), Cadet Week still remains and is one of the most popular youth weeks in East Anglia.

The Dragonflies celebrated their 21st anniversary in 1968 by going to Ireland to race against the Rothman Cup team, in their 14' Irish Dinghy Racing Association (IDRA) one-design class, a sister class of the Dragonfly. This has been repeated since then with the Irish also making the return visit. Later in 1970, the Squib Class was adopted fulfilling the need for a racing keelboat and as a replacement for racing yachts on an increasingly busy river. The yachts still race occasionally but less often than previously.

The International Cadet Class very sensibly introduced a new swimming rule which meant that competitors were now expected to be able to swim a short distance before being allowed to sail including those at Waldringfield. The beginnings of health and

Enterprises racing at WSC [518]

safety!

By 1974, the cost of blank cartridges was becoming too expensive and so it was decided that in future no gun would be fired for racing, but a hooter would be used instead. This had already been the norm on Sundays, as the Club was not allowed to fire guns on that day because the Clubhouse had been built on Church land and the Church wouldn't allow it. Easter Sunday was the exception, but racing didn't start until after Church. The '3 Cannon Gun Trophy' (suitably disabled) is now presented as a yacht prize.

After the number of Fireflies dwindled and the class was disbanded in 1978, the Laser class was introduced, initially with a fleet of 8. Other members set off on adventures across the Atlantic on their yachts. This set a trend for later years with several intrepid yachting members setting out for ever-increasing challenges. However many yacht owners preferred to stay closer to home with annual cruises to London and around the coast of the UK.

Rosemary Schlee had started organising sailing courses and John and Oriel Laws (Rosemary's daughter) changed these to RYA-accredited Courses.

During the Fastnet Storm of 1979 many Waldringfield boats were damaged including Charlie Taylor's Dragonfly which was wrecked on the Deben Bar. This event influenced the introduction of the Wayfarer class to Waldringfield by Rosemary Schlee. Charlie needed a boat to sail so he decided to be one of six to order a new Wayfarer from Seamark Nunn. Within 2 years they had a fleet of 12 boats. There is a good fleet of Wayfarers to this day.

The Lark class was adopted in 1984, mainly due to the enthusiasm of Ian Bowles, the Class Captain, and 16 Larks started racing. The fleet became quite strong with many crews (including many ex Cadets) going on to become National Champions.

In the 1988 season, 420 races were held for 3180 boats and 80 trophies had been contested. This also saw the 150th anniversary of Deben YC, one of the oldest yacht clubs in the UK. The Cadets took part in the sail past. Later David Moon and the Lark class also organised the first 24-hour race for dinghies. The format being that the dinghy has to be sailed by a team of sailors for a total of 24 hours and the team sailing the most laps wins. In principle, it sounds easier than it is in practice because a team is also required to make sure that the correct number of laps are recorded and that crews can swap over in a safe manner. Added to this are problems occurring on tidal waters, where some courses are not accessible at low tide and the often fickle winds overnight, but it did make for an

The Larks racing in 1986 [519]

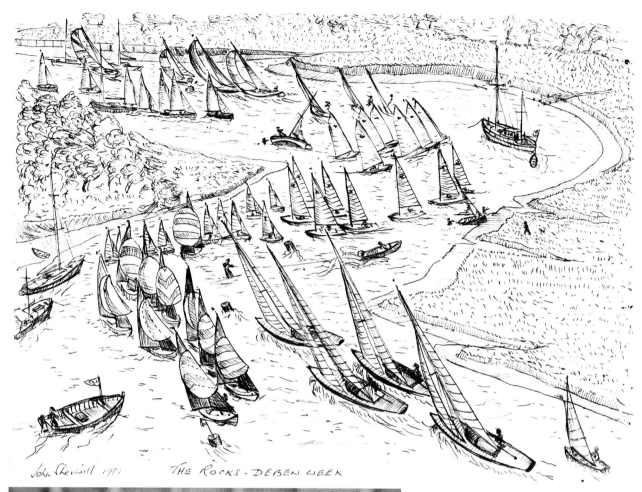

John Sherwill 1981   THE ROCKS · DEBEN WEEK

Ted Kaznica on Rescue [521]

Boats racing through the Rocks
by John Sherwill [520]

interesting race.

This picture of boats racing through the Rocks during Deben Week was drawn in 1981 by John Sherwill (1923-1990) who was an active member of WSC from 1964 until 1982 when he and his wife Pat retired back to their native Guernsey. His boat was the 1926 one-off wooden dayboat *Cockleshell* that he had sailed across the English Channel from Guernsey in 1959 and in which he raced in WSC's yacht handicap class. A lifelong sailor, John was also a skilled model maker and occasional artist. His enthusiasm shines through in this depiction of typical Deben Week activity – although somewhat more crowded than usual!

In 1995 Ted Kaznica, as a retirement present, was presented with a most beautifully inscribed scroll, thanking him for his work as Club Bosun. For

40 years he had followed races, relaying messages and instructions in his own inimitable language. A storm and tidal surge hit in 1993 causing many boats to float off downriver on a Sunday night high tide. Ted Kaznica was out on his own, throughout Monday, in his rescue boat rescuing and returning boats to Waldringfield, and that night a few hardy souls continued to search for the remaining lost boats, some not getting back until the small hours of the morning. He singlehandedly towed some back up from the Rocks, but some were retrieved later from as far downriver as Felixstowe Ferry.

He was the most memorable and longest-serving Bosun who was an ever-present rescue boat driver. He terrified the junior members from his large blue clinker-built displacement boat. He kept his eyes open for distress in all weathers and just quietly got on and 'did his thing'. History does not relate whether he ever passed his Powerboat Course or indeed whether he could swim! More of a caretaker than a Bosun, he remains immortalised by a framed poem on the wall of the Clubhouse. The club also gave him the rescue boat that he had lovingly maintained and helmed for so many years.

1998 saw the Cadet Squadron acquire their own rescue boat which could be used locally for training, or taken to events for support on the water to the increasingly mobile fleet. It was a rather large RIB that was called *Smuggler* reflecting the fact that it had been purchased from HM Customs and Excise who had acquired it from a smuggling gang after they were arrested in the Mediterranean. It proved to be very useful, but a little big for towing around the country, so this was eventually swapped for a slightly smaller RIB and *Smuggler* was then used by Lance Cooper for Club Rescue. It now became apparent how useful

The WSC 75th Anniversary mug [522]

50th Deben Week commemorative mug [523]

RIB's were for rescue and safety boat duties and the club gradually increased the number of RIBs in their possession to three – *Stingray*, *Avocet* and *Hooligan*. They still retained the displacement boats *Fynn Lass* and *Kirton Owl* for mark laying and other general activities and have *Boudicea* as Committee Boat for starting and finishing races on the water. *Stingray* has now been replaced by a new RIB called *Kingfisher*.

In 2009 Graham Harrison took over running the Sailing School section from Cathy Fish. He developed it into a more substantial enterprise, running more RYA courses including winter shore-based courses and acquiring more training boats. The courses were mainly open to club members and trained many RYA (Royal Yachting Association) Yachtmasters and Instructors as well as running VHF and Power Boat courses for rescue personnel. Many teenagers were set on the path to working abroad, with their new qualifications, for their gap years and onwards; some even turning it into a way of earning a living becoming paid yacht crew or skippers on superyachts for the mega-rich. Thus harking back to the Club's origins of paid professional crew.

RYA Sailing Course 2009 [524]

WSC new Wayfarer Mk4 dinghies purchased and
named in Rosemary Schlee's memory [525]

The club's 3 new Wayfarer Mk 4 dinghies purchased
and named in Rosemary Schlee's memory were
christened by Oriel (her daughter) with the names
Relentless, *Redoubtable* and *Resolute*, adjectives that truly
described Rosemary's indomitable character. Each of
the three boats were differently configured. Rosemary
Schlee pioneered teaching club members to sail and
her generous legacy of £10,000 enabled the Club to
continue that successful activity.

2010 also saw the 40th
Anniversary of the formation of
the Squib fleet on Sunday 13th June.
They celebrated with a weekend
of racing, a BBQ and singing to a
shanty band. Chris Thompson, who
had just turned 90, sailed with his
son in law Chris Baker in *Discord*
which had been in the family since
the fleet was founded. David Copp
had tentatively introduced the
Club's first asymmetric class – the
RS400 in 2004. It persisted for a
couple of years before disappearing
again. However, this paved the way
for another asymmetric class to be
introduced in 2016 – the RS200
class. This is felt to be more suitable
for the river and is also a very
exciting boat to sail especially in
windy conditions. It was also seen
to be more modern and tempting to
those sailors leaving the Cadet class and wanting to
continue to sail 2 handed boats.

2019 saw the 70th Anniversary of the Dragonfly
class and a visit from Ireland of the sister class IDRA
14 for a weekend of festivities including racing on a
very windy weekend. Local crews swapped into the
Irish boats to experience the joys of trapezing in the
tough conditions.

The weekend also included a meal and dance
evening and the unveiling of a new bench designed and
made by Spencer Wix, a stonemason of Woodbridge
and Dragonfly sailor.

Squibs racing [526]

RS200 introduced in 2016 [527]

Going Forward

Fleet racing is seen as a strength at WSC as this prevents racing becoming a mishmash of different types of boat. Fleets come and sometimes go. Currently, the racing fleets consist of Wayfarers, Squibs, Lasers, Cadets, Dragonflies, RS200s, Larks and Toppers. There is also still a yacht fleet, but they don't tend to race in the river much these days apart from the Cork Race but venture further afield to compete in events like the Haven Series, where yachts from many local clubs combine to race offshore. Handicap dinghy racing does take place on a limited basis as historical trophy races with traditional courses occur during the year and for the popular Wednesday evening series. This gives people a chance to bring out their more unusual craft if desired but also allows the fleets to race as one.

The latest plans are for an internal revamp of the main Club Room, which is beginning to look a little tired. This has remained largely unchanged since the 1982 extension was finished and will hopefully be finished in time for celebrations in 2021 for the Centenary. It is hoped that the Waldringfield Sailing Club will be set up for the challenges of the new century.

IDRA 14 sailing at the Dragonfly 70th Anniversary Worlds Regatta. Local Cadet crew, Ethan Davey trapezing, making a guest appearance [529]

The WSC Clubhouse decked out for the Dragonfly 70th Anniversary Celebratory Weekend in 2019 with the new Dragonfly bench in front [528]

The WSC Honours Boards

A glance at the Honours Boards in WSC reveals a significant level of success at national and international level. Pre-war stars like Cyril Stollery and Ken Palmer in 1935 with the National 12 class showed the way

and this pairing continued somewhat after the war. Cyril and Roger Stollery sailed with Mike Richardson in a Dragon and even completed Olympic trials but didn't make the cut. Mike went on to win the OK National Championships. Other local sailors also competed at this level, such as Bob Garnham in Olympic standard dinghies and Sharpies up to Offshore Class 1. He also crewed for Geoff Pattinson on many RORC Admirals Cup races in *Jocasta*, winning Class 1 three years in a row.

Jack Knights, a club member, sailed regularly at Waldringfield before going to University. Afterwards he was 3 times the British Finn champion and North American Finn Champion, He was reserve for the Great Britain Olympic Sailing Team for the Melbourne Olympics in 1956 and had a variety of other major successes in yachts both big and small. He became a respected writer and ran the London Boat Show.

A team of Ric and John Cordy, Gordon Harris and Ron Jackson, Derek Bell-Jones and Patsy Jackson/Graham Dale, won the East Coast Area Team Championship title at Ardleigh in Enterprises.

The Nationals Boards in 2020 [530, 531]

Jack Knights, *Yachts and Yachting* reporter [532]

Cutting a dash – Gordon Harris c. 1951 [533]

Gordon Harris went on to win the Pandora Nationals in 1975 with his son Ian and the Express Nationals in 1976 and then onto sail Wayfarers.

His children Emma and Ian learned their sailing through Cadets. Emma won the Lark Nationals in 2002 sailing for Waldringfield. Then Ian's children Jamie and Bettine who started their sailing career in Optimist dinghies took up Cadet sailing and won the nationals in 2015 and Jamie won again in 2016 as well as the World Championships representing Waldringfield.

The eighties and nineties saw some keen competition from Waldringfield in the OK class with Jonty Sherwill, David Rose

and David Carroll winning the National Championships between 1978 and 1997.

The Waldringfield Cadet Squadron, Squadron 35, had stuck to mainly local events until Ted Sudell got them competing at National and International levels. Chris Mason with his crew Mike Hutchinson won two races at the Nationals and attended the Cadet Worlds in Spain in 1986. Then Adrian Mills won races at the nationals in 1990 and Alan Krailing won the under-13 trophy. Together they sailed at the World Championships in Poland. They were followed by Neil Watson and Polly Baker in Argentina, and also the brothers Chris and Jonathan Fish, amongst others. Many of these young sailors went on to win Championships in other classes.

The Cadet Squadron was now going from strength to strength with Sam Carter (great great nephew of Captain Jack Carter of HMY *Britannia*) winning the 2000 Nationals and then World Championships in Poland. Ex-Cadet Katie Archer won the Laser Radial Ladies singlehanded Nationals in 1999 and was the first lady at the Laser Radial Youth Worlds in 2000.

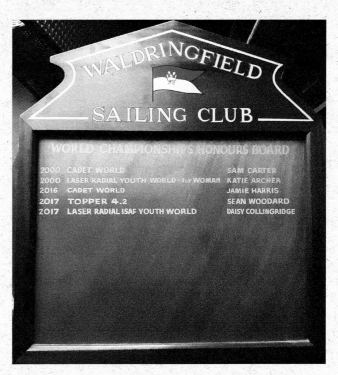

The World Championship Honours Board [534]

Sam Carter and crew with crew winning the World Championships in Poland in 2000 [535]

Stephen Videlo and James Jopling winning the Inland
Championships at Rutland 2004 [536]

Successful cadet sailors from Waldringfield village include Stephen Videlo who, taking after his uncle, aunt and father, was the reserve for the British Team with his brother Chris in 2003, came 5th in Australia with James Jopling as crew and then was beaten into second place by another British boat in the Worlds in Spain in 2005 sailing with Aaron Woolf. He won the Cadet Nationals 2 years running (2004/2005) and in the process beat the World Champion and thus gained some revenge. Stephen later went on to be part of a British team which won the ISAF World U21 Team Racing Championship in La Gandia, Spain in 2007. Interestingly his father Ian had sailed Cadets at Frensham Pond in Surrey – not Waldringfield – yet the boatyard that had built his World's winning Cadet in 1975 was Larkman's of Melton.

Subsequently Hamish Stone came 2nd at the Cadet World Championships in Hungary in 2006. Many other Waldringfield Cadets have also represented GB as part of the World Team. Another Waldringfield village ex-Cadet Tim Carter, went on to race 420s with James Hayward and then onto 470s and Nacra 18s as part of the Olympic training squad. He was a member of the America's Cup team Land Rover BAR (Ben Ainslie Racing) in its Communications and Commercial Team and is now part of the sailing team for the INEOS Team UK challenge for the America's Cup against New Zealand, due to take place in 2021. At the time of writing, training is on hold due to the Coronavirus pandemic, but the hopes are that it will resume in the near future, possibly in New 'Zealand'.

Tim Carter and Team INEOS for the next Americas Cup [537]

Cadet Squadron 35

'The "Cadet" is more than a dinghy. It is an academy at which one is introduced to the lessons of life as well as the skills and arts of sailing. The Cadet Class is more than an Association. It is a movement where children and parents mix, where lasting friendships are made, nationally and globally. It is a sharing of knowledge, skills, equipment, food, drink and lodging. It is a family, a big family, but a beautiful family.'

The Cadet Story by Guy Holmes
– Foreword by RG Holmes

Cadet no. 3 *Seahorse* with Ann Mossman, now Thubron [538]

The Cadet dinghy was designed in 1946 by Jack Holt as a boat that could be built at home on a family budget. At that time, there was a chronic postwar shortage of good quality wood and families were keen to spend more of their leisure time together. His design was small enough for youngsters to manage in and out of the water and made use of marine ply that had been developed during the war. The bow transom avoided the use of excessive bending and made the whole thing cheaper and easier to build at home. This design allowed children to participate in similar activities as their parents and provided them with a boat that looked and performed like a thoroughbred dinghy, yet was still practical enough for a beginner.

The International Cadet Class was formed in 1947. Since then, thousands of children have had their first introduction to sailing via the Cadet including several past and current Olympic Sailing medallists.

Crews will normally start at 8 or 9 years old and then begin to helm at 12 or 13 but this is largely dependent on size and ability. The class finishes for children when they turn 18.

The Cadet Squadron at Waldringfield was formed by Mr Mossman and Dr Palmer in 1950. They were 'Old Ipswichians' and were able to persuade the Ipswich School Headmaster to provide 4 cadet dinghies, 2 of which were built with the help of pupils. The first Waldringfield Cadet Week was held in 1956 and became a highlight of the summer holiday. Racing happened during the day and other social activities took place in the evenings such as beach games, discos and barbeques. Many sailing families owned beach huts or inherited them from past generations and they are still well used during the summer holidays, especially during Cadet Week, when 'tent city' often appeared on the site where the cricket and tennis used to be played.

1980 was a year of celebration for the Cadets, as the Waldringfield Squadron number 35 had its 21st birthday. Pauline and John Cooney were Squadron Leaders and a huge birthday cake was made for the traditional tea at the end of Cadet Week prize giving. Andrew Cooney designed the cake which was decorated with a Cadet (under spinnaker), showing '1980' on the sail.

1980 Cadet Week Silver Jubilee celebrations [539]

Anthony Mason (Commodore then and current) taking part in the old gaffers race in Cadet Week 1983 [540]

Rev John Waller and Ted Sudell putting the World to rights [541]

In 1984, the Cadet Squadron held its first Cadet Open Meeting and Fitting-Out Supper with the ex-cadets supervising.

Later that year, Ted Sudell retired as Chairman of the International Cadet Class, a post he had held since 1971. He had been involved with the Cadets since 1957, but in 1969 he singlehandedly raised £2,300 to send two British crews and their boats to Australia for the 1970 World Championships. He was very organised and focused his attention on planning efficient and professionally-run World Championships from then on. He also encouraged the local crews to start competing at National and International level. He travelled to many parts of the world, supporting Cadet World Championships over his tenureship and afterwards for fun. His son William, who had competed as a child together with his siblings, would take over the helm of the International Cadet Committee from 2001 to 2007, travelling to the furthest corners of the world. At the same time his wife Ali was on the British Cadet Committee which was chaired by Ian Videlo, also of WSC, during which time GB hosted the 60th Anniversary Worlds in 2007.

2009 saw the 50th anniversary of the Cadet Squadron with a special Cadet Week. Cadet Week still remains popular today with visitors from other Clubs also taking part. The format remains largely unchanged since it started, with cup racing over 5 days and social activities such as raft building, kite building and treasure hunts thrown in during the evenings.

The ex-Cadets still race for the 'Ex-Cadet' Trophy (singlehanded in Cadets) and it is hotly contested.

The Waldringfield Cadet fleet, starting place for many of the Club's top sailors, racing in 1988 [542]

There is also an 'Old Gaffers' Trophy race. This race is for a combined crew age of 70 with a helm aged over 35 but this does mean that certain competitors could qualify to race on their own. However, a crew of two is required!

These races also make for good entertainment as a commentary is provided by the Cadets and there is not much room to be had in the front of a Cadet! Laser Radials were introduced in around 2007 for the slightly older children or those who considered themselves too big for Cadets, but these have now been replaced with the two-handed, RS200.

A treasure hunt amongst the creeks and saltings arranged for after racing during Cadet week [545]

John Palmer related his memories of his first Cadet bought for £30 in 1956, CK702, which had no spinnaker, kicking strap or toestraps. The sails were blue cotton and a terrible shape but he bought a new set for £11. The boats were all plywood with inflatable buoyancy bags tied in under the decks. The sails had brass slides sewn onto luff ropes which went onto brass tracks on wooden masts and booms.

Encouraged by Ted, many Cadets started to travel further afield to National Championships and some even travelled to World Championships. Despite the recent overall decline in National Cadet numbers this trend continues today with the GB team of seven boats normally including at least one representative from Waldringfield, sometimes more. This has led to families travelling to many parts they would not ultimately have gone to, including Australia, Argentina, Poland and Hungary.

The numbers of squadrons and Cadets sailing in the UK has declined in recent years, but it is still a very competitive class especially internationally. Argentine sailors won 14 world championships in the 20-year period between 1991 and 2010 which just goes to show what an achievement Sam Carter's Worlds win was. The Cadet remains an ideal training boat and a good stepping stone to other classes. It is still well supported at Waldringfield and remains the main training class of choice for children at the club. Whilst maintaining the aim that sailing is first and foremost fun, improving your sailing by training and racing is seen as the end result. Much of the training is given by parents, ex Cadets and friends passing on their previous knowledge and experience of National and International sailing, and occasionally supplemented by guest trainers such as dinghy legend Michael McNamara, who has won titles over 45 years in classes from Wayfarers to National 12s.

60th Anniversary of Cadet Week, 2017 [544]

Cadet Squadron 60th Anniversary Cake being cut by Ann Thubron and John Palmer [543]

The Waldringfield Dragonfly

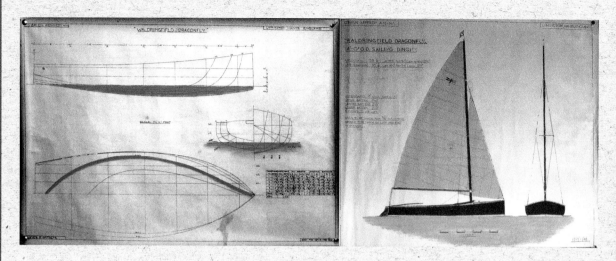

O'Brien Kennedy's plans for the Waldringfield Dragonfly [546]

Over the summer of 2019, this classy clinker-built sailing dinghy celebrated 70 years of racing on the Deben. The Dragonflies were joined by three sister dinghies from the Irish Dinghy Racing Association.

First launched in May 1949, the Dragonfly had been two years in gestation. Addressing the WSC committee in 1947, Mr Ernie Nunn's introduction of the notion of 'one-design racing' was enthusiastically received. It was agreed that the boat should be a Bermudan-rigged 14-footer, matching the speed of the popular National 12 and sufficient beam to 'take grandma sailing on Sundays'.

A design for a new 'Fuss-type' dinghy from the drawing board of Irish designer, O'Brien Kennedy was proposed by Ken Nicholls Palmer and readily adopted.

In September of 1948, interested members met in an (almost certainly) smoke-filled committee room to respectfully argue their cases for a whimsical selection of names such as 'The Deben', 'Jollyboat', 'Sandpipers', 'Peewits', 'Chameleons', 'Rainbows' and 'Fusspots'. At the vote, Mrs Heather Parker's proposal, seconded by Dr Palmer, that the new class should be 'The Dragonfly' was carried unanimously.

No fewer than 20 members had pledged a sum approximately equivalent to one and a half times the current working man's wage to purchase one of the new Dragonflies – £152.10s.to include sails, rowlocks, royalties and measuring fee. Two local boatyards – Nunn Bros and Robertson's were commissioned to build ten apiece.

Later that winter, the partly-built skeleton of a Dragonfly was transported to Ipswich and hoisted up to the first-floor ballroom of the Great White Horse Hotel to be star exhibit at the club's annual dinner and dance. A mere four months later, with numbers carved into 18 new transoms, a draw was held to allocate the new boats to their excited owners.

On June 11, 1949, the Dragonfly fleet – all four of them- came to the WSC line for their first race. By the end of that season, 16 Dragonflies had competed, Dr Palmer had won the newly donated Regatta Shield and one-design racing had come to Waldringfield. By 1963 there were 43 boats, numbering up to 45 (8 and 13 were never built) and 24 clear varnished hulls graced the Anchorage with a line of gold swinging prettily on their mooring trots. A fleet of 18 came to the line for the Deben Week Regatta of 1978 as the class approached its 30th anniversary.

Great characters emerged from the early postwar river rivalries. A driving force in dinghy racing, Cyril Stollery, commodore of the 'Democratic Sailing Club of Waldringfield' for 21 years, gained notoriety as 'someone who was always tinkering with his boat in pursuit of a bit more speed....to no great effect...'

Rules were always there to be stretched by some, such as Mr R Garnham mooring his boat at the top of the tide line in an attempt to get around the '48 hours afloat before competing' regulation and irascible dentist Ted Sudell filing a bit too much off his stern planking.

Tout Compris leading *Fantee* at Green Point [548]

But the guaranteed way to get among the trophies was to put local boy George Turner on the tiller of your Dragonfly. Brought up on the Deben and generally acknowledged to know the river better than anyone, George took the prestigious Regatta Shield a record ten times in the first 20 years. As a young apprentice George reputedly took more in prize money – helming his employer's boat in Deben Week – than he took home from a week at work.

More mature WSC members in 2019 would remember Dragonfly stalwart and renowned squeezebox player Charlie Taylor. Charlie's Dragonfly days came to a dramatic end in the North Sea at Felixstowe when he was plucked from the foaming froth of the Deben Bar. Sadly Dragonfly No. 2 could not be saved.

It had never of course been all about the racing. As a family club, members had resolved from the outset that they wanted a craft that would double as a 'comfortable day boat'. The enduring appeal of this 1940s classic is that it remains a splendid boat for just messing about on the river.

The class has had its less buoyant time – boats have disappeared from the area, others decaying to a state beyond repair and numbers on the moorings dropping to a handful in the 1990s. But hitting 70 the Dragonfly took flight again due largely to the efforts of two members of a family which goes right back to the beginnings. James Palmer, grandson of founding member Ken Nicholls Palmer (D18 & D42) gave the class the best possible shot in the arm in 2016 with the production of the brand new traditionally-constructed Dragonfly 46 *Phoenix*.

Meanwhile, John Palmer, dad of James, son of Ken, devoted countless hours in a workshop bringing three Dragonflies 'back from the dead' as well as helping and advising on the restoration of others.

The class has made a few concessions to modernity – spinnakers and metal spars are allowed – but the dozen or so lovingly-varnished hulls swinging elegantly on their moorings reflect not just the summer evening sun but a justly treasured piece of living Deben heritage.

Launch of the first Dragonfly, no. 17 *Stinger*, from AV Robertson's Yard, May 1949 (left to right: Frances Stollery, Roger Stollery, Cyril Stollery, Arthur Robertson) [547]

The PUNCH Dinghy

Rum Tum Tugger with Noel Fraser
in charge – 2013 [549]

This dinghy was conceived by Roger Stollery in 1980 on the beach at Waldringfield after a conversation with Judy Stinson, who wanted a boat in which to teach her grandchildren to sail. She had tried a Mirror dinghy but found it too tippy to sit on the windward side in light airs. Ideally, she wanted a traditional lug-sailed clinker dinghy, but there were none available.

Just at that time Roger's 6-year-old son, Peter, had been loaned an Optimist dinghy and found a great deal of confidence provided by the beamy square box sectioned shape. So the idea of an Optimist for 'grannies', which had room for grandchildren and which would be sufficiently stable for Judy, was born.

The other influence was the development of the 'swing rig' in the competitive racing environment of radio controlled sailing. At the time Roger was the only designer developing this 'innovative' swing rig and had converted his Mirror dinghy rig into a swing rig using very basic pieces of 2 x 2 timber, plywood etc. It was not a high-tech rig but it worked extremely well and made the normally flimsy Mirror rig much stronger, as there was no mast bending from the kicking strap. This version of the rig freed up the space in the Mirror for Susan and his two young children.

The prototype was PUNCH no. 4, launched in 1981, from which a couple of details were improved. There was no change to the design of the following half a dozen boats, which have been seen on the river. PUNCH no. 1, the first production dinghy, was built for Judy and was subsequently owned by Julia Stroud (née Waller) and now John Fish and family. During that first year, a young student saw its potential for disabled people. As she was about to be involved in teaching them, she persuaded her father to make PUNCH no. 5, which has since been owned by Rosemary Schlee and Martin McBeal.

PUNCH no. 8 was the last number to be built locally and all except 5 were built by Ray Gallington in Seamark Nunn's workshop in Trimley.

Everyone who has sailed them has really enjoyed the simple balanced rig, the stability and the ease of sailing them, and the very relaxed feel that the boat gives for kids of all ages! None more relaxed than the Fraser family who have got two and can occasionally be seen lounging on cushions in their PUNCHES; when they aren't rowing!

The Stollery family in the prototype
Knockout – mid-1980s [550]

Although PUNCH is only 3.3 m long, the same length as the Mirror, the space is more than that available in a Wayfarer. It is great for sailing up a creek, anchoring, having lunch and then sunbathing on the decks, bigger than the cockpit of many larger yachts.

For training, its advantage is that at the end of a session, if the instructor is satisfied with the proficiency of a student, he can let him or her sail the boat on his or her own. At the end of a sailing course in 1981, a student with only one arm was frustrated by not being able to sail the Wayfarer in which he had been training, on his own. He was absolutely delighted when lent a PUNCH, which he found so easy to sail on his own..

The BOTTLE Boat

Loud claims of 'water please!' were heard from Stephen Videlo 18 and several competitors, with the wind light and the tide strong boats needed plenty of space to round the windward mark [551]

Like the PUNCH dinghy, the idea for the BOTTLE boat was conceived in Waldringfield.

In the mid-1990s the cost of a starter boat for new radio racing competitors was getting expensive, in the order of £2,000. The inspiration was bottles of washing-up liquid. That developed into the idea of using two-litre fizzy drink bottles, joined by a carbon fibre moulding to include the keel and structure for supporting the cantilevered swing rig and the radio gear etc. As well as recycling the bottles, an upturned plastic coffee cup was used as the bow, the spars were seconds carbon arrow shaft and the sails were recycled shopping bags etc.

The first boat was produced in 1998 and worked very well with a standard inexpensive servo able to pull in the sails instead of an expensive winch. As the swing rig is balanced, which reduces the sheeting forces, this was achieved using an innovative power lever.

The performance was amazing for such a small boat made of recycled parts with a ready-to-sail price of under £200. Model yachts require small sails when the wind is blowing hard and in this case, the mast is split into 2 halves, with only just a small topmast to rig the smaller sails. All of these features allowed the design to achieve a Millennium Product award by the Design Centre, for one of the most innovative products at the turn of the millennium.

The first big event for the class was sailed on the River Deben at Waldringfield in October 2002 in the most amazing gale, which dragged one of the moored yachts onto the mud. However, 3 of the dozen BOTTLE boats entered, managed to survive and finish the racing in their small rigs. Every year since then, the BOTTLE boat championship has provided a great spectacle in front of the WSC Clubhouse with up to 20 entries and offers exciting racing for both competitors and spectators alike, with children able to compete on an equal footing against some of the best dinghy sailors in the club.

Flooding

'Dark at tea-time and sleeping indoors: nothing ever happens in the winter holidays.'

Arthur Ransome, *Winter Holiday*

The Quay during a flood event on 1st March 1949 [553]

Flooding has long been an issue in the River Deben but the frequency of these events is increasing with global warming causing a rise in sea levels. A lack of investment into flood defences has also led many river walls to deteriorate which means these flooding events can cause even more devastation if the walls breach and get washed away, as has already happened both north and south of the village.

The most famous flood in living memory will be the widespread East Coast Flood of 1953 when many were killed.

The late Andrew Haig remembered:

'I had come down from London for the weekend 31.1.53 – 1.2.53 to stay with my mother in Waldringfield. I went down to the Boatyard where Ernie Nunn told me a high tide was expected. I walked along to our hut (No. 27) and 'moored' it to a nearby tree with a thick rope. I related this to my mother who thought I was mad. When I revisited the hut the next day I was told High Water predicted for midnight did not actually happen to 5 a.m. My hut would have floated away had I not tied it up – I think 3 huts did float off down the Deben. The height of the water was about 3 feet from the ground of my hut.'

Ray Whyard, who has lived in the village all his life and was a child at the time, said that the flood reached up Cliff Road to the bend by the Maybush car park which makes a height of around 6.2m above mean sea level.

We have very few pictures of this famous event from Waldringfield's history except for one of the beach huts the following day.

Mr Spear's old hut on the river wall, which was the last hut downriver, was originally a hut made from two very large bomb packing cases that were acquired from Debach Airfield. It was built by the so called 'Yanks' during WW2, to entertain their lady friends before it came to Waldringfield; hence the lettering on the woodwork. Two families now share this hut and they still own pieces of the timber from the original hut showing the bomb box markings.

Evidently, the timber appeared in position one day and stayed until it moved during the 1953 floods.

In the late 1800s / early 1900s, Reverend Thomas Henry Waller recorded floods in his Perennial Diary:

26.3.1874: Very high tides water over the Walls.
30.1.1877: High tide, marshes flooded.
20.12.1897: High tide with gale, water nearly up road below Deben Villa, and great flooding all

The Spear hut during the 1953 flood [554]

Packing case from the original hut
showing bomb markings [555]

1993 Flood on the Quay [556]

along the coast.

*29.11.1897: High tide breaching river walls &
flowing to Shottisham Ford. Wall near Ramsholt
Creek afterwards repaired for £1,000 with
sandbags and again Nov 22nd 1903 broken thro'.
22.11.1903: High tide with NW. wind breaching
river walls and flowing to Shottisham Ford as on
Nov 29th 1897. High Water at about 1.45 a.m.*

1993 Floods at the Quay [557]

Geographical conditions dictate that the highest
spring tides in Waldringfield are likely to occur around
midday and midnight. If these coincide with a deep
low over the North Sea then a flood occurs.

In 1993, the water came over the wall and right
through the dinghy parks with many boats drifting
away. Some were found downriver as far as Felixstowe.

In 2007 the flood again came over the walls in
the middle of the night and many boats had to be
moved in the dark to higher ground. The Boatyard
also flooded but not enough to float the bigger boats.

The most extreme flood in recent memory
occurred in December 2013. Again, it was a night-
time phenomenon. A survey carried out by the
Environment Agency in 2013, before the floods,
predicted where the Deben was most likely to flood
allowing for a future sea-level rise to 2050, assuming
a wall could survive being overtopped by 300mm and
that the wall was kept in reasonable condition.

Floods in 2007. The water came over the wall
near the beach huts in the night [558]

However, in December that year, the inevitable
happened and an overtopping occurred. This again
occurred in the middle of the night.

By 10.30 pm the Quay was completely underwater.
The boats were beginning to float and required tying
down by the owner of Waldringfield Boatyard, Mark
Barton. Fortunately, there was no wind. Quay Lane
became flooded and local residents took shelter in the
Maybush.

Flood in Boatyard 9 Nov 2007 [559]

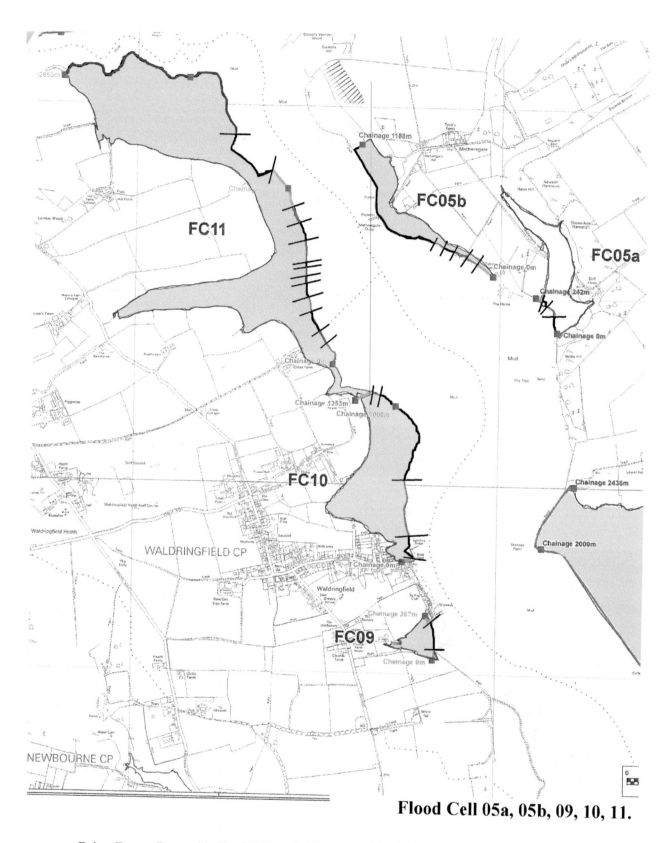

Flood Cell 05a, 05b, 09, 10, 11.

Deben Estuary Partnership Flood Cell survivability report March 2013, based on Environment Agency surveys, with shaded sections to show flood heights if river walls were to be breached [560]

The following morning, the full extent of the damage was apparent. There was considerable damage to property. Luckily, being December, the dinghy parks were empty of dinghies.

There were several places where the river wall was damaged enough for residents to feel that it would not withstand another event. Thankfully, it did not breach on this occasion. This proved to be in line with the Environment Agency Report.

After the flood, as many houses on the Quay and the Boatyard had flooded, a Flood Defence scheme was installed with help from Environment Agency. The scheme was funded, designed and constructed within 12 months. This was partly due to the basic groundwork already having been completed, but also to a partnership with a local group which allowed for good local engagement. This in turn, attracted alternative funding streams which produced a significant reduction in costs. The new flood gates were installed on the slipway, walls were built around all the houses on the Quay and the Boatyard and the mud walls to the north of the village were raised in height with clay extracted from the Dairy Farm Marsh.

The flood cell survivability map opposite shows the natural extent of the river before the river walls (purple lines). If the river walls were breached then the land behind would be flooded where it is shaded beige. The different coloured lines show the survivability category of the wall in 2013:

- **Black:** Will overtop and may breach during a 1:5 year event in 2012. Cannot survive a 1:5 year surge event in the year 2050.

- **Red:** Will overtop and may breach during a 1:20 year event in 2012. Can survive a 1:5 year surge event in the year 2050 with overtopping. Cannot survive a 1:20 year surge event in the year 2050.

- **Blue:** Will overtop and may breach during a 1:75 year event in 2012. Can survive a 1:20 year surge event in the year 2050 with overtopping. Cannot survive a 1:75 year surge event in the year 2050.

- **Green:** Will not overtop during a 1:75 year event in 2012. Can survive a 1:75 year surge event in the year 2050.

The survey of the river walls carried out in 2013, resulted in the new river wall which protects the housing and businesses on the Quay from flooding and this was tested in 2020 by another high surge tide, this time at midday.

The Quay at about 11 pm on 5th December, about an hour before peak high water. Mark Barton of the Boatyard rowed along the Quay to access properties [561]

The morning of 6th Dec 2013 after overnight flooding on the Quay. The water has receded at this point, but it was low tide at this time [562]

The morning of 6th Dec 2013 after overnight flooding. The haystack in the middle of the picture floated from near Sandy Lane, across the fields and wedged against the river wall. The fields behind the wall remained flooded [563]

Up & down river flooded areas overtopping walls which are below 3 metres Ordinance Datum Level

Overhead pictures showing the land that would be flooded if there were no river walls [564]

The February 2020 Flood

There is now a flood warning system in place by the Environment Agency which gives people fairly accurate forecasts of water heights predicted. The data from previous floods has allowed them to computer model the likely situation and is becoming more accurate each time.

This warning was received:

> 'River Deben, North Sea
> This message has been issued because there is a possibility of some flooding of homes and businesses between 11:30am and 1:30pm today, Monday 10th February. Tides are expected to be higher than usual due to the forecast weather conditions during spring tides. Areas most at risk are properties behind the river wall at Felixstowe Ferry, including the Golf Club, Newbourne, Ramsholt and isolated properties on the Deben Estuary. The detailed forecast for those that use it is for a peak level at Harwich of 3.07m AODN at 12:33pm, on Monday 10th February, which is 0.92m above tide tables, wind Force 7, SW. (m AODN is height above average sea level, for more information refer to local tide tables). There may be 2 separate high water peaks.'

Part of the Flood defence scheme on the Quay [565]

A flooded Quay, Feb 2020 [566]

The two peaks occur if the high surge tide doesn't quite coincide with the normal high tide. If the normal high tide and the surge high tide were to coincide, then another flood similar to 1953 is likely to occur. (In 2013, the peaks were about two hours apart.) Hopefully with better communications and early warnings now in place, it would not result in loss of life as in 1953.

In February 2020, the water came up the front of the gate across the Quay (see [566]). The Boatyard wall did its job but pumping was still required to extract some seepage (see [567]). The flood wall here wasn't raised and the water still overtops on a more regular basis with rising sea levels (see [568]). The new hut on the site of the Spear hut, despite being built on legs, still suffers when there are high surge tides (see [569]).

There are hazards other than just property flooding (see [570]). On this occasion, a channel mark chain broke and the mark floated away. Tony Lyon, the Harbourmaster had to retrieve it in his launch and tether it to the harbourmaster's hut until it could be repaired and replaced (see [571]).

Seepage being pumped from the Boatyard, Feb 2020 [567]

The river wall downriver of Waldringfield being overtopped Feb 2020 [568]

This is the site of the hut that floated off in 1953. Feb 2020 [569]

The other front row beach huts Feb 2020 [570]

The harbourmaster retrieving an errant channel marker buoy Feb 2020 [571]

Little egrets on the John Pretyman Waller reserve [572]

The Wetland Reserve

The Reverend John Waller had long envisaged a wetland nature reserve behind the wall on the marshland north of the village and this was created as the clay was extracted to raise the river wall after the 2013 flood. The area is now a haven for wading birds, ducks, little egrets and the endangered water vole.

It is hoped to encourage new bird species and also new plants, such as fritillaries and bee orchids. There is already widespread evidence of water-voles and otters and it is also envisaged that the area will encourage reptiles (such as adders and slow-worms).

The Coasts and Heaths AONB encompassing the River Deben was created in 1970 and, since 1992, the Deben Estuary has been designated as an SPA and a Ramsar site as it is home to nationally significant populations of overwintering waders and wildfowl. It forms 40% of all the saltmarsh in Suffolk. Just north of the village, the saltmarsh to reedbed transition

The Bird Reserve was created after the death of John Pretyman Waller to fulfil his vision of a freshwater nature reserve on Dairy Farm Marsh [573]

The wetland reserve from the air [574]

Mullet rings, formed when mullet are competing for food in shallow water [576]

zone is home to one of Britain's rarest snails, the 'Vertigo angustior' or narrow-mouthed whorled snail, protected by an SSSI.

Mullet used to be very common, always hiding under boats, but there were many years when they were not seen at all until recent returns from their distant travels in 2006.

A number of creatures have increased or returned to the area over the years as the river has become cleaner and as a result of the creation of reserves and protected areas. These include avocets, barn owls, marsh harriers, red kites (once nearly extinct in the UK), peregrine falcons, and even ospreys. Little egrets now nest regularly and have progressed from summer visitors to being here all year round. Terns nest downriver on the saltings. This is probably a sign of improving water quality as not so many years ago it was rare to see many fish in the river. Seals often cruise amongst the boats, popping up to survey everyone. They give birth on the mudflats in the quieter areas just to the north and south of the village. Seals have been known to catch quite large eels.

Many other nationally important animals find a home or stopover around the village.

The river in 2016 showing increased gull fishing activity. The gulls were fishing for small fry being hunted by the larger bass under the water [575]

Eight Decades of Dinghies

Deben Week 1955. This photo shows several Dragonflies, two Fireflies
(F 489 & F 1037) and two National 12s (N 393 & N 1276) [577]

History can be learned not only from people but also from objects. Sitting on Waldringfield Beach on a dinghy-sailing day offers an insight into more than eighty years of amateur sailing for pleasure. Over that period available materials have changed, new design ideas have evolved and different age groups and social classes have found their way onto the water. Welcoming the new has not meant jettisoning the old: if you train your eye to recognise some of these main dinghy classes adopted by the Waldringfield Sailing Club, you will be watching different generations of dinghies, still sailing and bringing their own moments of history with them.

In 1935, the only dinghy raced on a national basis was the expensive International 14, so in order to encourage dinghy sailing the RYA, in 1936, published the rules for a simpler and cheaper boat – the National 12. This allowed dinghies of any design as long as they conformed to the length, weight and sail area regulations. This is called a development class, encouraging new techniques and innovation. Today these dinghies are built from a range of materials, but early examples, as seen here, were traditional wood construction. After WW2 there was a strong move for greater social equality – dinghies were more likely to be a uniform design (like the Waldringfield Dragonfly) so that the challenge was for the most skilful sailor, not the person with the newest boat. The Firefly class was put into production immediately after World War II using the techniques of cold-moulding strips of plywood that had been used to develop the Mosquito aircraft. They were two-person dinghies used at the 1948 London Olympics.

The Cadet dinghy designed by Jack Holt in 1946 [578]

The modern Cadet built of fibreglass
with a alloy mast and boom [581]

The Cadet postwar dinghy class is a tribute to the new approach to sailing that considered it a family sport. This was the first class of dinghy designed for an older and a young child to sail together. Today Cadets can be built in GRP. For competitive sailing all crew members should be aged under 18 at 31 December. They are a recognised Junior Racing Class.

The Mirror was originally conceived as a two-man, build-at-home boat. It was designed by Jack Holt in 1962 so slightly later than the Cadet and Enterprise. It has distinctive red/orange sails and over 70,000 were built. Like the Cadet it has international appeal. They are slightly bigger than a Cadet which means that an adult can sail it with a junior more comfortably, especially for training, and there is no age limit.

Designed in 1956 by Knud Olsen, a Danish designer, OKs are built in wood or GRP and was originally intended as a preparation class for the Olympic Finn. They were regularly raced in the 60s and 70s but the success of the Laser class rather dampened this class. There are still some members who sail them nationally and internationally and will compete in Open Meetings at WSC.

The Mirror class hasn't been a major class at Waldringfield
as it has too many similarities to the Cadet [579]

Another popular racing dinghy the OK sailed since the 60s [580]

In the 1960s-1970s many wooden boats were superseded by GRP. The Squib is a keelboat designed in 1967 by Oliver Lee and introduced to WSC in the 1970s as a cheaper alternative to the Dragon. It is a strict one design boat with distinctive orange sails. Squibs are often used to cruise as well as race although they do not have a cabin so difficult to stay onboard overnight.

The Squib Class were introduced to WSC in the 1960s [582]

Larks: Alan and Helen Krailing (blue hull) with Harry and Gemma Pynn (white hull) [584]

The Lark is a two-person, non-trapeze sailing dinghy, designed in 1966 by Michael Jackson. All Lark hulls are made of glass-reinforced plastic (GRP). The Lark is a one-design class which leads to very close racing. These were introduced to appeal to the lighter, younger crews leaving Cadets, offering the excitement of a spinnaker (unlike the Firefly and Enterprise). The Club has a very strong history in Larks, producing many National Champions.

The Wayfarer is a wooden or fibreglass-hulled, Bermudan-rigged sailing dinghy of great versatility, designed by Ian Proctor in 1957. Originally wooden, GRP was introduced in 1965. They make very good training boats and although regularly raced they also enable families to day-sail together.

The Wayfarer introduced to WSC in 1980. Many race regularly in Saturday fleet racing [583]

The Laser, is a highly popular family of small one-design sailing dinghies using the same common hull and interchangeable rigs with different amounts of sail area. Bruce Kirby designed the Laser in 1970 with an emphasis on simplicity and performance. It is currently an Olympic Class and some of the WSC younger sailors have gone on to compete nationally and internationally. These are a good choice for those who like to sail alone and not be dependent on having a crew.

There are now a few of these more solid GRP Cornish Shrimper keelboats boats at WSC. They were designed in 1979 in Cornwall. They are normally used for day sailing on the Deben or for days out to other nearby rivers. They can also be trailer sailed which means they can be towed to another part of the country for holidays much more easily and cheaply than a yacht.

The Topper is an 11 foot 43 kg (95 lb) sailing dinghy designed by Ian Proctor in 1977. The boat is constructed from tough polypropylene, and is popular as a racing boat or for sail training. They are extremely simple to un-rig and to transport often by roof rack.

The fast, modern RS200 is an asymmetric spinnaker boat (an asymmetric spinnaker is flown from a pole coming out from the bow of the boat, called a bowsprit) which appeals to sailors who look for speed and excitement. The open transom allows the RS200 to virtually self-drain after a capsize and a moulded self-bailer removes any remaining water. The rise in popularity of asymmetric boats has seen the demise of some older designs, nationally and at Waldringfield.

The Laser singlehanded dinghy [587]

The Cornish Shrimpers are not regular races at WSC but do occasionally join in for the Regatta [586]

The recently introduced Topper [585]

The RS200 is now one of the larger classes at WSC [588]

A Last Look across the Anchorage

The Nunn family's *Rikasa* with safety boat *Kirton Owl* alongside and *Blazer* on the starboard quarter [589]

Dick and Dawn Larkman's grandson Steven in the Danish-designed *Kiwi* [590]

George and June Jones's great grandchildren setting off on their first cruise with their parents on board *Blossom* [591]

It's August 2020 and we take a last look across the anchorage. As ever the boats offer their own commentary. There are slightly fewer than we would normally expect to see on the water at this peak time of year, though the foreshore and the anchorage filled up quickly after the eerie emptiness of the spring. Perhaps people are enjoying what is here with a greater intensity – though normal WSC social life has not been resumed due to the continuing need to avoid proximity, especially in indoor spaces.

It has been an extraordinary period and it's not over yet. Those who want to recapture the feeling of the earlier 'lockdown' months would do well to seek out the video diary posted by cameraman and Waldringfield resident Dylan Winter. His current small yacht lies unobtrusively on her mooring, silently making the point that adventures of all sizes may take place in yachts of all sizes and there's no need to fetishize the craft or the designer if all you really want to do is get away on your own and explore. Many people followed Winter's earlier *Keep Turning Left* circumnavigation of the UK for his expert photography and perceptive commentary, not the glossy varnish work or speed though the water. It's yet another example of the astonishing development of the camera since TN Waller's time.

There is still glossy varnish on view at Waldringfield and classically lovely yacht design. The mid-20th-century Kestrel class has gone, as have the Dragons, but the Waldringfield Dragonflies are cherished. Waldringfield's oldest inhabitant, *Kestrel*, still survives from Queen Victoria's reign though the Edwardian yacht *L'Atalanta* and the sailing barge *Ena* (both from 1906) lie elsewhere hoping for new owners and restoration.

Ondine, *Vashti*, *Jesus* and *Oystercatcher* are among the mid-20th-century wooden boats which still moor here and others, like *Peter Duck* and *Persephone* (the very early Kim Holman-designed Stella), regularly sail through. The Deben remains a good river for wooden boats. There's renewed expertise and enthusiasm in the yards upstream and there's a rumour that the 1920s Cherub class may soon be racing down this way again.

Traditional [592]   Contemporary [595]   *Odin*: Best of both worlds? [596]

Remarkable new water craft, such as Stand-Up Paddleboards (SUPs) are seen at Waldringfield and they are occasionally used in new ways. The first Suffolk Pride Paddle set off from the Maybush this month – an event that would have seemed inconceivable to earlier residents such as Jack Jones, resentful at the necessity of denying this aspect of his identity.

One of the main messages of the river is continuity and change. Though there are no longer Wallers as Rectors of Waldringfield yet the family is still here and *Jesus* is a visible reminder of their history. Other village families are similarly tenacious though many of them – like the Nunns – have moved with the times in their choice of boat. Some of the Waldringfield History Group members, however, are more recent arrivals who look at it with fresh eyes and enjoy new types of yacht. There's evidence of many different tastes, personalities and purposes in the Waldringfield anchorage, despite the absence of the largest vessels for whom there is no longer space.

Perhaps though, as we stand on the foreshore from which the coprolite barges and the London muck deliveries have mercifully gone, we will see Arthur Ransome's *Nancy Blackett* or Clifford and Daisy Paterson's *Clytie* pause here. Ransome's stories continue to work their magic with successive generations and *Clytie* will be 100 years old in 2021. She is still owned and sailed by descendants of those same families who discovered the magic of the Deben and never entirely left.

Masters up the mast: Clifford and Daisy Paterson's great great grandson Josh Masters up *Clytie*'s mast [594]

The First Suffolk Pride Paddle, August 2020 [593]

2020 Vision

A Walk towards the Future...

Waldringfield in 2020 [597]

Not everything survives the passing of time [598]

In January 2020, Waldringfield History Group launched a project to record as many aspects of village life as possible during the year. Local community groups and the village school were all invited to participate. Village residents have been busy recording events, completing questionnaires and taking photographs. We hope that in twenty years' time, and again in forty and sixty years' time residents of Waldringfield will be asking about the past and using the information we have left for them to continue the story. Like every year before it, 2020, will be full of stories for future generations, from the early tidal surge and final visit of the mobile grocery shop to the devastating COVID-19 pandemic and subsequent 'lockdown.' This came into effect on March 23rd 2020 and affected everyone in one way or another.

On May 8th 2020, Waldringfield's strong community spirit came to the fore for the 75th anniversary of VE Day when many people decked their houses and gardens with flags and tried to mark the event as best they could under 'lockdown'.

The widely admired Waldringfield Village Hall, completed in 2002 with the help of a grant from the national lottery and much fund-raising from residents, was closed by the 'lockdown.' Under normal circumstances it is a focal point for village life and hosts a wide variety of

Greenaway pays tribute to the WW2 generation [599]

regular activities for those in the Parish and further afield. The popular village pub, the Maybush, suffered the same fate. Nobody was able to recall a previous time when the pub had been closed before during licensing hours. The two places of worship in the village were also obliged to shut. It is likely that the last time All Saints was completely closed was during the time of major refurbishment in 1865.

Over a century has passed since Waldringfield was industrial and probably very toxic to both humans and wildlife. Much of the wildlife has recovered as evidenced by the contributions to a popular village wildlife newsletter entitled 'What's About' which records local bird and mammal sightings. The sight of hundreds of Brent Geese in flight of a winter's evening, for instance, is something to behold and to register.

Fortunately, attitudes to the environment have changed since our 1881 walk. Egrets no longer lose their lives and feathers in favour of ladies' hats. Instead, they grace the shores of the Deben. The Waldringfield stretch of this tidal river estuary is home to a rich diversity of wildlife with important areas of salt marsh, mudflats and grassland including habitats for many species of plants, birds and mammals. The river has been designated a Special Protection Area (SPA), 'Ramsar' site and Site of Special Scientific Interest (SSSI) within the Suffolk Coast and Heaths Area of Outstanding Natural Beauty (AONB). The River Deben Association Saltmarsh Research Group was formed in January 2014 and a research project

was set up to survey the saltmarsh just upstream of Waldringfield in 2018. This was supported by the Environment Agency (EA) and Marine Management Organisation (MMO) and partially funded by the AONB Sustainable Development Fund. The aim of the project was to discover the causes of erosion of the Deben saltmarshes and to look for effective ways of regenerating them. To date, the survey has recorded some significant results, including the discovery that the rapid erosion of the saltmarsh edges inland from the river channel is believed to have been caused by shore crabs.

Winter in winter: Dylan Winter's yacht stays out in all seasons [600]

21st century farming has its own beauty [601]

The village has had an active Wildlife Group for many years and more recently, an environmental group known as 'Greener Waldringfield', a combined resource for local wildlife, gardening and other groups and individuals who share an interest in the environment and sustainability. The Church Field Trust was established in 2003 to manage the 5.2 acres of land given to the village by Dr Tom Waller, a local GP and former member of the government's Advisory Council on the Misuse of Drugs. Dr Waller campaigned tirelessly for better treatment and healthcare for drinkers and drug users. Church Field, formerly agricultural land, was given to the people of Waldringfield and the surrounding area for recreational use.

In 1971, British Telecom's main research facility was completed at Adastral Park on Martlesham Heath. Forty six years later, in 2017, Suffolk Coastal District Council (SCDC) granted an application for up to 2,000 dwellings with associated facilities on the land to the south and east of Adastral Park. This significant development will undoubtedly affect the future of the village, perhaps bringing additional people to the area to live and work, as well as more visitors to the river. The Parish Council and village community groups will continue to liaise with planners to ensure that the AONB is not adversely affected.

Each year, the warmer summer weather brings with it an influx of visitors from further afield and, as in many popular tourist destinations, problems have been known to arise with increased use of rubbish bins and discarded crabbing lines on the beach. Nevertheless, perhaps recognising their good fortune to live in such a beautiful place, many local people work hard to ensure that the village remains litter free and pleasant for visitors to enjoy. The verges are planted with bulbs and wild flowers by members of the community and the popular village school makes use of volunteers to accompany children on litter picks and to assist them with the maintenance of a garden and wildlife pond.

Efforts to reduce erosion [602]

Many visitors to the village are sailors who value the Boatyard, Sailing Club, launching facilities, sheltered anchorage and access to the delights of the rest of the Estuary and the North Sea. Perhaps a less obvious but moderately concerning issue as one looks out over the Waldringfield Fairway, is the eventual fate of some of the fibreglass hulls when they get to the end of their useful lives. The production of these boats started during World War II but did not hit the leisure market until the 1970s when little thought was given to environmental concerns. Their safe and environmentally friendly end has not been planned – there is a glimmer of hope that the fibreglass may be recycled safely for use as insulation in the construction industry.

After the flooding in 2013, the river wall was upgraded and in 2016, as a final phase in their three year programme of procuring improved flood defences for Waldringfield, the Waldringfield Flood Defence Group (WFDG), a community-led flood protection project, commissioned works involving the restoration of an area of fringing saltmarsh owned by the Crown Estate and stretching over a kilometre immediately north of the village. This work is now complete and visitors to the village should note the low level polder fence work (see photo [590] constructed from driven chestnut stakes supporting strapped bundles of hazel faggots.

There is now a brick flood defence wall around the properties on the Quay and a gate across the slipway. The flood wardens keep a close eye on warnings issued by the Environment Agency and react if called upon. The warnings are far more accurate these days thanks to computer modelling and there are fewer false alarms. These improvements kept the water back at the northern end of the village during the tidal surge in early 2020. However, the area on which the beach huts lie, remains unprotected. The remainder of the river wall, north of the village, was raised using clay and mud extracted from a scrape behind the wall thereby creating the wildlife reserve named in honour of Rev John Waller.

According to an Eastern Inshore Fisheries and Conservation Authority (IFCA) Finfish Report 2014, river fish stocks remain in a fragile position probably due to pollution and global warming but also possible changes to the saltmarshes which are important feeding grounds for young bass and mullet. Nightingales are now regularly heard in full voice, with barking muntjac deer and foxes. Badgers have become bolder with reports of them invading gardens at night. Barn owls are frequently seen hunting noiselessly over the meadows and the saltings. Little egrets, redshanks and herons patrol the dykes and shallows, and water voles, otters and kingfishers frequent the new scrapes and foreshore. The river walls now make an excellent place from which to view these creatures and marvel at the variety of species now thriving in this area.

The UK Office for National Statistics records that the population of Waldringfield was 464 at the time of the 2011 census. Estimated population in 2018 was 458. This may not have included all residents who own second homes in the village.

Despite everything, the River Deben remains ever-changing and captivating; a source of enjoyment and comfort to many. It is hoped that future generations will be inspired by the village of Waldringfield, its riverside setting and the wealth of history in this book.

The Waldringfield anchorage, the gold at the end of the rainbow! [603]

The Deben

Gives us much pleasure,
Boats sail their measure,
Against ebb and flow,
Against winds high and low,

Just walking the shore.
Knowing there is more,
Each day a different hue.
Each day a changing view,

Sands enjoyed by tots,
All spades, buckets and pots,
Birds that stay and feed.
Dabbling in the weed,

A veritable garden of Eden,
That's our dear old Deben.

Kit Clark

[604, 605, 606, 607, 608]

Appendix

The Waldringfield History Group

The chapter entitled 'The Story of the Glass Plates' tells how, in 2006, the discovery of a box of nineteenth century photographic glass plates led to the presentation at the Village Hall by Joe Clark and Stan Baston of 'A Walk around Waldringfield 100 Years Ago'. This, in turn, led to interest in forming the Waldringfield History Group (WHG). The initiative was taken in April 2007 by the late Sandy Wells. Ten other people attended, some of them sadly no longer with us.

The first formal meeting of the Group took place in September 2007. The late aAndrew Haig suggested a constitution which stated: 'The group shall be called Waldringfield History Group. Its objectives are to promote the study of the history of the village, tell villagers about it and record it for posterity.'

Joe Clark was elected Chairman and Bob Crawley the Hon Secretary. The Chairman agreed to arrange an introductory visit to the Suffolk Record Office (SRO) and the Hon Secretary agreed to set up a website.

It was noted that the late Noel Edgar, as village recorder, had already been instrumental in documenting some of the village history. A box of items and papers collected by him had been provided for the meeting by his widow, Jill and one of their daughters, Jackie Brinsley, a teacher at the Village School.

It was also noted that in 1989 an informal group, the 'Bygones' had produced a 'History Scrapbook' and had taken several cassette tape audio recordings (now on the website). There remains a beautifully written account of their proposed activities which refers to an even earlier group called the 'Waldringfield Society'. It appears to have taken several decades to get this history of Waldringfield under control!

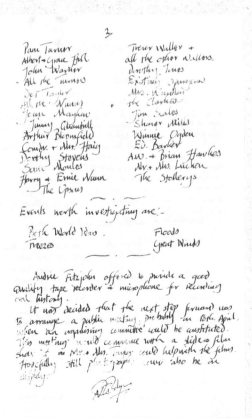

Pioneering Waldringfield Historians [609, 610]

Equally noteworthy was the fact that to mark the Millennium in the year 2000 Kit Clark and helpers had produced a three-volume album which featured a photograph and some details for most houses in the village. This valuable historical document has inspired the Group's latest ongoing project, 'Project 2020 Vision'. This is a collaborative effort to record village life in 2020 and to conserve the details for use as a digital time capsule in 2040, a village gift from the Present to the Future.

Project 2020 Vision header [611]

The early visit to the SRO proved fortuitous. A few months after the inaugural meeting of WHG, during an internet search for village related material, a record of the sale of Court Rolls for Waldringfield was discovered. This was both exciting in that the Rolls would contain information back to 1356, but also devastating in that they had been sold already to an unknown buyer for a price guided by a sale estimate of £3,000-£4,000. During the visit to the SRO it emerged that the Friends of the Suffolk Record Office were the 'unknown buyer' and that they had acquired the Rolls for £4,706.

Another stroke of early luck was the fact that the Tithe map of 1839, 6ft wide by 4ft deep and printed on linen, had recently been acquired by a village resident and that he was happy to provide access to it at any time.

One of the founding members of WHG, Margaret Lake, was interested in learning how to read and transcribe the Court Rolls and similar documents by studying paleography. She enrolled on a course and has continued her studies to this day. This is a long-term project which has resulted in the ability of the Group to acquire maximum information from old Wills and the like.

Another founding member, Bob Crawley, put his IT skills into creating and developing the WHG website, waldringfieldia.com, which, over the years, has accumulated a wealth of material, including many interviews and recollections in both text and audio form as well as cine films. There are thousands of entries which are searchable by text and organised into categories. There is a large collection of photographs many of which were provided to the WHG by residents and friends of Waldringfield. For the purposes of data protection, and of security, access to the website has to be password protected or arranged for a specific purpose through one of the officers. Access to the full website is a privilege of membership. Becoming a member requires an expression of interest, the payment of a modest annual subscription and an agreement to treat website data sensitively. Details for becoming a member are given at the end of this appendix.

Two more recent members, John and Caroline Ogden, have applied their interest and knowledge of military history to the preparation of Rolls of Service for the villages of Waldringfield, Hemley and Newbourne. The information for World War I has been the subject of an exhibition but, at the time of writing, the planned exhibition of the World War II Rolls is having to wait for the lifting of the COVID-19 lockdown. This military knowledge has been of immense value to the workings of the Group.

Between them the founding members, and those who joined later, possessed skills which enabled the Group to commit to a series of evening presentations and daytime exhibitions which are listed below. On occasions, when the chosen subject has coincided with the school curriculum, members of the Group have given talks in the Village School or invited the school to visit the exhibitions. All of the presentations are stored on the website. The majority were given as part of a series of the well-known Waldringfield Winter Talks.

- 2007: A Walk around Waldringfield 100 Years Ago (pre-dated formation of the WHG)
- 2008: The History of Waldringfield (the first WHG presentation)
- 2009: Waldringfield at War (A DVD of this talk is available for loan)
- 2010: Waldringfield at Work
- 2011: The History Exhibition in the Village Hall
- 2011: Waldringfield at Leisure
- 2012: The Titanic (presented in conjunction with the late Malcolm Crawford)
- 2012: Titanic Exhibition in the Village Hall
- 2013: The Post War years
- 2014: Sailing Barges
- 2015: Who Do We Think They Were?
- 2016: No presentation (all efforts put towards starting the book)
- 2017: I Spy?
- 2018: World War One Rolls of Honour (exhibition)
- 2019: From Closure to Conflict: A Village in Crisis
- 2020: World War Two Rolls of Honour (awaiting exhibition)
- 2021: A Present to the Future – 2020 Vision (ongoing project)

There is always a danger in naming names that others will appear not to be recognised for their extremely valuable contributions, be they recollections, drawings and paintings, nautical knowledge or skills in cartography, investigation, organisation, interviewing and, last but certainly not least, providing refreshment at our meetings.

The current membership list is as follows:

President:	Joe Clark	Past Members:	Mary Tucker
Chairperson:	Gareth Thomas		Stan Baston
Chairperson Elect:	Alyson Videlo		
Hon Secretary:	Jane Hall	In Memoriam:	Andrew Haig
Hon Treasurer:	Michael Atkinson		Audrey Ruffle
Members:	Amanda Sims		Gerald Tucker
	Bob Crawley		Jill Edgar
	Caroline Ogden		Judith Stinson
	Charles Croydon		Peter Kaznica
	Jackie Brinsley		Sandy Wells
	John Ogden		
	Liz Kennedy		
	Margaret Lake		
	Mike Nunn		
	Roger Stollery		

There are, of course, a number of active supporters including Joe Clark's wife, Kit and Kitty Moss who have undertaken paintings for the book. A collection of archaeological finds have been made over the years by detectorist Paul Tomlinson who has been very supportive.

For anybody wishing to become a member of the Waldringfield History Group it is possible to contact the Hon Secretary by email at Waldringfieldhg@gmail.com.

Acknowledgements

The Editors are immensely grateful for all the support they have received from Members of the Waldringfield History Group, both those now sadly missed and those present. They are listed in the Appendix, 'Waldringfield History Group'. This publication is very much a combined effort of the Group as a whole.

We are also indebted to all those who have provided photographs over the years since the inception of the Group in 2007. Wherever possible, we have accredited the photographs to their sources.

Some of the information in the book has been acquired from interviews which have been carried out over the last thirteen years. We are grateful to the interviewees for their time and their recollections.

Of course, a publication such as this depends on sponsorship and so our grateful thanks go to the following Sponsors:

Waldringfield Boatyard	Roberto Ices Ltd	Lewis Culf Ltd
Waldringfield Parish Council	Kingsfleet Wealth	Oak Garage Waldringfield
The Maybush	The Scarfe Charitable Trust	The Stollery Family
Waldringfield Sailing Club	Seamark Nunn	

During the last four years we have benefitted from advice and support from many, many other sources.

These include:

Walter Aldis	Seona Ford	Steve Lomas
John Archer, Elizabeth Hayley and family	Noel Fraser	Colin Low
Richard Barker	Fran Gifford	Tony and Christine Lyon
Paul Barrell	Michael John Gifford and family	Peter Maddison
Mark and Emma Barton	Ron Green	Lesley Mann
Stan Baston	Victoria Gunnell	Maggie Marriott
Jackie and David Beaton	Alex Haig	Anthony and Celia Mason
Leigh Belcham	Alexandra Hall	Jo and Paul Masters
Andrew Blaza	Peter Hall	Alan Matheson
Marian Bradley	Philip Hall	Jo McArdle
Linda Brook	Jeff Hallett	Sylvia and Martin McBeal
David Brown	Richard and Tabby Hill	Iain Morley
Andrew Brown	Tim Holt-Wilson	Dylan Moore
Tony Carter	Bill and Catherine Hughes	Kitty Moss
Kit Clark and family	Terry Hunt	Claudia Myatt
Mike Clark	Reverend Sarah Jenkins	Sarah Nevill
Anthony Cobbold and The Cobbold Family Trust	Sam Jennings	Andrew Nunn
Neil Collingridge, Sarah Northey and family	Julia Jones, Francis Wheen, Bertie Wheen and family	Rosemary Nunn
Steve Cooney	Ian Kay and Christine Fisher-Kay	James Palmer
Patrick Cooney	Roger Kaznica and family	John Palmer
Lewis Culf	Bernard Kufluk and family	Alan Powell
Charles Curry-Hyde	Jinny Kufluk (née Fraser)	Dorne Pretyman-Waller
Juliet Dearlove	Dawn and Dick Larkman and family	Margaret and Roy Quantrill
Cathy and John Fish	Matt Lis	Max Raffe
		Jonathan and Libby Ruffle and family
		Marion and Bim Sharpe

Jonty Sherwill
Geoff Sinton
Robert Simper
Penelope Smail and family
John and Alexis Smith
Martin Spall
Alan Stapleton
Dan Stinson
Ann and Rob Stock
Roger and Susan Stollery
Trish Sudell
William and Ali Sudell
Alison Thomas
Mark Thomas

Ann and Peter Thubron
Rebecca Todd
Paul & Mary Tomlinson
Roy Tricker
Adrian & Chris Turner
Christopher Videlo
Ian Videlo
Stephen Videlo
Peter Wain
Rosa Waller
David and Christine Ward
Sebastian Watt
Nickie and Charles Wellingham
Alma Wells

Martin Wenyon
Andrew White
David Whiting
Robin Whittle
Ray Whyard
Linda Wild
Linda and Jon Wilkins
Peter Willis
Charlotte Winn
Jill and Dylan Winter
Richard Woodman
Philip E West,
    `philipewest.co.uk`

Organisations:

East Anglian Daily Times
Felixstowe Family
    History Society
Ipswich Transport Museum
Martlesham Heath
    Aviation Society
Mersea Island Museum
National Historic Ships Trust

River Deben Association
Waldringfield Hut Owners
    Association
Waldringfield Fairway Committee
Waldringfield Parish Council
Waldringfield Sailing Club
Waldringfield Sailing Club,
    Dragonfly Class

Waldringfield Wildlife Group
Woodbridge Museum

Classic Kingfisher dinghy [612]

Select Bibliography

Arnott, WG *Suffolk Estuary*, Norman Adlard and Co Ltd (Ipswich 1955)

Arnott, WG *The Place Names of the Deben Valley Parishes*, Norman Adlard and Co Ltd (Ipswich 1946)

Basham, Winifred *Extracts from her Diary 1939-1945*, bbc.co.uk (21 July 2004)

Bender, Mike *A New History of Yachting*, Boydell and Brewer (Woodbridge 2017)

Benham, Hervey *Once Upon a Tide*, George G Harrap and Co (London 1986)

Berry, Sandra *The Cobbold Elliston Affair*, Number 11 Publishing (London 2007)

Bird, Vanessa *Classic Classes*, Adlard Coles (London 2012)

Carr, Frank GG *Sailing Barges*, Peter Davies (London 1931, edition used 1951)

Coldstream, John *Dirk Bogarde, The Authorised Biography*, Orion (London 2005)

Copinger, WA *The Manors of Suffolk*, TF Unwin (London 1905)

Cottam, Nick & Curtis, Tim *Life on the Deben* www.lifeonthedeben.com (Woodbridge 2019)

Dearlove, Juliet *Atlantic Children 1 & 2*, AuthorHouse UK (London 2010)

Francis, AJ *The Cement Industry 1796-1914: A History*, David & Charles (Newton Abbot 1977)

Finch, Roger & Benham, Hervey *Sailing Craft of East Anglia*, Terence Dalton (Lavenham 1987)

Foynes, Julian P *The Battle of the East Coast 1939-1945*, JP Foynes (Isleworth 1994)

Griffiths, Maurice *Post-war Yachting*, Hutchinson (London 1946)

Hazell, Martin *Sailing Barges*, Shire Publications (London 1976)

Hegarty, Cain and Newsome, Sarah *Suffolk's Defended Shore: Coastal Fortifications from the Air*, English Heritage. Royal Commission on Historical Monuments (London 2007)

Herbert, Sir Alan *The Singing Swan: A Yachtsman's Yarn*, Methuen (London 1986)

Holt-Wilson, Tim *Tides of Change: 2 Million Years on the Suffolk Coast*. Published as part of the Touching the Tide Landscape Partnership Scheme (2015)

Innes, Hammond *Hammond Innes' East Anglia*, Hodder and Stoughton (London 1986)

Innes, Hammond *Sea and Islands*, Collins (London 1967)

Ionides, C, Atkins, JB & Haig, AA *Floating Home and Born Afloat*, Chaffcutter, (Ware, Hertfordshire 2003, edition used 193/500)

Jones, GA *The Cruise Of Naromis: August in the Baltic 1939*, Golden Duck (Chelmsford 2017)

Kemp, John *A Fair Wind for London: Swansong of the Sailing Barges*, Sailtrust Ltd (Maldon 1983)

Kinsey, Gordon *Martlesham Heath*, Terence Dalton Ltd (1975)

Lloyd's Register of Yachts, Lloyds of London, editions used 1936, 1949, 1963, 1973

McGrail, Sean *Boats of the World from the Stone Age to Medieval Times*. Oxford University Press (Oxford 2002)

Phelps, Humphrey *Suffolk of One Hundred Years Ago*, Alan Sutton (Stroud 1993)

Plummer, Russell *The Ships that Saved an Army: A Comprehensive Record of the 1300 'Little Ships' of Dunkirk*, Patrick Stephens Ltd (Wellingborough 1990)

Price, Roger *Memories, World War Two through the Eyes of a 'Tweenager'* (9-15 years). WHG website (June 2012)

Redstone, Vincent *Burrough Memorials of Old Suffolk*, Sagwan Press (2015)

Robertson, E Arnot *Ordinary Families*, Cape (London 1933, edition used Penguin 1947)

Sharp, Nigel *Troubled Waters: Leisure Boating and the Second World War*, Amberley Publishing (Stroud 2015)

Simper, Robert *The Deben River: An Enchanted Waterway*, Creekside Publishing (Ramsholt 1992)

Simper, Robert *East Coast Sail: Working Sail 1850-1970*, David & Charles (Newton Abbot 1972)

Simper, Robert *The River Orwell and the River Stour*, Creekside Publishing (Ramsholt 1993)

Tooley, Peter *Operation Quicksilver*, Ian Henry Publications (Romford 1988)

Treadway, Martin *Harbouring the Dream*, Suffolk Yacht Harbour Ltd Levington (2011)

Tye, Walter *A Guide to Waldringfield and District*, Norman Adlard and Co

Ltd (Ipswich 1952)

Upfield, Arthur W *The Gifts Of Frank Cobbold*, ETT Imprint (2018)

Waller, Rev Thomas Henry *Perennial Diary*, courtesy of Joe and Kit Clark, Waldringfield

Wardale, Roger *Ransome at Sea: Notes from the Chart Table*, Amazon Publications (1995)

Wareham, Andrew *Lords and Communities in Early Medieval East Anglia*, Boydell Press (Woodbridge 2005)

Whisstock, Sue *A History of Whisstock's Boatyard*, Leiston Press (Leiston 2017)

White, Archie *Tideways and Byways in Essex and Suffolk*, Edward Arnold (London 1948)

'Myths, legends and stories are the signposts previous generations have left us' (from a quote by Fred Van Lente) [613]

Willis, Peter *Good Little Ship: Arthur Ransome, Nancy Blackett and the Goblin*, Lodestar books (2017)

We have benefitted from articles in the following newspapers and periodicals, among others:

Classic Boat; *Classic Sailor*; *East Anglian Daily Times*; various articles by kind permission of Tara Cross; Archant Newspapers (see reference section on WHG website for details); The Ipswich Archaeological Trust; various (see reference section on WHG website); *Journal of the Institution of Civil Engineers*; *The Marine Quarterly*: River Deben Association Newsletters (now *The Deben*); *Suffolk Magazine*; *Yachting Monthly*; *Yachts and Yachting* and the publications of the Waldringfield Sailing Club; *Waldringfield Sailing Club 1921-1996, Anniversary Tidings*; *Tidings Magazines 1967-2002*; *Golden Anniversary Tidings*; *Waldringfield Sailing Club Newsletters 1998-2001, 2014-2019*; 'The Club Line', *2019/2020*; *WSC History 25 Years 1971-1996* (various authors).

Detailed references will be found in the source notes on the website (`whghistorybook.shortcm.li/sources`) and, where appropriate, in the text notes for the relevant chapters or pages.

Websites:

adls.org.uk
ancestry.co.uk
bernardoconnor.org.uk
cadetclass.org
cementkilns.co.uk – Dylan Moore. 2017
churchofengland.org
classicboat.co.uk
cobboldfht.com
cwgc.org
earlyphotography.co.uk
findagrave.com
findmypast.co.uk
forces-war-records.co.uk
gro.gov.uk

heritage@suffolk.gov.uk
historicengland.org.uk
ipswichat.org.uk
longlongtrail.co.uk
nationalarchives.gov.uk
nationalhistoricships.org.uk
pillboxes-suffolk.webeden.co.uk
riverdeben.org
royalharwichyachtclub.co.uk
shct.org.uk
suffolkarchives.co.uk
yachtingmonthly.com
wikipedia.org

List of Illustrations

AB1	Adrian Bird	DS	David Stearne
AB2	Andrew Blaza	DT	Daniel Thrun
ACM	Anthony & Celia Mason	DW	David Whiting
ACT	Adrian & Christopher Turner	EADT	East Anglian Daily Times
AF	Audrie Fitzjohn	EK	Elizabeth Kennedy
AS	Alexis Smith	EN	Ernie Nunn
AT	Ann Thubron	FAG	Findagrave.com
AV	Alyson Videlo	FC	Free Clipart
BC	Bob Crawley	FSRO	Friends of Suffolk Records Office
BG	www.billiongraves.com	GR	Guillaume Rolland
BH1	Bill Hughes	GS	Geoff Sinton
BH2	Brian Hammet	GT	Gareth Thomas
BK	Bernard Kufluk	HC	Hammond Collection
C	Collins	HE	Harriet Earle
CC1	Charles Croydon	HF	The Hughes Family
CC2	Colonel Colby	HK	Hazel King
CCH	Charles Curry-Hyde	INEOS	Tim Carter and Team INEOS
CF	Cathy Fish		
CM	Claudia Myatt	IS	The Ipswich Society
CMF	Cambridge Museum of Folk	ITM	Ipswich Transport Museum
CV	Christopher Videlo	IV	Ian Videlo
DB	David Brown	JB	Jackie Brinsley
DDL	Dick & Dawn Larkman	JC	Joe Clark
		JD	Juliet Dearlove
DEP	The Deben Estuary Partnership	JF	Jones Family Collection
DM1	Dunwich Museum	JH	Jane Hall
DM2	Dylan Moore	JK	James Kidner
DR	David Ruffle	JO	John Ogden

JP1	James Palmer	RS2	Roger Stollery
JP2	John Palmer	RW	Robin Whittle
JPM	Jo & Paul Masters	SB	Stan Baston
JS	Jonty Sherwill	SCM	Susan & Chris Morton
KC	Kit Clark	SE	Susan Edwards
KM1	Kim Mayhew	SF	The Sudell Family
KM2	Kitty Moss	SHS	Suffolk Horse Society
LB	Leigh Belcham	SIAH	Suffolk Institute of Archaeology and History
LM	Lesley Mann		
MA	Michael Atkinson		
MB	Mark Barton	SJ	Sam Jennings
MH	Martin Hazell	SK	Siem Kroes
MHAS	Martlesham Heath Aviation Society	SL1	Steve Larkman
		SL2	Steve Lomas
ML	Margaret Lake	SN	Sarah Nevill
MM	The Mersea Museum	SRO	The Suffolk Record Office
MN	Mike Nunn		
MS	Maureen Shepherd	TC	Tony Carter
NBT	Nancy Blackett Trust	TNW	Thomas Naunton Waller Collection
NSC	Neil & Sarah Collingridge		
		UK	Unknown
OSO	Ordnance Survey Office	VM	Vivian Mason
		WC	Wikipedia Commons
PH	Penny Hunt	WF	Waller Family Collection
PK	Peter Kaznica		
PS	Penelope Smail	WHG	The Waldringfield History Group
PT	Paul Tomlinson		
PW	Philip West	WM	Woodbridge Museum
RD	Robert Deaves	WSC	The Waldringfield Sailing Club
RG	Ron Green		
RS1	Robert Simper	WSCDC	WSC, Dragonfly Class
		YY	Yachts & Yachting

1.	RS2	21.	CV&RS2	41.	RS2	61.	SL2	81.	WHG
2.	CV&RS2	22.	CV&RS2	42.	DT	62.	KC	82.	WHG
3.	CV&RS2	23.	CV	43.	RS2	63.	JB	83.	EADT
4.	RS2	24.	RS2	44.	RS2	64.	AV	84.	MN
5.	JC&KC	25.	RS2	45.	RS2	65.	WHG	85.	WHG
6.	JB	26.	WHG	46.	RS2	66.	IS	86.	JFC
7.	JH	27.	RS2	47.	FC	67.	WHG	87.	JFC
8.	JH	28.	RS2	48.	JB	68.	WHG	88.	JFC
9.	HE	29.	AV	49.	CC2	69.	PT	89.	DR
10.	JH	30.	WHG	50.	GT	70.	WHG	90.	JH
11.	SB	31.	JP2	51.	WHG	71.	SB	91.	JH
12.	RS2	32.	WHG	52.	SIAH	72.	AV&JH	92.	WHG
13.	JO	33.	CV	53.	WHG	73.	WHG	93.	WHG
14.	WFC	34.	WHG	54.	WHG	74.	KM2	94.	JH
15.	TNWC	35.	RS2	55.	FSRO	75.	WHG	95.	DB
16.	WM	36.	WHG	56.	AV	76.	AV	96.	WHG
17.	WM	37.	WHG	57.	JB	77.	WHG	97.	DB
18.	DR	38.	AV	58.	JB	78.	WHG	98.	JPM
19.	RS2	39.	CV	59.	WHG	79.	SK	99.	DW
20.	AV	40.	RS2	60.	DM1	80.	WHG	100.	DW

101.	DW	121.	WHG	141.	WHG
102.	WHG	122.	JFC	142.	WHG
103.	JFC	123.	ITM	143.	OSO
104.	JFC	124.	JFC	144.	WHG
105.	JFC	125.	WHG	145.	GT
106.	JFC	126.	MN	146.	DR
107.	JFC	127.	DDL	147.	WHG
108.	JFC	128.	JFC	148.	AV
109.	JFC	129.	DDL	149.	WHG
110.	JFC	130.	LM	150.	WHG
111.	JFC	131.	SE	151.	WHG
112.	BH2	132.	AB2	152.	AF&AV
113.	JFC	133.	SRO	153.	JFC
114.	JFC	134.	SE	154.	MH
115.	JFC	135.	SE	155.	WHG
116.	JFC	136.	EADT	156.	RG
117.	JFC	137.	AV	157.	RG&MM
118.	SN	138.	OSO	158.	RS2
119.	RS2	139.	GT	159.	JFC
120.	NSC	140.	WHG	160.	RS1

Text Notes

A great deal of research over several years is included in this book. The text notes that follow are intended to answer specific queries that people might feel as they read through, particularly about some of the people mentioned who might have been household names in their time but less well known today. More specific sources and detailed finding aids are listed on an open access page on the Waldringfield History Group's website: `whghistorybook.shortcm.li/sources`

So much information has come from Waldringfield residents, past and present, and their friends. These are listed in the Acknowledgement section

We hope you will find the Bibliography useful to support quotations and to enlarge on topics. To gain full access to all the resources of the History Group and their website waldringfieldia.com it is necessary to be a member. Email the Hon Sec at: `Waldringfieldhg@gmail.com`

Wonderful Waldringfield

p6 Many Waldringfield groups (including the History Group) and village activities are gathered on the website: `waldringfield.onesuffolk.net`

To Begin at the Beginning

p11 The Waldringfield History Group website (`waldringfieldia.com`) has a members' area and an open area email (`waldringfieldhg@gmail.com`) for information how to join.

The Ever Changing River

Material for this chapter comes from many sources and specifically 'Further Reminiscences of Jill Atkins' (RDA - River Deben Association - Spring 1995)

'Pre-war Reminiscences of the Deben' Jim Turner (RDA Autumn 1996)

'Deben River Wall Heritage' Robert Simper (RDA Spring 2010)

Waldringfield's stretch of the river now flows from below Cross Farm. Previously the riverside boundary was closer to Waldringfield. It was possibly moved in the 1970s when boundaries came under review, but maybe earlier. Some more recent Council maps still showed the boundary as it was in 1904 but these were incorrect.

Photographer, Chris Baker, adrift in his dinghy making the best of the early morning light [614]

Waldringfield before the Written Word

p26 Archaeology being an interest but not a specialism for any WHG member, we are grateful to Dr Iain Morley, Academic Coordinator of the School of Anthropology, University of Oxford, for checking the contents.

Michael Atkinson, member and Treasurer of WHG, extracted from the *Proceedings of the Suffolk Institute of Archaeology and History 1903-2007* a list of archaeological finds relevant to Waldringfield. These are listed in the sources section on the website. There is also a comprehensive list of finds to be found on the `heritage.suffolk.gov.uk` website.

The Maybush

p49 Ronald Carl Giles (1916-1995), often simply referred to as 'Giles', was a cartoonist best known for his work for the *Daily Express*. For many people Christmas was not complete without the Giles Annual. He never actually sold his creations, preferring to donate them to friends and to charitable organisations, like the RNLI, of which he was Life President, and which continues annually to issue charity Christmas cards bearing his work.

Owd Boys

p55 On the back of George Jones's photo of Bob Button there's a note that he was locally famous for being able to drink nine pints of beer without needing to relieve himself.

The Old Maltings

p56 Although known as Cliff House and renamed the Old Maltings in the 1930s by the Heath family, the house is often referred to locally as simply the Maltings. This is because there was an actual maltings (brewing) business carried on here by John Hill during the 19th century. There are entries in The Perennial Diary of Thomas Henry Waller (1832-1920) which refer to the Maltings although at this time, the house itself was Cliff House. Occasionally this may give a feeling of inconsistency in our text.

The Cobbold Family ran the Cliff Brewery on Cliff Quay, Ipswich. The original Cobbold brewery had been set up in Harwich but, in 1746, in order to benefit from a better source of water, Thomas Cobbold (1708-1767) relocated the majority of the family brewing business to Ipswich. The current building is a tower brewery by William Bradford. It became a Grade 11 listed building in 1989.

p61 'Everson's Shed'. David Green (RDA Spring 2011)

The phrase 'hot bed of spies' was quoted in the obituary of Sir Clifford Copland Paterson in the *Journal of the Institution of Civil Engineers* (November 1948)

p62 'Deben Reflections'. Anne Whiting (RDA Spring 2015)

p65 Jack Jones's comments were written on the back of the studio photograph.

p66 Norman Scarfe (1924-2014), born in Felixstowe, was a historian, author and local activist. Among his many achievements was the founding of the Suffolk Records Society and authorship of the *Shell Guide to Suffolk* and other county guides.

Jonathan Trowell (1938-2013) was an internationally successful artist and draughtsman whose landscape painting is more usually associated with Norfolk.

'Jack Francis Jones, Naval Architect'. Julia Jones (*Classic Sailor* December 2015).

'Jack Jones designed yachts to look after their owners' Julia Jones (*Yachting Monthly* January 2016).

p66 Stewart Platt wrote the story of *Celandine* in *My Three Grey Mistresses* Atlantic Transport (2002).

p67 Brian Hammett was closely associated with the Cruising Association and used *Avola* to follow in the wake of Arthur Ransome's *Racundra*. He produced two modern editions of Ransome's Baltic cruises which were published by Fernhurst Books.

Alan Gurney (1936-2012) is remembered as one of the most innovative designers of his generation, with Chay Blythe's *Great Britain II* among his notable commissions. He was also an author and a pioneer of high latitude sailing.

p68 The East Coast Sail Trust (ECST) continues to support the barge *Thalatta* and to take groups of children to sea `thalatta.org.uk`

The East Anglian Group of Marine Artists (EAGMA) is limited to 25 members and exhibits at least twice a year both in London and in East Anglia.

The Kestrel Class

p72 Gunter rig is a fore and aft sail set behind the mast. The lower half of the sail is attached to the mast, and the upper half is fastened to a spar which is approximately vertical and reaches above the top of the mast.

Bermudan rig consists of a triangular sail set aft of the mast with its head raised to the top of the mast; the front of the sail runs down the mast and is normally attached to it. The lower part of the sail is usually attached to a horizontal boom controlled by a sheet (rope).

A Walk Along the River in 1881

p84 The Cement Cottages are commonly known as such in the village as they were built by the Cement Works for their employees. They are however also referred to as the Concrete Cottages because of the innovative material used in their construction. Both descriptors are used in our text.

Working Boats

p88 Thomas Churchyard (1798-1865) was born in Melton. He trained as a solicitor, and worked in the law for many years, but his real interest was landscape painting.

p96 Sailing Barge *Ena* is currently decaying in a barge graveyard in the River Medway at Hoo. In 2002, *Ena* was featured on the Channel 4 television programme Salvage Squad - available to watch online. In 2011, it was reported that she was up for sale on eBay with the bidding starting at £85,000. But despite the high profile televised effort made to restore her, her future looks bleak, abandoned alongside wrecks at Hoo and buffeted by the elements and tides.

Wildlife at Waldringfield

p106 The *Magna Carta* of 1215 includes a clause stating the Barons' demands for the removal of the King's (and other) weirs: 'All fish-weirs shal be removed from the Thames, the Medway and throughout the whole of England, except on the sea coast'.

p106 Simpers of Ramsholt have developed both a shell fish and sea-fishing business on the Deben and adjacent coast. In recent years this has included the Woodbridge Shuck Festival.

p107 William Cobbett's *Rural Rides*, though not including Suffolk, give a vivid picture of rural poverty in the 1830s as does Ronald Blythe's *Akenfield*, 100 years later.

The Impact of the Great War

p125 'Remembrance 2018: Pioneering WW1 aerial photographer William Walden Hammond'. Vicky Gunnell (*Suffolk Magazine* November 2018)

Zeppelins had been developed in Germany at the

Channel buoys and other markers by the harbourmaster's hut [615]

end of the 19th century. In World War I they were used for reconnaissance but also bombing missions including London and several East Coast towns. L48 was just one month old and the first of a new class when it was brought down by British aircraft.

Waldringfield's Links with HMY 'Britannia' (Royal Cutter Yacht)

p126 King George V's dying wish was for his beloved yacht to follow him to the grave. On 10 July 1936, after *Britannia* had been stripped of her spars and fittings, her hull was towed out to sea and sunk by a Royal Navy destroyer.

The Waldringfield Anchorage, 1900-1939

p128 Edward Fitzgerald (1809-1883) was an English poet and writer, born in Bredfield, near Woodbridge and friendly with writers such as Tennyson and Thackeray as well as the artist Thomas Churchyard. His most famous work is the English translation of the *Rubáiyát of Omar Khayyám*.

p129 'Driven by desire' James Palmer's *Kestrel* (*Classic Boat* February 2014).

Hervey William Gurney Benham (1910–1987) was the pioneering proprietor of Essex County Newspapers, an author of books on Essex and the East Coast (many focused on traditional vessels) and a significant benefactor of local charities.

Arnold Bennett (1867-1931) was a prolific and successful English novelist and journalist who, though famous for novels set in the Staffordshire potteries, lived on the Essex coast from 1912-1920 where he became an enthusiastic sailor.

p132 Transcriptions of the original Logs of *Enigma* were loaned to WHG by the Palmer family.

p133 Later *Enigma* reminiscences - A longer account is available in 'Boats of the Deben' - *Enigma* - David Bucknell and John Palmer. (RDA Autumn 2011).

p139 'Pre-war Reminiscences of the Deben'. Jim Turner (RDA Autumn 1996).

A Carpet-slippered Cruise

p142 Arthur Ransome's yacht *Nancy Blackett* is owned by the Nancy Blackett Trust which enables members to get involved in her maintenance and enjoy sailing her. She is laid up at Robertson's Boatyard every year. For more information contact: nancyblackett.org

A Focus on the Foreshore

p154 Archie White from West Mersea was a writer and artist who advocated the joys of river and creek-sailing rather than high seas adventure.

The Boatyard and Boatbuidling

p156 'Deben Reminiscences'. John Adams (RDA Autumn 1997).

p162 Mike Clark's recollections were recorded by Claudia Myatt and published in *Marine Quarterly* Summer 2020.

The Beach Huts

p168 'An Introduction to the History of Waldringfield Huts'. Linda Wilkins (RDA Spring 2016).

p170 For a detailed explanation of a 1918 Nissen Hut, please visit the reference section.

p171 Flag officer - A Naval Officer above the rank of Captain, as a fleet Admiral, Vice Admiral, Rear Admiral or Commodore, is entitled to display a flag indicating his or her rank. Yacht and sailing clubs commonly term their executives 'flag officers'.

Waldringfield's Contribution to the War Effort

p190 The icon used in this chapter is from detective novelist Margery Allingham's *The Oaken Heart*. Her description of WW2 from her Essex village has similarities with Waldringfield's experience.

p194 Martlesham Heath was once the site of the Aeroplane and Armament Experimental Establishment and therefore, after the Royal Aircraft Establishment at Farnborough, it was the most important RAF base in the country. It was moved to Boscombe Down in 1939. The Martlesham Heath Aviation Society (MHAS) has a museum in the old control tower at Martlesham. Further details can be found here: mhas.org.uk

A Walk along the River in 1944

p205 The date of D-Day was June 6th 1944, but Hitler was slow to respond as he may still have believed that the main focus of the operation was the Pas-de-Calais area and that the Normandy landings were a diversion. The first V1 (doodlebug) was launched against London on June 13th 1944.

Wing Commander Roland Beamont (1920-2001) was a British fighter pilot for the RAF and a test pilot during and after WW2. In June 1944 his unit was stationed in Kent and from 16th June was charged with intercepting the V1s.

Tadeuz Szimanski was a Polish officer flying with the RAF. He is believed to be the first pilot to flip a V1. June Scott's family opened their home in Kent to officers from abroad who had nowhere to spend their leave or to convalesce after injury. Szimanski became a family friend.

Post-WW2 Yachting

p210 'The Life and Designs of Kim Holman' (*Classic Boat* January 2008)

p213 Sir Francis Chichester (1901-1972) was a British pioneering aviator and sailor who named his *Gypsy Moth* yachts after the aeroplane he previously flew. In 1966-67 he became the first person to sail single-handed around the world by the clipper route.

Ralph Hammond Innes (1913-1998) was a British novelist who wrote over 30 novels. He lived in Kersey in Suffolk after WW2 and travelled extensively to research his books. His wife Dorothy was an actress.

p214 Uffa Fox, (1898-1972) was an English boat designer and sailing enthusiast who was a friend of Prince Philip and often raced with him at Cowes. One of his WW2 achievements was designing airborne lifeboats and his post war designs were notable for making use of materials developed during the conflict.

'Dressing overall' consists of stringing International Maritime Signal flags onto a ship from the front (bow) to the back (stern) via the top of the mast (or masts).

p215 Sir Percy Wyn-Harris (1903-1979) was an English mountaineer, colonial administrator, and yachtsman. He served as Governor of the Gambia from 1949 to 1958. From 1962-1969 he sailed round the world in his yacht *Spurwing* which was based on the Deben.

p216 Fran Gifford's talk at the Tamesis Club, John Dunkley (*Yachts & Yachting* February 2011).

p214 *Duet* was built in 1912. She was originally owned by the explorer August Courtauld and then his son Rev Christopher Courtauld. Today she is owned by the Cirdan Sailing Trust who run residential holidays for small groups of people, often disabled. cirdantrust.org/fleet

p217 The Felixstowe Master Mariners Club is an active organisation which meets at the Felixstowe Ferry Sailing Club and whose objective is to foster comradeship among master mariners and raise money for nautical charities: mastermariners.uk

The Caravan Site

p222 Today, there are two caravan sites with easy access to Waldringfield and the river. Low Farm (stayatlowfarm.com) is on the Ipswich Road at the entrance to the village and the Moon and Sixpence moonandsixpence.co.uk is on the Newbourne Road.

Deben Week

p224 Greasy Pole: Caitlin Smail related how one year in the final she and her opponent, Tessa Young, secretly agreed to a truce and to not knock each other off, so as to share the prize.

George Jones wrote or contributed to the *Yachting Monthly* coast notes for many years, though he was often more focused on the Essex area rather than Suffolk.

A Walk along the River in 1871

p228 The population of Waldringfield increases significantly in the holiday season. As the 10 year census is taken in April the figures are probably an underestimate.

p230 The names Blumfield, and Bloomfield crop up repeatedly when looking at ownership of the land freed up by the closure and demolition of the Cement Works. In 1947 Israel Vernon Bloomfield of Ilford owned Atbara in Deben Lane, having obtained some of the land by gift from Miss EA Bloomfield in 1924. Miss Bloomfield also owned land adjacent, where Heron's Kiln is now, in Deben Lane. The 1924 Deed for Atbara also refers to Ernest Victor Bloomfield of Forest Gate as the purchaser.

Peter Ducks, Pandoras and Plastic

p241 The Sail Training Association is now known as the Tall Ships Youth Trust: tallships.org

Waldringfield Sailing Club (WSC) Post-WW2

p243 Bob or Robert Hill was the father of Albert Hill who was the landlord of the Maybush. His brother Henry was landlord of the Fox at Newbourne and father in law to Ernie Nunn. Prior to running the Fox, Henry had a distinguished naval career winning a Conspicuous Gallantry Medal at the Gallipoli Landings in 1915. Robert and Henry's uncle, John Hill was a tenant at Cliff House.

p246 *The River Deben Magazine* Oct 2011 has an account of Bob Ruffles taking the barge *Ena* up river for the Clubhouse opening and being unable to turn her in the anchorage so needing to go right through until he could drop anchor and swing round.

The history of the 'Old Lady' on the Clubhouse as far as we know it, is as follows: in 1923 Mr AW Stollery asked Mr EA Nunn to remove this figurehead from a boat called the *Annabel*, an old trading boat which lay rotting in the creek beyond the Dinghy Park. This was done and the figurehead was placed in the garden of Gorse Cabin where it remained for many years. When the extension was made to the Clubhouse in 1949, Mr Goddard renovated and painted the figurehead and it was placed on the gable of the extension between the Port and Starboard Lights which were given by Mr Nunn. Later Mr Goddard re-painted and renovated the figurehead. Her earlier history is not known but the hairstyle and ruff suggest Elizabethan days. After the rebuilding in 1982, she was moved indoors as there wasn't a suitable place for her outside.

OOD is the Officer of the Day and is in charge of racing, starting and finishing.

p251 Rosemary Schlee had been part of the Club for many years. She raised huge amounts of money towards the building of the Club House. She ran the first Sail Training Course, organised some disabled sailing and the first 'Taster Day', and introduced Wayfarers to Waldringfield. She also ran the highly successful Oxfam B&B scheme for which she was awarded the MBE in the late 1990s. She was a frequent sailor well into her seventies in her Wayfarer, especially during Wednesday Evening Racing, often getting ready to race when everyone else was reluctant to go because of adverse weather conditions.

p252 *Cockleshell* is still going strong in her 95th year, now owned by John's son Jonty and kept on the River Hamble, Hampshire. In 2016 she inspired the founding of the Hamble Classics Regatta and has been a regular Wednesday evening racer for an unbroken 30 years at Hamble River Sailing Club, which celebrated its centenary in 2019. The complete *Cockleshell* story can be viewed at: cockleshell.org.uk

p255 Irish Boats at Dragonfly 70th. Julia Jones (Classic Sailor November 2019)

The WSC Honours Boards

p256 Jack Knights was born in 1929 and won a half blue for sailing in 1952. He had a variety of other major successes in yachts both big and small. He won several dinghy national championships, as well as the 'Round the Island' race at Cowes. He was the yachting writer for the *Daily Express* and was closely associated with the London International Boat Show until his death on 26 January 1981, aged only 51. A Jack Knights Memorial Race is held at Cowes every year.

Cadet Squadron 35

p258 ISAF is now called World Sailing.

p259 There is an old Pathe News video of Cadets at the Burnham Nationals in 1959 showing these boats as described: youtu.be/7a7J9N_8s-E

Another from 1988 features many local Waldringfield sailors and shows how the boats evolved over the years while the basic concept of having fun still remains.

The Waldringfield Dragonfly

p262 George O'Brien Kennedy's autobiography *Not All at Sea* (Morrigon 1987).

p264 & p265 The PUNCH dinghy and the BOTTLE boat are innovative designs from Roger Stollery.

Flooding

p271 AONB: Area of Outstanding Natural Beauty
p273 SSSI: Site of Special Scientific Interest.

2020 Vision

P281 SPA: Special Protection Area – The Ramsar Convention on Wetlands of International Importance is an international treaty for the conservation and sustainable use of wetlands. It is named after the city of Ramsar in Iran, where the Convention was signed in 1971.

p283 IFCA: The Inshore Fisheries and Conservation Authority.

More information:

whghistorybook.shortcm.li/sources

Index

Black-tailed godwits in flight [616]

Looking East [617]